C000255681

INSIGHTS INTO Vedanta

INSIGHTS INTO Vedanta

TATTVABODHA
तत्त्वबोधः

Transliteration, word-for-word meaning, translation, and commentary

by

Swami Sunirmalananda

Sri Ramakrishna Math
Chennai, India

Published by
Adhyaksha
Sri Ramakrishna Math
Mylapore, Chennai-4

© All rights reserved
First Edition 2005

IV-2M 3C-8-2011
ISBN 81-7823-229-4

Cover Design:
Mr Tomaz Lima and Lucia Lima, Brazil.

Printed in India at
Sri Ramakrishna Math Printing Press
Mylapore, Chennai-4

Publisher's Note

We place before you INSIGHTS INTO VEDANTA, an English translation of *Tattvabodha* with a running commentary, based on Sri Ramakrishna and Swami Vivekananda's teachings. Sri Sankaracharya is the putative author of this work. This book has not been translated for a long time into English. Now our publication fulfils that need.

Tattvabodha is apparently a simple text, and the purpose of the author is to acquaint the lay reader with Advaita. But the text is profound. Though the book appears to merely mention the different aspects of Advaita Vedanta, it anticipates discussion and deep thought.

A thoroughgoing study of Advaita Vedanta in the light of Sri Ramakrishna and Vivekananda's teachings has been a long-felt need. The translator has made a humble attempt towards this end. He has divided the topics into chapters and has commented on each idea in detail, chiefly using the words of Sri Ramakrishna and Swami Vivekananda.

Swami Sunirmalananda, the translator, is a monk of the Ramakrishna Order. He was the editor of *Prabuddha Bharata,* an English Monthly of the Ramakrishna Order, between January 1999 and December 2001. Also, he was an *Acharya* of the Monastic Probationers' Training Centre at Belur Math. Presently, he is the Assistant Minister at the Ramakrishna Vedanta Centre, Brazil. He has got a simple style and has done this translation well.

One reader-friendly feature he has adopted is giving not only the text in Devanagiri and transliteration in English but also word for word meanings. So even those with only a nodding acquaintance with Sanskrit can understand the text correctly. What is more, on each verse he gives a running commentary wherein he explains the thrust of the verse as illustrated by the observation of Sri Ramakrishna and Swami Vivekananda in relevant contexts. Several drawings and charts have been included to aid comprehension.

We hope the reader will be acquainted with the numerous aspects of Advaita through this book.

Sri Ramakrishna Math, Chennai
February 2005

CONTENTS

Key to Transliteration and Pronunciation

	Sounds like
अ	a-o in son
आ	ā-a in master
इ	i-i in if
ई	ī-ee in feel
उ	u-u in full
ऊ	ū-oo in boot
ऋ	ṛ-somewhat between r and ri
ए	e-ay in May
ऐ	ai-y in my
ओ	o-o in oh
औ	au-ow in now
क	k-k in keen
ख	kh-ckh in blockhead
ग	g-g (hard) in go
घ	gh-gh in log-hut
ङ	ṅ-ng in singer
च	c-ch (not k) chain
छ	ch-chh in catch him
ज	j-j in judge
झ	jh-dgeh in hedgehog
ञ	ñ-n (somewhat) as in French
ट	ṭ-t in ten

	Sounds like
ठ	ṭh-th in ant-hill
ड	ḍ -d in den
ढ	ḍh-dh in godhood
ण	ṇ -n in under
त	t -t in French
थ	th -th in thumb
द	d -th in then
ध	dh -theh in breathe
न	n -n in not
प	p -p in pen
फ	ph-ph in loop-hole
ब	b -b in bag
भ	bh-bh in abhor
म	m -m in mother
य	y -y in yard
र	r -r in run
ल	l -l in luck
व	v -v in avert
श	ś -sh in reich (German)
ष	ṣ -sh in show
स	s -in sun
ह	h -in hot
	m-m in sum
:	h -ḥ in half

Translator's Note

By the grace of the Divine Mother, we present a translation, with commentary, of *Tattvabodha.*

Tattvabodha in its Sanskrit original is a mere booklet. To translate it should be easy. But a simple translation would not do because this little book contains the whole of Advaita philosophy in a gist form. In about 50 paragraphs, the author of *Tattvabodha* has discussed all aspects of Advaita using the question-answer method. A mere translation will be doing injustice to the book.

One way of translating the text is to follow the beaten track—transliterate, translate, and explain important terms in footnote in small type. But footnotes generally become cumbersome, and readers tend to ignore them. Further, this would only add to the long list of not-for-the general-reader books. So we adopted a slightly different method.

We divided the whole book into about 53 chapters, based on the topics it deals with. Instead of explaining difficult and important terms in footnotes, we have made use of the narrative. Hope the reader will find this method easy to read and understand.

In discussing different topics we have Sri Ramakrishna and Swami Vivekananda explaining various concepts in detail on several occasions. In fact, the book is full of their words. Sri Ramakrishna and Swami Vivekananda are imperative now, because they are the ideals of the age, have passed all stages of sadhana and attainment, are the best exemplars of religion, spirituality, Advaita and Vedanta, know every nook and corner of spiritual life, and are rational, scientific, and universal in their approach to everything.

Further, they have come to teach the world. So they are the best interpreters of important Advaitic terms. Some diagrams and tables have been added by the translator for easy comprehension.

Owing to the pedantic love for details and technicalities, Vedantic scholars have made Vedanta in general and Advaita in particular quite unpopular. No one but a few rare souls touch Vedantic and Advaitic texts—which are generally in terse Sanskrit and, if translated, in impossible-to-understand format. Swami Vivekananda, however, came to make Vedanta practical and popular. He called upon everyone to 'carry the light and the life of the Vedanta to every door, and rouse up the divinity that is hidden within every soul.' So stories and anecdotes too are added, rarely though, to help the student.

Quotations from Sri Ramakrishna are from *The Gospel of Sri Ramakrishna* [referred to as *Gospel* here] by M, translated into English by Swami Nikhilananda and published by Ramakrishna Math, Mylapore, Chennai. Swami Vivekananda is quoted from *The Complete Works of Swami Vivekananda* in 9 volumes, published by Advaita Ashrama, Mayavati, and referred is to as *Complete Works*. Other books are mentioned fully. References to page numbers of quotations are mentioned at the end of each chapter.

I

THE INSPIRATION

A Boy Goes to Yama

Long, long ago there was a little boy by name Naciketa. His father sent him to the Kingdom of Death. The Emperor of Death, Yama, was out. So the boy waited for the emperor for three days. Returning from his tour, Yama saw Naciketa, and was sad: 'Ah! I made a little child, a brāhmaṇa child to add to my sorrow, wait at my doorstep for three days—unfed and uncared for! I must atone my mistake.' Turning to Naciketa, he said: 'My child, I give you three boons. Ask anything you want.'

For the first boon, the intelligent boy said that when he returned home his father should recognize him, love him, and must not fear him. There were several boons in one boon. Seeing the child returning from the jaws of death, the father might assume he was a ghost and drive him away, or get scared. So the boon. That was granted. Then the boy asked about going to heaven: he wanted to know what means were to be adopted to go to heaven. Yama explained patiently, to this little boy, everything about heaven and ways to attain it.

The boy asked the third boon now. Naciketa asked Yama: 'Sir, some say something survives after the death of the body, while some others deny it. What is the truth?' Yama was worried now. 'My child, this is a big question for you. Ask for horses, houses, kingdoms, etc. Do not ask for such a thing.' The boy was adamant. Yama had to yield. At last Yama told him that after the death of the body, something indeed survives. And that is the Atman. He told the boy that the body is merely like the chariot while the Atman is the owner of the chariot, who sits in it. 'Isn't the mind charioteer then?' 'No, it is not. The intellect is the driver. The mind is the reins that control the horses; and horses are the senses.' And so on. The boy returned home satisfied, and brought the knowledge of the Atman to the world.

This is the wonderful story of the *Kaṭha Upaniṣad.*

A mere boy, Naciketa, brought home the best knowledge ever received.

Six Children Go to A Sage

Six little boys—Sukeśā, Śaibya, Sauryāyaṇī, Kauśalya, Bhārgava, and Kabandhī—went to a great sage of olden times. The name of that great sage was Pippalāda. Sage Pippalāda was a profound personality, versed in all the sciences, and a man of realization. These boys wanted to know certain important things from him. The sage was happy to see the boys. But he told them: 'My dear children! Everything needs discipline. If you wish to know higher truths, you must have some qualifications. So lead a life of faithful service, devotion, and purity for one full year. Then you will be ready to receive knowledge. Come prepared and ask any number of questions you wish.'

The boys happily did that. That was the love of knowledge in ancient times. The six children returned after a year of prayer, study, meditation, austerity, etc. Their minds were tuned to higher truths now. The sage, pleased with them, answered all their questions. The questions too were daring ones: 'Where do people come from?' 'Where do the gods, if they are there, bring forth beings from, keep, and take back to?' 'We all breathe, true. But where does life-force or *prāṇa* come from?' 'In this body, who is it that dreams?' and so on. The sage answered all of them with love and care. The boys were satisfied. Those answers form the famous *Praśna Upaniṣad*.

The Other Children

Uddālaka, Śvetaketu, Aruṇi, Satyakāma—all these names are popular in the Upaniṣads. They are not names of big sages with huge beards. They were little children, little children at that, wanting to know the Truth ardently. No one discouraged them from knowing the Truth. Then there were women—Gārgī Vācaknavī, Maitreyi, and so on. They were all discoverers of Truth. There were the working-class people too—Raikva, for instance.

All this shows that spiritual life or seeking the Truth is not only for the elite few, the elders, or those who have 'nothing else to do.' Knowledge is not meant only for the *brāhmaṇas* either. It is for everyone, at any stage of life—the younger, the better. It is for anyone who seeks the Truth ardently, but seeking is necessary. To wish to give up falsehood and seek the Truth is indeed natural for thinking ones.

Seeking has been highlighted in such a way in the scriptures that the metaphor given borders on a hyperbole. One of the scriptures says that the aspirant should pant for the Truth just like a person, whose head has caught fire, pants for water.

Gautama Siddhārtha gave up his kingdom, wife and child, esteemed position, health, and everything else for Truth. So he became the Buddha. Dhruva, a little child of five, went to the forest to seek God. St Francis gave up everything for God. Catherine was a queen but gave up everything for God. Kevin was a king before he became a hermit. Mahāvīra was a king before becoming a Jaina Tīrthankara. Purandara Dāsa and Kanaka Dāsa of the Dāsa tradition of Karnataka were rich and powerful men before becoming God's servants. Such is the spirit of seeking shown by the great.

In fact, to hold on to the world and not to show interest in spiritual life and the Truth are unnatural. Sri Ramakrishna says:

Therefore I say again that work is only the first step. It can never be the goal of life. Devote yourself to spiritual practice and go forward. Through practice you will advance more and more in the path of God. At last you will come to know that God alone is real and all else is illusory, and that the goal of life is the attainment of God.[1]

II

ADVAITA: AN INTRODUCTION

Vedanta and Us

What is Vedanta? 'Veda' means 'knowledge', and 'Anta' means 'the highest.' Vedanta, therefore, stands for the highest knowledge.

There are many nuances of truth. 'Someone is sitting there,' is true. 'Rama is sitting there,' is also true. 'Rama is sitting on the bench there,' is a greater truth. 'Rama, age 30, is sitting on the bench in that park and reading a book,' is a still greater truth.

Evidently, gradations in truth reveal the clarity of comprehension of something. That which is very hazy and unclear is only half-true, while that which is perfectly and absolutely clear is the highest truth.

Vedanta teaches us the highest truth and nothing short of it. That highest truth is about ourselves. The ordinary truth is that we are so-and-so. The higher truth is that we are human beings called Rama, Jack, Jill, etc. The highest truth is that we are Reality alone, called Brahman in Vedanta, and nothing else. And this is the teaching of Vedanta.

Vedanta and the Cosmos

We should remember at the very outset that the Truth of Vedanta is not a mere intellectual exercise but a vibrant experience. Anyone, anywhere, anytime, can experience this Truth. The Truth experience is for all, and our goal of life is to experience that.

While telling us that we are neither Jack or John but the Reality itself, Vedanta also teaches us the highest truth about the universe we live in. The ordinary truth about the universe is that there are countless galaxies and milky ways and stars and planets; and that we live on this little planet with our relatives and friends and others. A little higher truth is that all these countless planets and stars and trees and living beings are permutations and combinations of some five elements alone. The highest truth, however, is that everything is Brahman or Reality alone.

Vedanta and God

Vedanta teaches us about the one thing we have been believing in since the beginning of time: God. That there are many gods and goddesses to satisfy our numerous needs is a lower truth. That there is a supreme God, who is the creator of the universe, is a higher truth. But the highest Truth is that there is only one Reality—called variously as God, Brahman, etc—which is what exists. All else is a mere false manifestation. That Reality is vast and endless, and so is called 'The Vast' (Brahman).

Thus Vedanta deals with all the phases of life, which, when deduced, comes down only to three: God, the universe, and ourselves. The whole of Vedanta is a serious, practical, and *real* discussion about the mutual relationship between these three apparent realities.

Myself, the world around me, and God—these are the only three things that concern me. What is the relationship between one another—between me and the world, the world and God, and myself and God? Advaita Vedanta says that all the three are but manifestations of only One. One alone exists; the rest is unreal. But Vedanta also proposes several other models or viewpoints about Reality. By 'Vedanta,' one generally means Advaita Vedanta. Yet this is a generalization only.

Benefit of Vedanta Study

Why should we study Vedanta? Swami Vivekananda asks the same question and answers it in a beautiful way:

'What, then, is the use of Vedanta and all other philosophies and religions? And, above all, what is the use of doing good work? This is a question that comes to the mind. If it is true that you cannot do good without doing evil, and whenever you try to create happiness there will always be misery, people will ask you, "What is the use of doing good?" The answer is in the first place, that we must work for lessening misery, for that is the only way to make ourselves happy. Every one of us finds it out sooner or later in our lives. The bright ones find it out a little earlier, and the dull ones a little later. The dull ones pay very dearly for the discovery and the bright ones less dearly. In the second place, we must do our part, because that is the only way of getting out of this life of contradiction. Both the forces of good and evil will keep this universe alive for us, until we awake from our dreams and give up this building of mud pies.'[2]

Vedanta Removes Suffering

Misery should go and bliss should come—this is the goal of all living beings. We are endlessly in search of bliss everywhere. Why are we in search of happiness and bliss? We are in search of bliss because that is our essential nature. We are seeing only a faint shadow of that supreme Bliss and hence this craving for bliss. Vedantic Brahman, the only Reality, is nothing but Bliss. To attain It, therefore, should be our goal.

Secondly, suffering should go. There are three types of suffering, according to the Sāmkhya philosophy: suffering from oneself, from natural forces, and from other beings. In spite of all our efforts we cannot eliminate suffering. If we drive it out from one place, it comes to another. Suffering will never go because it is existential—it is one with existence. We must transcend this limited existence in order to overcome suffering. Limitations will go when we know the truth about ourselves. Truth alone can liberate us from existential suffering. The knowledge of the Truth brings us true and lasting happiness. Why does this knowledge bring happiness? For the simple reason that falsehood can't bring true happiness. To see many in that One, to imagine ourselves and others in that One, and to imagine suffering, misery, etc, in that One, is all called falsehood. This is ignorance.

Every truly rational and scientific individual should study Advaita Vedanta for his or her own benefit. And what is that benefit? The benefit is to become free from all limitations, sorrows, sufferings. The simplest truth about ourselves is this: that what we think we are, *we are not!* Yet we do not want to believe this. Vedanta is not esoterical. It is compassionately telling us what we are, that is all. Yet we are not listening to it. The chief teaching of Advaita is that our so-called individuality is false.

Advaita Vedanta is the highest view of Reality, born of experience. Advaita is a matter of experience, not theorization. Śrī Śaṁkarācārya had to propound Advaita, and the truth of Brahman being the sole Reality, because of numerous reasons. He had to establish true religion and reject claims that everything is 'nothing'. Śaṁkara overstressed oneness of Truth and falsity of everything because that was the experience of countless sages and himself, and that was the highest truth propounded by the Vedas. However, it is wrong to say that Śaṁkara rejected the universe as unreal in every sense. When the soul experiences the highest, then there is no duality. When the soul is in the state we are in, everything is real. This is the Advaitic position. Suppose we dislike the idea that the world is unreal. Yet it is a fact. 'Truth does not pay homage to any society, ancient or modern. Society has to pay homage to Truth or die. Societies should be moulded upon truth, and truth has not to adjust itself to society,' says Swami Vivekananda. So Advaitic truth is the highest. The highest but not the only correct view, because Truth can never be limited.

Sri Ramakrishna always says that one can never say God is this much alone. And Truth is beyond thought and words. What Truth is, should only be experienced. So there are other views of Reality as well. When once the individual *realizes* that he or she is that Infinite Truth, he or she can't explain that Truth in words. This is what sages and saints tell us.

There are theories and theories about the universe—like the Big Bang, for instance. All such theories are always challenged, and many tumble too. But the Advaita theory of Vedanta has remained untarnished since time immemorial because it is founded on experience.

Vedanta: Technical Details

Vedanta is the end portion of the Vedas. The authorship, date, and other details of the Vedas are being debated. Whatever the debate, every sane individual can understand that the Vedas could not have been composed in a short time of, say, a few thousand years, considering them to be compositions. According to the religious tradition, the Vedas are created by the supreme Being, Brahman, for the benefit of humanity. They are eternal truths and become manifest in every age according to necessity.

The Vedas are divided into four groups, as the chart shows. **Mantra** is primarily a collection of hymns and prayers, addressed to numerous gods and goddesses, seeking everything under the sun. **Brāhmaṇa** is primarily a collection of sacrificial detail—rules and details regarding the performance of numerous sacrifices. **Āraṇyaka** is primarily a continuation of the sacrificial ideas, but it also contains ideas about the Atman, Brahman, and so on. These are the beginnings of the purely spiritual element of the Vedas.

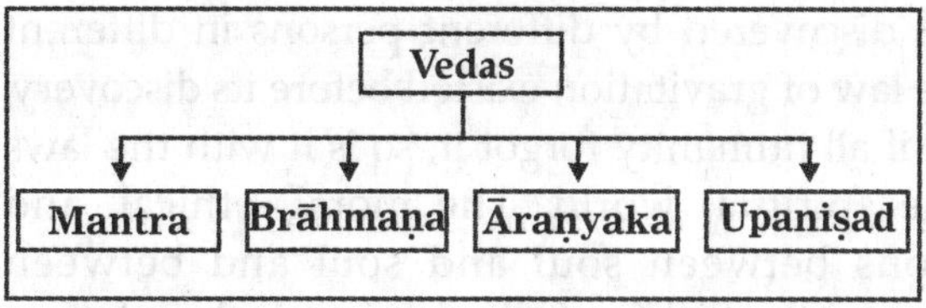

The first three divisions of the Vedas, then, are primarily about this world and the next—seeking happiness, prosperity, destruction of enemies, food, cattle, progeny, and so on in this world, and heavenly pleasures in the next. Gradually, the Vedas take us to the highest. Thus we come to the Upaniṣads. The **Upaniṣad** is the repository of spirituality. It is the highest knowledge—knowledge of the Atman and Brahman. Atman is Brahman—this was the fundamental discovery of universal implications, made by Indian sages. The Upaniṣads lead us to liberation from bondage.

The Upaniṣads, as sacred literature, are called Vedanta. They are the *veda-anta*—end portions of the Vedas. They are both physically and spiritually the end portions. Physically they are situated towards the end of each Veda. Spiritually, they teach the highest truths—the truths that liberate the suffering and bound living being and take him to the threshold of supernatural and everlasting bliss.

Who Wrote the Vedas?

'The Hindus have received their religion through revelation, the Vedas. They hold that the Vedas are without beginning and without end. It may sound ludicrous…how a book can be without beginning or end. But by the Vedas no books are meant. They mean the accumulated treasury of spiritual laws discovered by different persons in different times. Just as the law of gravitation existed before its discovery, and would exist if all humanity forgot it, so is it with the laws that govern the spiritual world. The moral, ethical, and spiritual relations between soul and soul and between individual spirits and the Father of all spirits, were there before their discovery, and would remain even if we forgot them,' declares Swami Vivekananda. [3]

The ancient sages of India discovered these truths and transmitted them to posterity by word of mouth. Their medium was Sanskrit. They created science after science—phonetics, grammar, lexicon, metre, astrology, and so on—to protect the supremely sacred knowledge of the Vedas. Thousands of lives have been dedicated for the study, propagation, and living of the Vedas. Countless Indians have shed their blood for the sake of the Vedas. Innumerable sages and saints have withstood hunger and thirst, cold and heat, humiliation and defamation—for propagating sacred knowledge.

Each syllable and each intonation of the Vedic Sanskrit was important. Thousands of years rolled by but the Vedas remained the same without the slightest change. Different schools rose up, and comparison between them has proved this fact. At last, when writing was discovered, the Vedas came to be noted down. This is how we have got them.

Truths were scattered in different directions. There came a great sage by name Vyāsa, who took up the arduous task of compiling the Vedas. Vyāsa divided the Vedas into four groups, and thus we have the four Vedas:

Each of the four Vedas has several Upaniṣads attached to it. Thus there are at least 108 known Upaniṣads, of which 12 are very important. These ten are important because Śrī Śaṁkara has commented on them. They are: Īśa, Kena, Kaṭha, Muṇḍaka, Māṇḍūkya, Bṛhadāraṇyaka, Chāndogya, Praśna, Aitareya, and Taittiriya. The others which are important are Śvetāśvatara, Jābāla, Muktika, Kaivalya, Mahā-Nārāyaṇa, etc.

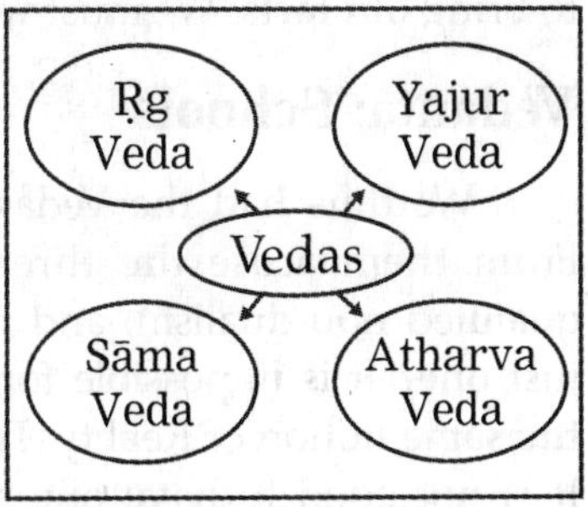

Teachings of Vedanta

What do the Upaniṣads teach? सर्वासां उपनिषदां आत्म-याथात्म्य-निरूपणेनैव उपक्षयात् (*Sarvāsāṁ upaniṣadām ātma-yāthātmya-nirūpaṇenaiva upakṣayāt*), says Śrī Śaṁkara. That is, 'All the Upaniṣads exhaust themselves in discussing the Atman.' This is because, that Atman is the only Truth and that is the only element worth discussing. Everything else is impermanent, superimposed, and misery-producing. What is called the Atman in the individual is called Brahman in the collective. Atman is Brahman. This is the fundamental teaching of the Vedas.

Since the Upaniṣads are a huge literature, and to master one would take several years, Vyāsa brought out a book in gist form. That was the *Brahma Sūtras. Brahma Sūtras* is a collection, in four chapters, of the essential truths about Atman and Brahman and spiritual life in general. It is a compendium on the sadhana, attainments, and every aspect of spiritual life. So *Brahma Sūtras* too has been called the Vedanta.

Seeing the various schools of thought and problems concerning religion, there arose Bhagavān Śrī Kṛṣṇa, who gave the *Bhagavad Gītā* to the world. This is also Vedanta.

Thus we have three texts, called the 'Liberating Trio' (*prasthāna traya*) which are called Vedanta: the *Upaniṣads, Brahma Sūtras,* and *Bhagavad Gītā.* The period of none of these is known. Whatever is done is guesswork, depending upon some stray facts. But there are seekers these days, who are working hard to bring out facts. We must wait and see.

Vedanta: Schools

We thus had the Vedas and Vedanta—the three works. From them arose the three schools of thought—dualism, qualified non-dualism, and non-dualism. Why three and not just one? It is impossible for all of us human beings to have the same notion of Reality. The same coat cannot fit everyone. It is not good to have one single idea. Variety is always the ideal. So there are diverse opinions about God, ourselves, and the cosmos. Some say God is only in the image. Some others say God is up there in heaven. Still others say God is in one's heart. There are others who say God is all-pervading. So there are opinions. The quarrel arises when we think our idea of God alone is right, and others are wrong. The so-called fights, killings, wars, and so on in the name of religion are all concerning external, lesser details. The essentials are the same. This was Sri Ramakrishna's discovery. Swami Vivekananda says:

'Now I will tell you my discovery. All of religion is contained in the Vedanta, that is, in the three stages of the Vedanta philosophy, the Dvaita, Vishishtadvaita and Advaita; one comes after the other. These are the three stages of spiritual growth in man. Each one is necessary. This is the essential of religion: the Vedanta, applied to the various ethnic customs and creeds of India, is Hinduism. The first stage, i.e. Dvaita, applied to the ideas of the ethnic groups of Europe, is Christianity; as applied to the Semitic groups, Mohammedanism. The Advaita, as applied in its Yoga - perception form, is Buddhism etc.

Now by religion is meant the Vedanta; the applications must vary according to the different needs, surroundings, and other circumstances of different nations. You will find that although the philosophy is the same, the Shaktas, Shaivas, etc. apply it each to their own special cult and forms.'[4] While Sri Ramakrishna followed all the paths and found them leading to the same goal, Swamiji too had many supernatural experiences to this effect.

Dvaita or Dualism, *Viśiṣṭādvaita* or Qualified Non-dualism, and Advaita or Non-dualism are the three possibilities of looking at Reality—in a broad sense. You can say that God and you are absolutely different, that you are a part of God, or that you are one with God. These are the three ways of looking at ourselves, the cosmos, and God. We are separate and God is separate. We are parts of God. Or we are God. Swamiji has time and again declared that the highest concept is to know that God alone exists, that we are Brahman. The following diagram shows the three views of Reality.

The Three Views

In the diagram, the first is dualism, which says that God, soul, and cosmos are three different things.

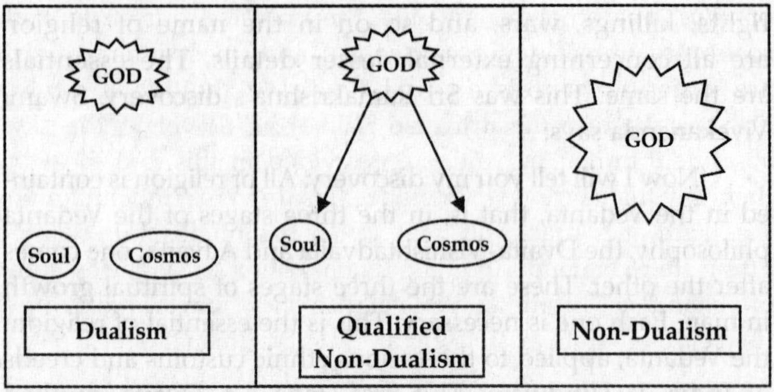

The dualism is in thinking that God is separate and soul as well as the cosmos are separate. The next is qualified non-dualism, which too accepts the soul and the cosmos, but as the qualities of Brahman. They are there if God or Brahman is there. According to the third, Advaita, the ultimate analysis says that Truth alone remains.

Swami Vivekananda was asked once: 'What does the Advaitist think of cosmology?' He responded: 'The Advaitist would say that all this cosmology and everything else are only in Maya, in the phenomenal world. In truth they do not exist. But as long as we are bound, we have to see these visions. Within these visions things come in a certain regular order. Beyond them there is no law and order, but freedom.'[5]

These three philosophies were there in the three texts of Vedanta. They had to be systematized and put forth in a comprehensive way. That work was done by Śrī Śaṁkara, Rāmānuja, and Madhva—in that order. Thus we have the three schools of thought—perfected to the last point.

Advaita: What it is

'Advaita' is a negative term. It means 'not-two'. Advaita is a state of Reality, a matter of experience, and not theory. There is One without a second, which is to be experienced.

That which is eternal is only One. That alone is eternal

or *nitya.* The other realities like the universe, ourselves, and so on are unreal, temporal (*anitya*) and, most interestingly, are superimpositions on that One. We should, however, not mistake that the universe is like the flower in the sky, absolutely unreal. Advaitins are divided in this, but most of them say that since we experience this universe until attaining the Truth, it is practically real. But it has no absolute reality. This is the Advaita position. Sri Ramakrishna says: 'The essence of Vedanta is: "Brahman alone is real, and the world illusory;" I have no separate existence; I am that Brahman alone.'[6]

We experience either the world or God—not both simultaneously. For us now, the universe alone is real, and God is unreal. After realization, God alone should become real and all else a mere superimposition—like covering the table with a tablecloth.

The Cause of Ignorance

The question is, how did this superimposition of the temporal take place on that one Eternal Truth? Superimposition is the work of ignorance. Where did this ignorance come from if there is only one Reality? To this question, Vedantins reply that if we knew the Reality, there wouldn't have been ignorance at all. So the question of ignorance does not arise. However, since millions see this universe, it has a practical reality. For such, there has to be something called ignorance. A child sees a palace in dream, wakes up, and asks his mother, 'Mother, whom does that palace belong to?' The mother cannot convince the baby that it was a dream. So a story is told. Similar, say some Advaitins, is our case with ignorance.

We need not know the cause and position of ignorance. We should only transcend its influence. Further, if we knew ignorance, we would not have been within its hold at all. We better cared for the removal of ignorance and attainment of that One, instead of worrying about its origin, lifespan, etc.

Swami Vivekananda was also asked the same question.

'Why does Maya or ignorance exist?'

Swamiji: '"Why" cannot be asked beyond the limit of causation. It can only be asked within Maya. We say we will answer the question when it is logically formulated. Before that we have no right to answer.'

This, then, is the way Truth is viewed by a great group of philosophers of India. They have been a very strong group. Maybe Advaita or Oneness is only a matter of experience—the highest experience. Hundreds of sages and saints have, down the ages, experienced this Advaitic oneness. The latest among them were Sri Ramakrishna, Holy Mother, and Swami Vivekananda. So that is the truest experience. Since Brahman as the absolute Truth is a matter of immediate experience, and is indirectly known through the Vedas, it has to be explained and told. But it is difficult to express that. This problem confronts the Advaitin. Yet the brilliance of Śrī Śaṁkara has made it possible to refute all counter-arguments and propound the theory of ignorance and Oneness of Reality. This is the last word of Vedanta, they say. This viewpoint is considered to be the most ancient, perfect, and correct worldview.

History of Vedanta

After the Upaniṣads came into existence—whenever it was—there was the *Brahma Sūtras*. Then came the *Bhagavad Gītā*. These are the source-works of Vedanta.

A host of Vedanta teachers appeared from time to time on the Indian soil. Some names are still famous, though their works are no longer there. Among them are Aśmarathya, Auḍulomi, Ātreya, Kārśakṛtsna, Bādari, Bodhāyana, and Kārṣṇajini. These Vedanta luminaries have not left any trace of their literature but quotes from their works are extant. To the next group belong those whose works are known: some of them are, Bhartṛhari, Ṭanka, Dramiḍa, and other Vaiṣṇava Vedantins. Upto these luminaries, there is no knowing when and where they all lived. It is defnitely certain that most of them were pre-Christian.

Then comes one of the doyens of Advaita, Gauḍapāda. He was perhaps one of the pioneers to say that the cosmos is unreal—a superimposition—and that Brahman alone is real. His book, *Māṇḍūkya-Kārikā,* an independent treatise based on the *Māṇḍūkya Upaniṣad,* is read with devotion even now. After him comes Śrī Śaṁkara. Many scholars have taken immense trouble to fix the date of Śrī Śaṁkara's birth as 788 AD. Śrī Śaṁkara had four disciples—Padmapāda, Troṭaka, Sureśvara, and Hastāmalaka. All these were stalvarts of Advaita. After them came Vācaspati Miśra, Prakāśātma Yati, Vimuktātma Yati, Śrī Harśa, and others. This marks the end of the 10th century AD.

Among the later luminaries of Advaita were Citsukhācārya, Amalananda, Appayya Dīkṣita, Madhusūdana Sarasvatī, Sadānanda Yogindra, and so on. These great men lived between the 12th and 18th centuries.

Viśiṣṭādvaita Vedanta had Rāmānuja during the 10th century. He was followed by a circle of extraordinary devotee-Vedantins, who condemned the idea of the falsity of the universe and Brahman being the sole Reality in no uncertain terms. The tussle went on and then came Madhvācārya in the 13th century with his Dualism. This was the exact opposite of Monism. Of the greatest adherents and exponents of dualism were Vyāsarāya, Vādirāja, and others.

A great contribution towards the harmonization of dualism, monism, and qualified monisim came in the 17th century from Mādhavācārya, who wrote *Sarva-darśana-Sañgraha.* His brother, Sāyaṇa, wrote a commentary on the Vedas, and has become immortal. There were other Vedantins after them who tried to harmonize the faiths.

At last came Sri Ramakrishna in the 19th century, who harmonized all the different approaches in a wonderful way. This message was to be spread all over the world, and the task fell on his disciple, Swami Vivekananda, who said that the three schools—advaita, dvaita, and viśiṣṭādvaita—were three ways of looking at Reality. Rather, they were three stages.

Sri Ramakrishna's Harmony

We should read from *Sri Ramakrishna, the Great Master* by Swami Saradananda to know how Sri Ramakrishna brought the three views of Vedanta together:

> **Question**: Was not then the Master a true follower of the doctrine of non-dualism? Did he not accept the full implication of the non-dual doctrine founded by Sankaracharya, in which the very existence of the universe has been denied? For the Master, you say, upheld a difference in the Divine Mother Herself (Svagatabheda) and saw Her existence in the two different aspects of Nirguna as well as Saguna.
>
> **Answer**: No, it is not exactly that. The Master accepted all the three doctrines of nondualism (Advaita) qualified non-dualism (Visishtadvaita) and dualism (Dvaita). But he used to say, "These three doctrines are accepted by the human mind according to the stage of its progress. In one stage of the mind dualism finds acceptance; the other two are then felt to be wrong. In a higher stage of spiritual progress the doctrine of qualified non-dualism is regarded as true; one then feels that the Reality, which in Itself is eternally devoid of attributes exists in sport as always possessed of attributes. One then cannot but feel that not only is dualism wrong but there is no truth in nondualism also. Finally, when man reaches the ultimate limit of spiritual progress with the help of Sadhana, he experiences the Nirguna nature of the Divine Mother and remains in oneness with Her. All the ideas, such as I and You, subject and object, bondage and liberation, vice and virtue, merit and demerit, are then all merged in the One."[7]

Swamiji's Harmony

Swami Vivekananda concludes the experiences of Sri Ramakrishna in this manner: 'We have seen that it began with the Personal, the extra-cosmic God. It went from the external to the internal cosmic body, God immanent in the universe, and ended in identifying the soul itself with that God, and making one Soul, a unit of all these various manifestations in the universe. This is the last word of the Vedas. It begins with dualism, goes through a qualified monism and ends in perfect monism.'[8]

There was a question-answer session on 25 March 1896 at the Harvard University, USA. Swami Vivekananda was in the chair.

> The questioner asked Swamiji: 'Is the Advaita antagonistic to dualism?'
>
> Swami Vivekananda replied: 'The Upanishads not being in a systematised form, it was easy for philosophers to take up texts when they liked to form a system. The Upanishads had always to be taken, else there would be no basis. Yet we find all the different schools of thought in the Upanishads. Our solution is that the Advaita is not antagonistic to the Dvaita (dualism). We say the latter is only one of three steps. Religion always takes three steps. The first is dualism. Then man gets to a higher state, partial non-dualism. And at last he finds he is one with the universe. Therefore the three do not contradict but fulfil.'[9]

Works of Śaṁkara

In order to teach us what this Advaita worldview is, and in what way it is beneficial to us, the greatest proponent of Advaita, Śrī Śaṁkara, wrote several great works. Of them, his commentary on the *Brahma Sūtras* is considered a masterpiece in Sanskrit literature; especially, the introductory commentary, called *Adhyāsa Bhāṣya;* it is a marvel. Then there are other commentaries—on the *Bhagavad Gītā,* and the ten Upaniṣads. Apart from these commentaries, Śaṁkara is said to have written several independent works like *Vivekacūḍāmaṇī, Upadeśa Sāhasrī, Ātma Bodha,* and so on. Of all the books of Śaṁkara, perhaps the smallest and the most beautiful work that is **attributed** to him is *Tattvabodha.*

III

THE SUPPOSED AUTHOR AND THE BOOK

The Supposed Author

Perhaps Śrī Śaṁkara is the author of *Tattvabodha*. *Śrī Śaṁkara Digvijaya* is the only source book of Śaṁkara's life. Following tradition, we may say this much about Śrī Śaṁkara. Śaṁkara was born in Kalady, Kerala, in 788 AD. His parents were Śivaguru and Āryāmbā. Born in a Brahmin family, Śaṁkara learnt Sanskrit and numerous scriptures within a short time. Gaining an intellectual grasp of the Truth from these scriptures, the boy developed a passionate desire to know and realize the Truth. For this, he wanted to become a monk. The father had passed away when he was a mere baby, and his mother would not permit the boy of eight to become a monk. Divine intervention forced her to permit him, and Śaṁkara left home. He went to the banks of the River Narmada, and found his spiritual master in Govindapāda. That sage bestowed the supreme mantra on him, and he attained the highest realization. Sri Ramakrishna comments that after realization, Śaṁkara retained the ego of knowledge in order to teach the world. Thus began the ministry.

The next part of Śaṁkara's life was spent in showing the falsity of pseudo religions, arguing against false practices and heavenly pleasures, and establishing the truth of the Oneness of God. He had to travel all over India of those days on foot, meet religious leaders and scholars, and discuss Advaita. There used to be heated debates, and everywhere Śaṁkara was the winner. Thus he conquered all quarters. He then established four monasteries in the four corners of India for the protection of dharma. He reorganized monasticism and introduced the 'ten-traditions' *daśanāmī sampradāya*. He had four wonderful disciples, who were true to their teacher in learning and attainments. Śaṁkara had begun writing commentaries to sacred texts like the *Bhagavad Gītā* as a young monk, and continued this work till the end. Through his commentaries, Śaṁkara brought out the importance of these scriptures before humanity. When he gave up his body, they say Śaṁkara was only 32 years old. He is said to have passed away in the Himalayas.

The Importance of Tattvabodha

Numerous books are being written about Advaita Vedanta. Apart from Śrī Śaṁkara's original commentaries, there have been a considerable number of secondary works. Of them, explanations of Śaṁkara's commentaries form the major portion. Then there are independent treatises by many later Advaita scholars, chiefly in terse Sanskrit. *Advaita Siddhi, Khaṅdana-Khaṅda-Khādya, Anubhūti Prakāśa, Iṣṭa Siddhi, Citsukhī,* and so on are some examples.

If Advaita is to be a practical philosophy—and not a mere theory—leading us from bondage and suffering to liberation, it must be *comprehensible* to us. Such a grand truth about Reality should not be just an intellectual wonder. Ordinary people should be able to understand and assimilate the philosophy. How to do this was a big question in the minds of traditional Advaitins themselves. Thus there were a few attempts to write some general treatises, called *prakaraṇas,* in Sanskrit. A *prakaraṇa* treatise deals with the whole subject in a simple and brief manner. Of such simple works, the famous book *Vedānta Sāra* by Sadānanda Yogindra (17th century) is one. This book gives us the entire philosophy of Advaita in just a few paragraphs.

Though *Vedānta Sāra* is no doubt a simple work compared to other big works on Advaita, it still has its difficulties. There are beautiful English translations available, no doubt, like the one by Swami Nikhilananda; but the technical way in which *Vedānta Sāra* deals with the subject matter may dishearten the 21st century student.

Then there are the other simple works, attributed to Śaṁkara himself, like *Viveka-cūdāmaṇi, Ātma-bodha*, etc. These, however, are not meant to teach the basics of Advaita to the beginner; they are no doubt grand and inspiring works. Yet another work, Dharmarāja Advarindra's *Vedānta Paribhāṣā*, is not at all for the beginner. Thus there's a need for the 21st century reader, which needs to be fulfilled.

Tattvabodha: The History

How to introduce Vedanta to the beginner in modern times then? Śaṁkara has attempted a beautiful method: that of simple questions and answers. Though the author of *Tattvabodha* is said to be Śaṁkara himself, there are doubts, as usual. In case of almost all works bearing the name of Śaṁkara, the doubt about authorship remains. Any book on Advaita is easily attributed to Śaṁkara! But the safe rule is to follow popular opinion. Whoever the author, *Tattvabodha* is a wonderful attempt so far us modernists are concerned. It tells the beginner, in very simple words, the essentials of Advaita Vedanta using the coveted question-answer method.

Translations

Tattvabodha was translated into English long, long ago—in 1877—by one L. Simha (from Sialkot), says Karl Potter.[10] There was also a Hindi translation by Ram Swarup Sharma, in very old style and without any detail, and published in 1897. Potter cites Belvelkar[11] and says that *Tattvabodha* may not be Śaṁkara's work at all. However, Potter prefers to give a gist of the book under Śaṁkara.

We have not just translated the book here. Using the work, we have tried a detailed narration, which the reader may find useful.

References

1. Gospel, p. 453

2. Complete Works, Vol. 2, pp. 98-99

3. Complete Works, Vol. 1, pp. 6-7

4. Complete Works, Vol. 5, pp. 81-2

5. Complete Works, Vol. 5, p. 299

6. Gospel, p. 593

7. see Sri Ramakrishna the Great Master, pp. 439-444

8. Complete Works, Vol. 2, p. 252

9. Complete Works, Vol. 5, p. 297

10. See Karl Potter, *Encyclopedia of Indian Philosophies* (Delhi: Motilal Banarsidass Pvt Ltd, 1981), Vol. 3, p. 331

11. Karl Potter, op.cit.

Insights into Vedanta

TATTVABODHA

Chapter 1

ADORATION OF THE TEACHER

Benediction

There is a beautiful mantra in the *Śvetāśvatara Upaniṣad* (6.23): 'Spiritual truths mentioned in the Vedas will reveal themselves to one who has intense devotion to God, and has equal devotion to the spiritual teacher also.' The guru or spiritual preceptor has an exalted position in Indian thought. The guru is the helmsman. The guru is the real guide. The guru is like a signpost to Light. He unlocks the gates to knowledge and, thereby, removes the ignorance of the seeker. The guru is the destroyer of ignorance. Guru is God Himself. All scriptures and saints are of one voice in praising the spiritual teacher. Sri Ramakrishna repeatedly says that one achieves everything if one has faith in the words of the teacher. So the guru is vital to spiritual life.

Like most other traditional Indian works, *Tattvabodha* too begins with a benedictory verse—the adoration of the teacher. It is imperative to salute the spiritual teacher before undertaking any new venture. Such a tradition is prevalent in other spiritual traditions also.

Along with the guru, the supreme Being, or the chosen deity of the writer, is also saluted. Such an invocation is intended to seek the Lord's grace and blessings for success in the endeavour as also to surrender the fruit of one's deeds to Him. The author or the one who ventures into a new project is necessarily a spiritual seeker and his or her sole concern is to know the Supreme. In the Indian tradition, anything that is done is done for one's spiritual benefit alone. And all works lead to that one supreme goal if done in the right spirit.

In *Tattvabodha*, we find an invocation to the guru but not one to the Lord. This is in order, because it is an Advaitic text, and Advaita gives little importance to gods and goddesses. For, according to this system, there's only one Reality, called Brahman.

The Benedictory Verse

वासुदेवेन्द्र–योगीन्द्रं नत्वा ज्ञानप्रदं गुरुम् ।

मुमुक्षूणां हितार्थाय तत्त्वबोधोऽभिधीयते ॥

Vāsudevendra-yogindraṁ
natvā jñānapradam gurum;
Mumukṣūṇāṁ hitārthāya
tattvabodho'bhidhīyate.

Yogindram to the greatest of yogis; *gurum* (and) the teacher *vāsudevendram* called Vāsudevendra; *jñānapradam* (who is) the bestower of knowledge; *natvā* having bowed down; *hitārthāya* for the benefit of; *mumukṣūṇām* the seekers of liberation; *tattvabodhaḥ* the book called *Tattvabodha; abhidhīyate* is being written or prescribed.

Having bowed down to my revered teacher, Vāsudevendra, who is the greatest of yogis and the bestower of knowledge, I write this book called *Tattvabodha* for the benefit of those who are seeking liberation.

The Guru

In this invocatory verse, the author of *Tattvabodha* calls his guru 'the greatest of yogis,' *yogīndra*. Tradition says that Śaṁkara's guru was Śrī Govindapāda. Here he is called Vāsudevendra. So it is doubtful if the world-renowned Śaṁkara himself wrote this book. But it is also true that poetic nuances can change Govinda into Vāsudeva, because both are names of Śri Kṛṣṇa. *'Indra'* stands for the greatest. If Śaṁkara is not the author of the work, then some other saint must be saluting his own guru by the name Vāsudevendra.

For good or bad, ancient Indian authors have always tried to remain incognito. All their works were offerings to the Lord and for the good of the world. In their zeal to hide themselves absolutely, these holy writers did not even leave hints about themselves. Hence we do not know who the authors of most of our scriptures were.

Anyway, the author salutes his spiritual teacher and begins writing the book.

Knowledge

The guru has been called *jñānaprada* or 'giver of knowledge.' *Jñāna* means knowledge. How does the guru teach? There are no set methods for the spiritual teacher. He may use any method to destroy his disciple's ignorance. The one thing that drives the teacher to help the disciple is compassion.

In the *Chāndogya Upaniṣad* ((4.3.9), there is a beautiful story about devotion to the guru. Satyakāma was a poor woman's son. Jābālā, the woman, was a maidservant. Once, the little boy had the desire to learn. He asked his mother: 'Mother, I wish to become a novice (*brāhmacārī*). Tell me my family lineage.' Jābālā told him: 'My child, I do not know your ancestry. In my youth I was preoccupied in many household duties, and with taking care of guests, when you were born. Call yourself Satyakāma Jābāla, by my name. That will do.'

Satyakāma, armed with that information, arrived at Gautama's hermitage. Gautama was a famous teacher of those days. Seeing the boy approach him to be his disciple, Gautama asked him the natural question: 'To which family lineage do you belong, dear boy?' This boy, surprisingly enough, repeated the exact words of his mother. The sage remarked wisely: 'Ah, you are definitely a brāhmaṇa. This is because, none but the brāhmaṇa can make such a damaging statement about himself.'

Gautama initiated Satyakāma, and gave him a duty. In those days, the spiritual masters were such great souls that they had their own ways of teaching their disciples. Gautama wanted a new way of teaching his disciple. He wanted the boy to learn everything from nature. So he gave the boy 400 lean and starving cows and asked him to graze them. The boy thought that since his teacher had accepted him, he will serve his master. In what way? Until the herd of cows became a thousand, he would not return to the master.

So Satyakāma lived a number of years in the forest. During those years, the boy learnt numerous truths. One day, the bull of his herd told him: 'Satyakāma, take us back to the teacher's house now. We are a thousand.' Satyakāma said: 'Revered Sir, I shall do so.' Why did Satyakāma address the bull 'Revered Sir'? He understood that it was the deity of *vāyu* or air, which was addressing him through the bull. Vāyu taught him one quarter of Brahman. Then the fire god Agni taught him another quarter. The third quarter of Brahman was taught by a swan. Finally, the fourth quarter was taught to Satyakāma by a *madgu* (diving bird). Thus two birds and two deities taught Satyakāma the four quarters of Brahman, says this Upaniṣad.

When Satyakāma returned to his guru's hermitage, he was an illumined soul, and the teacher declared him so.

Knowledge can be both secular (*aparā*) or purely spiritual (*parā*). The *Muṇḍaka Upaniṣad* gives details about which one is *parā* knowledge, and which ones are *aparā*. It says that of all types of knowledge, Self-knowledge is the highest, and is the foundation of all other types of knowledge (*sarva-vidyā-pratiṣtha*). This is because, the Upaniṣad says that by knowing the Self, we know everything. The *Śvetāśvatara Upaniṣad* (5.1) says that knowledge is nectarine, and brings immortality.

It is the spiritual knowledge that destroys ignorance (*ajñāna*) enveloping our soul. Our true nature, the Atman, is hidden behind this veil of ignorance. Knowledge destroys ignorance and liberates us from limitations and suffering. This liberation is the goal of Advaita. Aruṇi, the illumined father, tells his brilliant son Śvetaketu that beings come from Truth, live here as worms, insects, tigers, lions, and so on, and think that this alone is true. They have to return to Truth but they are ignorant of it. In order that ignorance is removed, one should know who one is, and hence Aruṇi gives the best teaching to his son when he says: 'You are That.' This dialogue is in the *Chāndogya Upaniṣad* (6.10.2-3). Such is the teacher, who worries about the disciple and helps him get liberation.

Prada means 'giver'. The guru is the bestower of knowledge inasmuch as he paves the way for the removal of ignorance.

The Seeker of Liberation

Several vital concepts of Advaita have been mentioned in this verse. The first of them is the concept of guru or spiritual teacher. The second is *jñāna,* and the third is *mumukṣutvam* or the desire for liberation. *Mokṣa* means absolute freedom from ignorance and limitations. One who desires to attain *mokṣa* is a *mumukṣu.* The quality of desiring for liberation is *mumukṣutvam.* This book will discuss this concept of liberation further in subsequent verses.

The author remarks here—at the very outset—that this book is for seekers of liberation. All of us are seeking liberation—in one way or another. Knowingly or unknowingly, all of us are wanting to be free from limitations and suffering. Most of us do not know the process, while some can know by the grace of God. By the grace of God we get hold of books on Vedanta, or meet with monks and nuns who are leading higher lives, and they show us the path.

Thus all of us are seeking liberation from suffering, ignorance and limitations. After reading books on Vedanta, we must do that consciously—this is what is expected of us.

Tattvabodha

Tattva is Reality and *bodha* is enlightenment. Unable to describe God who is beyond thought and words, the Vedas have attributed certain positive qualities to Him or It. However, the best way they think of describing Reality is by simply calling it *tat* or 'That'. *Tattva* means 'about Reality'. The word *tattva* has a few other meanings, as evident in the case of Sāṅkhya philosophy, which says that *tattvas* mean the 24 cosmic principles.[1]

Advaita Vedanta is clear; it says, 'Know that *you* are the *Tat* or Truth, and be free.' When we say 'I am; you are, it is,' etc, we are wrong. When we say 'I am That,' we are right. This book is meant to train us for attaining that knowledge.

Why Should We Be Vedantins?

Every earnest student of Vedanta should read Swami Vivekananda's lecture titled 'Freedom of the Soul'.[2] Delivered in London on 5 November 1896, this lecture—quoted in part below—gives us a clear idea why we should be Vedantins.

> It is weakness, says the Vedanta, which is the cause of all misery in this world. Weakness is the one cause of suffering. We become miserable because we are weak. We suffer because we are weak. We die because we are weak. Where there is nothing to weaken us, there is no death nor sorrow. We are miserable through delusion. Give up the delusion, and the whole thing vanishes. It is plain and simple indeed. Through all these philosophical discussions and tremendous mental gymnastics, we come to this one religious idea, the simplest in the whole world.
>
> The monistic Vedanta is the simplest form in which you can put truth. ... I have reason to believe that it [monism] is the only remedy there is.[3]

Suggested Reading:

1. 'Discipleship', by Swami Vivekananda. [In his *Complete Works*, Vol. 8, pp. 106-121].
2. 'Guru or Spiritual Teacher', by Swami Gambhirananda.

3. Swami Vivekananda, *Jnana Yoga* [in his *Complete Works*, Vol. 1.]

4. Śaṁkara, *Viveka Cūḍāmaṇi*, verses 56-62, and 69-82.

References

1. Sāṅkhya of Kapila is the oldest philosophical system of India. Elementary ideas of this school have been included in the book.

2. Complete Works, Vol. 1, pp. 188-202

3. Complete Works, pp. 198-9.

Chapter 2

TEACHER AS SUPREME BRAHMAN

Tests of the Teachers

The first story is from Baghdad. Abu Bakr Shibli was an important officer near Baghdad. Circumstances made him think deeply about life and its impermanence. He had heard about Junaid, the great spiritual teacher of Baghdad. He ardently wished to be Junaid's disciple. But was it easy to please the teacher? After much effort, Shibli got audience with the spiritual master. The teacher saw the young man, and it was moments before Junaid decided that here was a potential jewel. Yet Junaid was not to be pleased easily. 'So you have come here to be my disciple. Good. But to be my disciple is difficult. And to love both God and the world is not possible. The world is too much in you. For the next one year, go about the streets and beg food.'

That was a shock for Shibli because he had been an officer, and to beg on the streets was painful. But he obeyed. He would somehow manage to beg every day, but would get nothing at all. He would return empty handed, but full of pain over the insults hurled by the public at him. One year of such an ordeal, and then there was another test waiting. 'The soul has to be purged before it can become God's companion. Before entering the spiritual world, go and beg pardon from all those whom you might have insulted while in office,' said Junaid. Shibli thought that was easy. But it took him more than a year's time to complete the task. When he returned, Junaid was there again, asking him to beg once more. This time Shibli did this gladly. He would get heaps of food this time, but he would give everything away.

The test was over. 'These were not tests but purging your soul. Now you are ready to receive the Lord,' said Junaid.

'Can you Beg?'

The second story, told using the exact words from the *Life of Swami Vivekananda* by his Eastern and Western disciples, is about Hathras Railway Station on the way to Hardwar. Swami Vivekananda sits there, evidently rather weary and in need of food. His figure catches the eye of the Assistant Stationmaster, Sharatchandra Gupta. After an exchange of greetings, Sharat asks him, 'Swamiji, are you hungry?' The Swami replies, 'Yes, I am.' 'Then please come to my quarters,' says Sharat. The Swami asks him, with the simplicity of a boy, 'But what will you give me to eat?' Promptly quoting from a Persian poem, Sharat replies, 'O beloved, you have come to my house! I shall prepare the most delicious dish for you with the flesh of my heart.' The Swami is delighted to hear this reply and accepts the invitation.

Sharat says, 'Sir, teach me wisdom.' The Swami answers him with a Bengali song, 'If you wish to attain knowledge, go and cover your moon face with ashes; otherwise find your own way.' Sharat immediately replies, 'Swamiji, I am at your service. I am ready to renounce everything and follow you.' Saying these words he disappears, to return divested of his official clothes, with ashes on his face. 'Here I am, Swamiji; what do you want me to do?' Later, the monk demands, 'Can you beg from door to door?' 'Yes,' comes the bold reply. The Swami is greatly pleased to see his courage and determination. He asks Sharat: 'Then take my begging-bowl and go and beg food for us from the porters of the station.' No sooner is the order given than Sharat goes to beg from his own subordinates. Having collected some food he brings it to the Swami, who in turn blesses him heartily, and accepts him as his disciple. This story, retold from the life of Swamiji in those very words, is about the life of Swami Sadananda.

'One Only'

The Infinite or Supreme is Itself the guru according to the Advaitin.

'Advaita' means 'one only.' That One alone exists, and the rest is all superimposition on that One, owing to ignorance. Advaitins say that Reality cannot be explained or understood, but *experienced* and realized. This is because, when we try to *understand* It, we become That.

In spite of this so-called difficulty, we must somehow explain It. The reason is, we cannot experience that Brahman or Reality all on a sudden. Discipline, mental purity, study, and so on are necessary. In order to start striving towards that goal, we need to hear about the Truth, cogitate and understand It intellectually, discover that we are leading false lives, and strive to become true. These three steps comprise the sadhana of Advaita. They have technical names and mean hearing about the Truth (*śravaṇa*), thinking about it (*manana*), and contemplating on it (*nididhyāsana*). 'Hearing' is mentioned because in olden times there were no books. Further, spiritual truths are best heard.

How to hear about the Truth if someone who knows It doesn't tell us? We must therefore approach the teacher with reverence in order to hear about the truths of spiritual life. Gurus are not easily available. The aspirant should strive and pray, say the scriptures, for the guru. If the aspirant is sincere, the guru will come at the right time.

The Vedas: Our Eternal Teachers

The Vedas are the experiences of illumined sages. These sages have realized that Brahman is the only Reality and everything else is a mirage. They have, fortunately enough for us, recorded their experiences. It is as if Brahman Itself has revealed some of It to us! So Vedas are called 'truths born of Brahman.' There were times when the Vedas were heard and understood; there were no books.

Words are powerhouses. How is that? When we listen to some word, we think we have understood it. The meaning is conveyed, we say. The meaning is conveyed because, we assume that the letters of the word were in order. But words by themselves cannot convey meaning. The same thing may have one word as its signifier now, and another a hundred years later. The thing, however, remains. There is an eternal connection between name and form. So there should be something behind the word, which conveys meaning. That something should be permanent. That something permanent is called the potency of the word. That is called *sphoṭa,* and this power enlightens the listener about the meaning or import of the word. While ordinary words awaken ordinary meanings, extraordinary words awaken extraordinary meanings. The Vedas are not only extraordinary but are supernatural. So the Vedas are not mere words but potential powerhouses. Hence the Vedas are called 'Word-Brahman' (*śabda brahman*). The Vedas are a valid means of knowledge, accepted by all positive schools of Indian philosophy.

It is through the Vedas alone, then, that we can know Brahman initially, before experiencing It. We cannot experience Brahman with our five senses, we cannot guess It, but we can read about it in the Vedas. So the Vedas or *Śabda* is the best means of knowledge to know Brahman. Hence the Veda, the manifest form of Brahman, is our first guru. This knowledge, however, is indirect (*parokṣa*). Experience alone is the highest knowledge and that is direct (*aparokṣa*). Through experience alone can we be liberated, not otherwise. Sri Ramakrishna used to say that books are only directors. They can never lead us to the threshold of Truth. Wringing a book about rainfall will never give us even a drop of water. If we think that we are learned because we have read a few books, we are worthless. Mere punditry is of no consequence.

Therefore the guru should be resorted to, say our scriptures. Who is the guru? He is a personification of realization and knowledge. He is pure. He is compassionate.

There is a problem here. If all that exists is One Reality alone, who will be the teacher, and to whom? Who will learn from whom? This is true from the absolute standpoint. Some have criticized Śankara, saying that if the world is unreal, whom is he teaching? This great sage did not deny the world in the relative sense. So in the relative sense everything is true. When we are individuals, when we think we are enjoying or suffering, when we think we are the doers of all our deeds and enjoyers of all our fruits of action, we are in ignorance. This is the chief problem. In order that we should overcome this problem, the Infinite Itself, which becomes Īśvara, comes as the guru and tells us about knowledge, Brahman, etc. This it does through the Vedas. There is also a second option. We hear about Brahman, and about the Vedas themselves, from illumined personalities. These illumined personalities, because they have attained Brahman, are Brahman themselves.

Will We Become Brahman?

If our guru is Brahman Itself due to the attainment of knowledge, shall we too become Brahman alone? The Vedantins reply: 'You will not *become* Brahman. You are Brahman Itself already! Ignorance (*ajñāna*) has enveloped knowledge. So you think you are limited.' The central concept of Vedanta is that one whose ignorance disappears and knowledge manifests itself will become Brahman Itself.[2] We become what we really are.

Swami Vivekananda says: 'Our reality, therefore, consists in the universal and not in the limited. These are old delusions, however comfortable they are, to think that we are little limited beings, constantly changing.'[1]

What about our Individuality?

The question then comes about our individuality. What will happen to our individuality? Will we become like the thin air when we attain Brahman? Will we become like burnt camphor or water vapour? This doubt comes to all of us, ordinary aspirants.

Swami Vivekananda replies:

> People are frightened when they are told that they are the Universal Being, everywhere present: through everything you work, through every foot you move, through every lip you talk, through every heart you feel.
>
> People are frightened when they are told this. They will again and again ask you if they are not going to keep their individuality. What is individuality? I should like to see it. A baby has no moustache; when he grows to be a man, perhaps he has a moustache and beard. His individuality would be lost if it were in the body. If I lose one eye, or if I lose one of my hands, my individuality would be lost if it were in the body. Then, a drunkard should not give up drinking because he would lose his individuality. No man ought to change it for fear of this.
>
> There is no individuality except in the Infinite. That is the only condition which does not change. ... We are not individuals yet. We are struggling towards individuality and that is the Infinite, that is the real nature of man. He alone lives whose life is in the whole universe, and the more we concentrate our lives on limited things, the faster we go towards death.[3]

Therefore in order to become true individuals we should study Vedanta and practise it. The first step towards this is approaching the guru. This is the theme of the second verse.

नित्यं शुद्धं निराभासं निराकारं निरंजनम् ।
नित्यबोधं चिदानन्दं गुरुं ब्रह्म नमाम्यहम् ॥

Nityaṁ śuddhaṁ nirābhāsaṁ
Nirākāraṁ nirañjanam|
Nityabodhaṁ cidānandaṁ
Guruṁ brahma namāmyaham||

Nityam eternal, *śuddham* pure, *nirābhāsam* without false appearances, *nirākāram* formless, *niranjanam* stainless, *nityabodham,* ever-knowing, *cidānandam* full of consciousness and bliss, *gurum,* the teacher, *brahma* who is Brahman, *namāmyaham,* I salute.

I salute Brahman in the form of the guru, who is eternal, ever-pure, without false appearances, formless, stainless, ever-knowing, full of consciousness, and blissful.

Nityam

Nityam, 'eternal' or 'everlasting'. That which does not change in any way, at any period of time, is *nityam.* Time is a human concept; rather, a concept of living beings. Brahman, the only Reality, is beyond time and space. Indians had discovered long ago that time and space are relative concepts, creation is only a projection of what was there earlier, etc. So in the case of Brahman, past, present, and future are meaningless. Eternal also means that the highest conception human beings can have about something is that it *is* there. Incidentally, all the so-called qualities which the Vedas use to describe Brahman are only used to give some idea about Reality to human minds. Brahman is beyond thought.

Śuddham

'Pure.' There is only one Reality, nothing else. That Reality is all-pervasive, everlasting. It is therefore beyond all concepts like purity, impurity, etc. What is impurity? Impurity is desire, and its consequent sin. God is beyond desire because nothing but He exists. So He is pure.

Nirābhāsam

'*Ābhāsa*' means 'false appearance'. *Nirābhāsa* is its opposite. All that we perceive through the five senses is unreal (*mithyā*). Now, since there is only one Reality, is Brahman appearing as this universe then? Yes and no! Owing to *ajñāna* or ignorance, we are superimposing name and form on Reality.

Such a super-imposition has been called *adhyāsa*. Superimpositon has been defined wonderfully well by Śankara, who says that superimposition is seeing something which is not there (*atasmin tad-buddiḥ*). There is no snake in that dark corner, but we become scared that there is one. When light is brought there, we see that it was only a piece of rope. This is superimposition of something on something else. Another word nearer to superimposition is *vivarta* or false appearance. *Vivarta* means confusing rope for a snake, Brahman for the cosmos. The cosmos, according to Vedantists, is not an actual creation, since in the absolute state it is not there. It is a *vivarta* of Brahman. In spite of superimposing so many worlds on Brahman, He or It isn't affected in the least. So It is *nirābhāsam*.

The great Advaita text, *Vivekacūḍāmaṇī,* says: 'What appears in ignorance as true does not remain so after discrimination but becomes one with the Reality—not separate from It. So this world is nothing but the Atman, just as we do not find the snake in the rope when we know the real nature of the rope.'[4]

Nirākāram

'Formless.' Name and form are attributes given by living beings to Brahman. The Advaitic concept of Reality, which we have repeated so many times by now, is that Brahman alone is the Reality. It is beyond thought and words. So It is formless. Ignorant people say they do not believe in God because He cannot be seen by them. 'Where is He?' they ask. It is difficult to understand that discipline is needed to know higher truths, let alone achievements like passing exams. Sri Ramakrishna's words are very aptly quoted here:

> No one can say with finality that God is only 'this' and nothing else. He is formless and again He has forms. For the bhakta [devotee] he assumes forms. But He is formless for the jñāni, that is, for him who looks upon the world as a mere dream. ... Do you know what I mean? Think of Brahman, Existence-

Knowledge-Bliss Absolute, as a shoreless ocean. What He is cannot be described. Who will describe Him? He who would do so disappears. He cannot find his 'I' anymore.[5]

Niranjanam

Anjanam means 'stain'. That which is stainless is *niranjanam.* What can stain That which is alone is?

Nityabodham

'Eternally known.' *Bodha* means enlightenment, awareness, etc. Brahman is eternally known—because It is not an object of knowledge. It is knowledge itself.

Cidānandam

Brahman cannot be described. But three terms have been used to give some clue about Its nature. These are, being (*sat*), consciousness (*cit*) and bliss (*ānanda*). Here Brahman has been called *cit* and *ānanda.*

Guruṁ Brahma

That Reality, which gives knowledge through the Vedas, teaches through the human medium also. And finally, It teaches through one's own mind, for according to Sri Ramakrishna, the mind alone will become the teacher in time. So Brahman Itself is called the guru. In spite of the Vedas' being our eternal teachers, we seek human gurus and such gurus should essentially have three qualities according to Vedanta: (a) they should be well-versed in the Vedas (*śrotriya*); (b) sinless (*avṛjina*); and (c) not conquered by desires (*akāma-hata*). That is, they should be illumined souls.

An illumined soul, according to Vedanta, is called a *jīvanmukta*, 'free-while-alive'. He or she may discard the body at any moment, but some retain it in order to teach the ignorant regarding spiritual truths. Sri Ramakrishna says that they retain their egos of knowledge. Such people become gurus. When they desire to drop off the last bondage, the body, they do so, and become liberated, *videha-muktas*.

In this verse, Śaṁkara is saluting one such guru, his own being Govindapāda. He calls the guru Brahman Itself because, but for the body, there is nothing that can separate the illumined soul (*brahma-jñāni*) and the Reality.

Namāmi Aham

'I bow down.' The author of our work bows down to his spiritual master who has been eulogised with so many qualifications. Surrendering to the guru is the first and foremost means to attain the highest. Guru is the guide, the leader, and the sure director to spiritual illumination. And he guides souls only out of compassion, as he does not need anything from the world at all. In the *Bhagavadgītā*, we see Arjuna becoming confused and assailed by numerous depressing thoughts. When he surrenders to Lord Kṛṣṇa, he is guided well.

Conclusion

In the first two verses, several important Vedantic terms have been mentioned: guru, Brahman, *jñāna, ajñāna, mumukṣu, mokṣa, jivanmukti, nirākāra, nitya, satcitānanda* etc. Further, we have discussed *vivarta, adhyāsa, mukti,* and so on also.

After having saluted the guru, which is essential for any endeavour to succeed, the author begins with the subject of his work.

Suggested Reading

1. *Vivekacūḍāmaṇī*, verses 475 to 500.

References

1. See Complete Works, Vol. 2, p. 79.
2. *Brahma-veda brahmaiva bhavati*
3. Complete Works, Vol. 2, pp. 79-80.
4. Śankara, *Vivekacūḍāmaṇī*, verse 388.
5. Gospel , p.148.

Chapter 3

ABOUT THE WORK

The Four Questions

After the invocatory verses, Śaṁkara, the putative author of *Tattvabodha,* begins with the subject proper. There are a few questions involved in the writing of any work. Hindu scriptures are extremely careful about this particular point. So they ask themselves: (a) Who is the book for? (b) What is its subject matter? (c) What is the connection between the book, and the idea that the reader is searching for? (d) What is the use of reading this book? These are the four questions asked. Nowadays we see a wild variety of books landing on bookshelves. Books come and go, depending on the worth of information they carry. Bestsellers of today are nonentities tomorrow. Some books, like the Bible, *Gītā*, and others, are everlasting. Then there are books which carry value for hundreds of years and then disappear. Reading such books is not

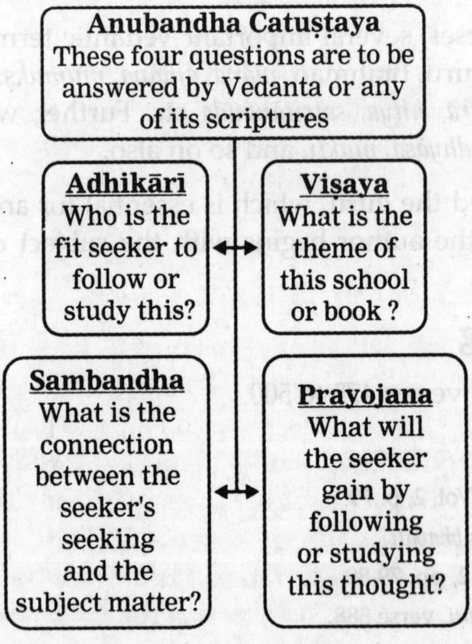
Anubandha Catuṣṭaya
These four questions are to be answered by Vedanta or any of its scriptures
Adhikārī
Who is the fit seeker to follow or study this?
Viṣaya
What is the theme of this school or book ?
Sambandha
What is the connection between the seeker's seeking and the subject matter?
Prayojana
What will the seeker gain by following or studying this thought?

for mere reading only; such books are for practice. The authors therefore anticipate ideal qualities in the aspirants.

Any Sanskrit classic will address itself with these questions at the outset. These four questions are technically called *'anubandha catuṣṭaya'* (the four pre-conditions). The Sanskrit terms used for the four questions are the following: (a) the fit seeker is called *adhikārī;* (b) the subject matter is called *viṣaya;* (c) the connection between the book and the seeker's desire to know is *saṁbandha;* and (d) the use of the book is called *prayojana.*

Adhikārī, The Suitable Seeker

Sadānanda Yogīndra, the author of *Vedānta Sāra*, a beautiful prosework on the fundamental tenets of Advaita Vedanta, gives a description of the fit seeker. He says: 'An aspirant for Advaita knowledge (i) is one who has read the Vedas quite well, and has understood them more or less; (ii) has performed daily, obligatory and expiatory actions with devotion (see chapter 47 for details about these three types of action) and, therefore, has become pure; (iii) has carefully avoided desire-born deeds and sinful deeds. Moreover, the aspirant has developed the faculties of discrimination between the real and the unreal, and dispassion for the unreal. Having repeatedly exercised the faculty of concentration on the Real, he has subdued the senses. Finally, he has an earnest and pulsating desire for liberation. This desire is likened to having burning coal on his head.

Not all of us are such ideal seekers. Some of us have not even begun our spiritual journey. What shall we do then? Though the ideal is such, if we are sincere and eager to know, we are welcomed by scriptures to study them and emulate ideas. As we go on with our struggle, the qualities like dispassion will become manifest in us soon, and they will make us *mumukṣus* or seekers of liberation from limitations. Sri Ramakrishna assures us: 'Let me tell you that the realization of the Self is possible for all, without any exception.'[1]

The preparatory steps towards Vedantic realization are: to seek holy company, read sacred works, perform good deeds without attachment for the fruits of such deeds, renounce evil and all that we can think of as being obstacles to sadhana, and, have the sword of discrimination always at hand. Through all such preparations, the mind becomes finely tuned to higher ideas and ideals. At present, owing to the world being too much in our minds, it cannot resonate to higher tunes. It needs purity to comprehend such higher ideas. This is the idea of the present verse.

साधन–चतुष्टय–सम्पन्न–अधिकारीणां मोक्ष–साधनभूतं
तत्त्वविवेक–प्रकारं वक्ष्यामः॥

Sādhana-catuṣṭaya-sampanna-adhikārīṇāṁ mokṣa-sādhana-bhūtāṁ tattva-viveka-prakāraṁ vakṣyāmaḥ.

Adhikārīṇāṁ the fit seekers; *sādhana catuṣṭaya-sampanna* (who are) rich in the four sadhanas; *mokṣa-sādhana-bhūtāṁ* those aids to liberation; *tattva-viveka-prakāraṁ* which are like the knowledge of the Self; *vakṣyāmaḥ* we shall speak of.

We shall narrate the method of attainment of Self-knowledge that is followed by those able aspirants, who are armed with the four sadhanas, which leads to liberation.

Tattva-viveka Prakāra

Tattva is 'Reality'. *Viveka* is 'discrimination', and *prakāra* is the 'method'. All the three terms together would mean 'method of attaining Self-knowledge.' As we saw earlier, knowledge can be of various kinds: from secular to spiritual. But that which liberates us from the hold of suffering is alone called true knowledge.

How to attain that knowledge of the Self is the theme of this book, and of Vedanta in general. In this verse, the author mentions the first of the four basic guidelines or principles: he mentions the fit aspirant, *adhikāri*. We have discussed *adhikāri* before. An *adhikāri* is a *mumukṣu*, who is full of dispassion for the world and discriminates between the Real and the unreal. He performs his daily devotions with earnestness, studies scriptures with devotion, concentrates his mind on the Eternal Self, and is free from blemishes.

The second issue raised in the beginning of this chapter was, what is the subject matter of this book, or of Vedanta itself? It is Self-knowledge or Brahman-knowledge, which leads to liberation from suffering. The third question is about the connection between the seeker's desire to know Vedanta, and the book's teaching it. Yes, what the aspirant seeks is what the book teaches. Finally, the use of studying this book, or Vedanta in general. It is liberation. May be one does not attain *mokṣa* by merely reading the book, but one attains it through sadhana after approaching the guru. This book tells us how to do it.

Thus the *anubandha catuṣṭaya* or the fourfold questions regarding the validity of this work are taken care of.

Mokṣa Sādhana

Mokṣa is liberation from limitations and that is the goal of Advaita. Liberation can be attained only through the attainment of Self-knowledge, and by no other means, says Advaita. Without Atman knowledge, there can be no *mokṣa*. According to Indian thought, there are four goals of life: Righteousness *(dharma)*, Wealth *(artha)*, Progeny *(kāma)*, and Liberation *(mokṣa)*. For the householder, the first three are the initial ideals, but finally, the last one is the ideal for all. A householder should follow dharma and, through righteous means, earn wealth to serve those in the other three ways of life, and have able progeny to continue the lineage. After the son is able enough to carry on the duties of the household, the father should retire to the forest and strive to attain liberation. This is the grand scheme of Hinduism.

The four *anubandhas* or questions of Self-knowledge, mentioned in the beginning of this chapter, are aids to the attainment of *mokṣa.* Of the four, the qualifications of an *adhikāri* or fit aspirant are important. It is only by practising all that the aspirant is told to, that we too can become fit seekers of liberation. Especially, the four sadhanas to be mentioned now.

Adhikāri

The fit aspirant (*mumukṣu*) for liberation is the *adhikāri.* The forthcoming chapter describes the preparations undertaken by the aspirant to come to such a stage in detail. All of us may read Vedantic works. All of us may be interested to know what Vedanta, or Advaita Vedanta, is. But not all of us have that tremendous hankering for liberation as the fit aspirant has. The aspirant, *adhikāri,* is so burning with the desire for liberation that, the moment his guru instructs him, he attains illumination; that is, his ignorance vanishes and he attains Brahman-knowledge.

Sādhana Catuṣṭaya

We discussed *anubandha catuṣṭaya—adhikārī, viṣaya, sambandha and prayojana.* These four pertain to the book, or to Vedanta itself. Now there is the *sadhana catuṣṭaya:* the four sadhanas of the aspirant. These are discrimination (*viveka*), dispassion (*vairāgya*), self-control (*śama, dama,* etc) and hankering for liberation (*mumukṣatvam*). These will be elaborated in the next chapter.

Recapitulation:

a. The spiritual teacher (guru) gets paramount importance in Advaita Vedanta.

b. *Moksa* (or *mukti*) is the only goal of Advaita Vedanta. *Mokṣa* means freedom: freedom from limitations, suffering and bondage.

c. *Jñāna* is the only means to the attainment of freedom.

d. *Jñāna* is not acquired: it is already there. It's covered by *ajñāna* or ignorance. Ignorance of the sincere seeker goes through sadhana and guru's grace.

e. The Reality is only One, called Brahman; all else is illusion, born of ignorance.

f. *Ajñāna* has made us think of ourselves as limited, and has created all this illusion. We are That alone.

g. *Ajñāna* covers *jñāna* and by discrimination, dispassion, etc, it goes.

h. Some sadhanas are needed to overcome ignorance. These sadhanas will be discussed in the future.

References

1. Gospel, p. 256.

Chapter 4

THE FOURFOLD QUALIFICATION

Jump for Life!

Chandrashekhar Azad was one of the famous freedom fighters of India. Anyone who sees his photograph will be thrilled to see this muscular man, twisting his moustache. His dictionary did not have the word 'fear'. The story is told of him that one evening he was relaxing on his terrace. A young widow from the neighbourhood came and stood there. For a moment Azad could not understand her purpose. Suddenly, when she began to speak, he understood that she had some bad intention. The woman was standing near the stairs. Azad saw that he could not get away by that way. Therefore, in order to save himself, he jumped out of the terrace and landed on the ground, several feet below. Perhaps he wounded himself. But for him it was better than being disturbed by a woman.

Azad was particular in telling his fellow freedom fighters to keep away women and lead pure lives. If a freedom fighter feels that purity is needed in order to fight, what to speak of those freedom fighters fighting for the freedom of their Atman!

The Necessity of Practice

'The fact is that one does not feel the longing to know or see God as long as one wants to enjoy worldly enjoyments. ... The soul becomes restless for God when one is through with the enjoyment of worldly things. Then a person has only one thought—how to realize God. He listens to whatever anyone says to him about God,' says Sri Ramakrishna.[1]

Worldliness and godliness cannot go together. One has to be renounced for the sake of the other. Vedanta helps us remove the incrustations of ages. The so-called individual in us goes, or becomes cosmic—so to say. However, in order to attain to such an exalted state, in order to be freed from all limitations, in order to be the Truth itself and enjoy everlasting bliss, certain qualities or qualifications are necessary. When ordinary secular knowledge demands qualifications, why not supernatural knowledge? What these qualifications are, is being discussed in this chapter.

Vivekananda on Practice

The qualifications for this supreme attainment are simple. They do not need much effort. We struggle so much to pass exams. To attain Self-realization, illumined souls assure us, is not that difficult at all! Swami Vivekananda says that spiritual illumination 'shines of itself in a pure heart, and, as such, it is not something acquired from without: but to attain this purity of heart means long struggle and constant practice. ... But such truths never appear in the mind of an uncultured and wild savage. All these go to prove that hard Tapasya, or the practice of austerities in the shape of devout contemplation and constant study of a subject is at the root of all illumination in its respective spheres.'[2]

The Effort

What are those practices which lead to such mental purity? The aspirant follows all the six disciplines that have been discussed in the previous chapter. Through all such noble acts the aspirant becomes qualified to practice a set of four higher spiritual practices. These higher practices are called qualifications and are mentioned in the following verse:

साधन–चतुष्टयं किम्?

नित्यानित्यवस्तुविवेकः ।

इहामुत्रफलभोग–विरागः।

शमादिषट्कसम्पत्तिः।

मुमुक्षुत्त्वम् च इति ॥

Sadhāna-catuṣṭayaṁ kim?
Nityānitya-vastu-vivekaḥ| Ihāmutra-phala-bhoga-virāgaḥ|
Śamādi ṣaṭka-sampattiḥ| mumukṣutvam ca iti||

Sadhāna-catuṣṭayaṁ kim? What are the four spiritual practices? *Nityānitya-vastu-vivekaḥ* discrimination between the eternal and the non-eternal; *Iha* here; *amutra* hereafter *phala* fruit (of actions) *bhoga* desire to enjoy *virāgah* renunciation; *Śamādi* self-control etc; *saṭkasampattiḥ* six treasures.

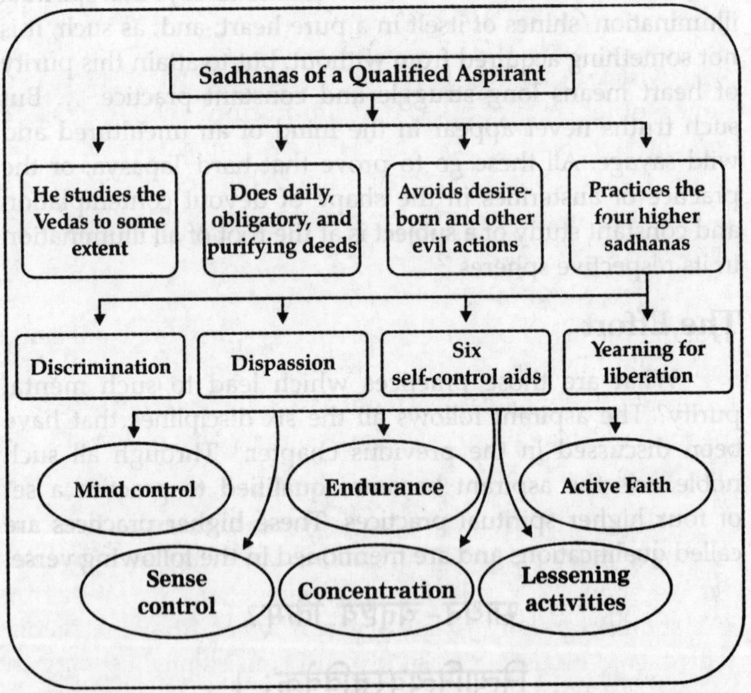

What are the four sadhanas of the aspirant?

Discrimination between the real and the unreal; renunciation of all the fruits of action leading to enjoyment here and elsewhere; the six treasures like self-control; and longing for liberation.

In this section, Śaṁkara has mentioned four sadhanas for the aspirant seeking Advaitic realization. These are: (1) Discrimination; (2) Dispassion; (3) The six treasures like self-control; and (4) longing for liberation.

Please note that each of the sadhanas will be taken up one after the other by the author in the forthcoming chapters. We shall, however, discuss them here. Why are these termed higher spiritual practices? They are higher because their practice requires a trained mind.

Nityānitya-Vastu-Vivekaḥ

Nitya is 'eternal', *anitya* is its opposite; *vastus* are sense-objects; *viveka* is discrimination. The first ever qualification of a seeker of the Self is discrimination. He should know what is lasting and what is not. When we intend seeking something that is eternal, we should not, at the same time, hold on to that which is transitory.

All knowledge that our five sense organs bring to us is about the external universe. We receive that knowledge and, generally, do not discriminate: we become slaves to the external world. We easily identify with the external world, its people and things, and say 'This is mine,' 'That is done by me' and so on.

Nothing that is created is permanent; it may be destroyed the next moment. Nothing created can bring us happiness. So we should not run after the mirage, say the Vedantins. We should carefully isolate the real water from the mirage. This has to be done constantly and consistently, keeping the sword of discrimination at hand always.

Though we read so much about discrimination, it is so difficult to practise it. Somehow our 'I-ness' and 'my-ness' come to the fore and we get entangled. Sri Ramakrishna says: 'Yes, discrimination about objects. Consider—what is there in money or in a beautiful body? Discriminate and you will find that even the body of a beautiful woman consists of bones, flesh, fat, and other disagreeable things. Why should a man give up God and direct his attention on such things?'[3]

The practice of discrimination leads to liberation from delusion. We imagine people love us; we imagine objects of enjoyment bring happiness to us; we imagine the world to be beautiful and a great source of joy. It is all untrue, declare saints. The more we discriminate thus, the more we understand that all joy really proceeds from ourselves, and not from others or objects of the senses. This will awaken us from slumber.

'When we receive blows, say they are not blows but flowers; and when you are driven about like slaves, say that you are free.' This, Swami Vivekananda says, is the teaching of the world to us. 'We may try to cover our old and festering sores with clothes of gold, but there comes a day when the cloth of gold is removed, and the sore in all its ugliness is revealed. … Religion begins with a tremendous dissatisfaction with the present state of things, with our lives, and a hatred, an intense hatred, for this patching up of life, an unbounded disgust for fraud and lies,' says Swamiji.[4]

Iha-amutra-phala-bhoga-virāgaḥ

Through discrimination, we understand that this world is impermanent, and that we should not get attached to it. But there is the belief in higher worlds: if this world is impermanent, there are heavens, we think. By performing good deeds we acquire merits, and may wish to enjoy bliss in higher worlds like heaven. But heavenly pleasures too are temporary, and after our merits are exhausted, we shall have to come back to take birth, may be, in extremely lower bodies—like plants, insects, etc. Imagine the suffering of being ants and insects once again! Who knows when we shall get the precious human birth again. The discriminating intellect shudders at such a thought, and shuns all pleasures as nothing. Such a person knows for sure that Brahman or Atman alone is real, and all else is unreal.

We may say so many things, but attachment for the world does not go. How to give up attachment for the world? Swamiji suggests two ways: 'Here are the two ways of giving up all attachment. The one is for those who do not believe in God, or in any outside help. They are left to their own devices; they have simply to work with their own will, with the powers of their mind and discrimination, saying, "I must be non-attached". For those who believe in God there is another way, which is much less difficult. They give up the fruits of work unto the Lord; they work and are never attached to the results. Whatever they see, feel, hear, or do, is for Him. For whatever good work we may do, let us not claim any praise or benefit. It is the Lord's; give up the fruits unto Him. Let us stand aside and think that we are only servants obeying the Lord, our Master, and that every impulse for action comes from Him every moment.'[5]

Renunciation of lower ideals to attain higher ones is the essential hallmark of a spiritual seeker. Whether one accepts the formal vows of *sannyāsa* or not is not the question. But the seeker assumes inner *sannyāsa*, and renounces everything that appears to him to be an obstacle to the realization of the Self. It appears to be a terrifying idea to give up things we love. We need not give up; the so-called loved ones will themselves give us up in time because worldly love is so superficial. Again, the things of the world will themselves tell us they are not to be depended upon.

Sri Ramakrishna says: 'One who has only a mild spirit of renunciation says, "Well, all will happen in the course of time; let me now simply repeat the name of God." But a man possessed of a strong spirit of renunciation feels restless for God, as the mother feels for her own child. ... He has inward resolution.'[6]

Florentus Rodville, the author of *The Imitation of Christ*, prays thus: 'O my God, let not flesh and blood prevail over me; let it not overcome me; let not the world and its transitory glory deceive me; let not the devil overreach me by his devices.'[7]

Rabbi Stephen Wise is said to have commented thus: 'Let something so high and noble come into your life that it shall be expulsive of everything low and mean.'

Śamādi Ṣaṭka Sampatti

'The six virtues like self-control.' There are six treasures: (a) *Śama*: control of the mind; (b) *Dama:* control of the senses; (c) *Uparati*, equipoise of the mind; (d) *Titīkṣā,* forbearance; (e) *Samādhāna*, concentrating the mind on Truth; (f) *Śraddhā* active faith in the teacher and scriptures.

Though *dama* is generally mentioned second in the list of six, it has been dealt with first here because this is the primary discipline.

a. *Dama*: The seeker of Truth should first of all give up all that is untrue. How does he do this? He closes the doors—the sense organs—leading to the world. Can one ever close the senses? No, we ordinary persons cannot; but sages can. We can control them. The senses run wildly towards their respective objects, but they are not independent. It is the will that is supreme. So the seeker should control the senses through the regulation of the will. Whatever leads to eternal misery should actively be rejected by the senses. Gradually they become withdrawn and indrawn. Like horses, their natural tendency is to run outwards. A sincere seeker controls them with effort and directs them at will.

b. Śama: *Śama* is mind control. The senses are ruled by the mind. By its control, the senses too come under control. The controlling of our senses will be aided by such a practice.

c. *Uparati:* What should we do with the senses and the mind which are controlled? We turn them inwards—this is the advice given to us. The senses and the mind, if not given a higher turn, will revert back to the world. They must be turned inwards. When we do this repeatedly and bring the mind on to the Self, 'Above all things, and in all things, my soul, rest always in the Lord…,' as the *Imitation of Christ* prays.[8]

d. *Titikṣā:* Forbearance has been considered a paramount virtue of the seeker of Truth. The world perhaps does not want to lose fools who had been its slaves for so long. So it tries its utmost to bind us down—through positive and negative means. The seeker will have, therefore, to endure everything patiently—good or bad. The seeker should attain to such a state that heat and cold, pleasure and pain, suffering and joy—all should become the same to him or her; that is, he or she should absolutely ignore them and concentrate on the Atman. '[When the Light shines forth] the flesh that has been mortified shall triumph more than if it had always been nourished in delights. Then will the lowly habit shine and fine clothing appear dingy. … then constant patience will be of more use than all the power of the world. … He who loves God with his whole heart fears neither death, nor punishment, nor judgement, nor hell…,' says the *Imitation of Christ*.[9]

All the above four disciplines demand consistent and constant practice. All of them should be practised together. Lord Kṛṣṇa says in the *Gītā* (6:35) that constant practice (*abhyāsa*) and detachment (*vairāgya*) are the only means of success in life. Why do our senses always run outwards? In the *Kaṭha Upaniṣad* (2.1.1), Yama tells Naciketa that the Lord of Creation Himself created our senses as going outwards. So they run outwards to their respective objects. The hero strives to bring them back to the Self.

e. *Samadhāna*: 'Tranquility of the mind'. This can never be attained when it runs after external things. It can attain peace only when it is in its *sāttvic* state—the state of perfect calm.

Through constant discussion, reading, hearing, thinking and meditating on the Self and Truth, the seeker establishes a strong undercurrent of peace within. This is the advice of all saints.

f. *Śraddhā:* *Śraddhā* is not merely faith; it is faith in higher values plus intense effort to attain what is believed in. Swami Turiyananda, who has translated *Vivekacūḍāmaṇi* into English, was Sri Ramakrishna's disciple, and an illumined soul. He translates verse number 25 of the work thus: 'A firm conviction, based upon the intellectual understanding that the teachings of the scriptures and of some of one's Master are true—this is called by the sages the faith which leads to the realization of the Reality.'

Swamiji's Summary

'These are the marks of the true Jnana Yogi: (1) He desires nothing, save to know. (2) All his senses are under perfect restraint; he suffers everything without murmuring, equally content if his bed be the bare ground under the open sky, or if he is lodged in a king's palace. He shuns no suffering, he stands and bears it—he has given up all but the Self. (3) He knows that all but the One is unreal. (4) He has an intense desire for freedom.' These are the words of Swami Vivekananda.[10]

Mumukṣutvam

'The longing for liberation.' This is the final requisite of a seeker. Whatever other qualities may be there in him, if this supreme quality is not there, there is still no hope of realization. This longing is in itself the end-product of the other sadhanas. Sri Ramakrishna gives a beautiful illustration of longing: 'I say that God can be realized if one feels drawn to Him by the intensity of these three attractions: the child's attraction for the mother, the husband's attraction for the chaste wife, and the attraction of worldly possessions for the worldly man.'[11]

Viveka, vairāgya, saṭ-sampatti, and *mumukṣutvam,* these are the four requirements or qualifications of a seeker of Truth. Armed with these qualities, he goes to the teacher, and with the latter's help, conquers ignorance *(ajñāna).*

Swami Vivekananda says:

> Only by going to the centre, by unifying ourselves with God can we escape the delusions of the senses. When we let go the eternal fever of desire, the endless thirst that gives us no rest, when we have for ever quenched desire, we shall escape both good and evil, because we shall have transcended both. The satisfaction of desire only increases it, as oil poured on fire but makes it burn more fiercely. The farther from the centre, the faster goes the wheel, the less the rest.
>
> Draw near the centre, check desire, stamp it out, let the false self go, then our vision will clear and we shall see God. Only through renunciation of this life and of all life to come (heaven etc.), can we reach the point where we stand firmly on the true Self. While we hope for anything, desire still rules us. Be for one moment really "hopeless", and the mist will clear. For what to hope when one is the all of existence?
>
> The secret of Jnana is to give up all and be sufficient unto ourselves. Say "not", and you become "not"; say "is", and you become "is". Worship the Self within, naught else exists. All that binds us is Maya—delusion.[12]

Suggested Reading:

1. 'Steps to Realization,' by Swami Vivekananda in *The Complete Works* (Vol. 1, pp. 405-416).
2. *Vivekacūḍāmaṇī,* Verses 14 to 30.
3. *Bhagavad Gītā,* Chapter 2.
4. *Vedānta Sāra,* Sadānanda Yogīndra

References

1. Gospel, p. 272.

2. Complete Works, Vol. 4, p. 436.

3. Gospel, p. 82.

4. Complete Works, Vol. 2, pp. 122-4.

5. Complete Works, vol. 1, p. 102.

6. Gospel, p. 166.

7. The Imitation of Christ, Book, 2, chapter 26.

8. Imitation of Christ, Book 2, Chapter 21.

9. Imitation of Christ, Book 1, Chapter 24.

10. Complete Works, Vol. 8, p. 10.

11. Gospel, p. 846.

12. Complete Works, Vol. 8, p. 22.

Chapter 5

DISCRIMINATION

The Snake-Rope

'How did you ever climb up this building?' asked Tulsi's wife. He replied: 'You were careful enough to let a rope down the window. I caught hold of it and climbed up. I entered through the window. You know how mad I am after you. I could not stay at home without you. So I came here, crossing the turbulent river....' 'Fie on your so-called love! If only you had even a little attraction for God that you have for this filthy body, you would have achieved much. Give up this false attachment for something that is impermanent, and concentrate on God. This alone will help you.'

Tulsidās stood downcast. He did not know what to say. His wife had opened his eyes. The golden moment had arrived. Tulsidās renounced everything and left his wife and home for good. The snake-rope example of Vedanta had indeed served its purpose in breaking Tulsi's delusion.

The Impermanence of Everything

In the previous chapter the author mentioned the four qualifications of a seeker. In this chapter he takes up the first qualification—discrimination.

That which comes, goes. That which is born dies. That which is a composite decomposes. That which is created is destroyed. That which is the fruit of something will vanish.

Thus everything we see, taste, smell, sense, hear and perceive are transient. The universe is a creation, and so it will perish. The mind is also a creation, and that too will perish. Our so-called intellect, our ego—all will go.

What is it that lasts forever? It is the Self—the Atman alone. There are no parts or composite things here. This Atman is the only thing that exists, and that alone is to be known, say the scriptures repeatedly.

The Three Basic Scriptures

Vedanta has three basic scriptures, called *prasthāna traya* 'the three helps to liberation.' These are the *Brahma Sūtras*, the *Bhagavad Gītā,* and the Upaniṣads. These three are the essential scriptures of Vedanta, and consequently, of Hinduism itself. The culmination of the Vedas, in every sense of the term, is Vedanta. Vedanta means the Upaniṣads. Since there are many Upaniṣads, and the ideas of the Upaniṣads are scattered everywhere, Sage Vyāsa wrote the *Brahma Sūtras*. Then there was the greatest harmonizing scripture of the world, the *Bhagavad Gītā*.

All these scriptures exhaust themselves in telling us of the third constituent of our personality, the Atman. They tell us again and again that we are not the body and mind, but the Self. Again, this Self is the One Reality that exists, they assert. Scriptures are our only means of knowing this intellectually. And then there is personal experience (*anubhava*).

In recent times, this direct experience has been very clearly stressed. Sri Ramakrishna, Holy Mother, Swami Vivekananda and other disciples of Ramakrishna have all experienced the highest Truth and shown that it is possible to achieve that goal. Sri Ramakrishna says:

> As a result of the discrimination that Brahman alone is real and the world illusory, the aspirant goes into samādhi. Then, for him, the forms or attributes of God disappear altogether. Then he does not feel God to be a Person. Then he cannot describe in words what God is.

And who will describe it? He who is to describe it does not exist at all; he no longer finds his "I". To such a person Brahman is attributeless. In that state God is experienced only as consciousness by man's inmost consciousness.[1]

This experience comes to the sincere seeker, say our scriptures, who has the four qualifications. The first of them is discrimination between the real and the unreal. Says *Tattvabodha:*

नित्यानित्य–वस्तु–विवेकः कः?

नित्यवस्त्वेकं ब्रह्म, तद्व्यतिरिक्तं सर्वम् अनित्यम्।

अयमेव नित्यानित्य–वस्तुविवेकः ॥

Nityānitya-vastu-vivekaḥ kaḥ ?
Nitya-vastu-ekaṁ brahma, tad-vyatiriktaṁ sarvam anityam| Ayameva nityānitya-vastu-vivekaḥ ||

Kaḥ What is?*nityānitya-vastu-vivekaḥ* discrimination between the Real and the unreal; *Nitya-vastu-ekaṁ brahma,* the Eternal is only one, Brahman; *tad-vyatiriktaṁ* other than That; *sarvam* everything else; *anityam* impermanent; *ayameva* this indeed is *nityānitya-vastu-vivekaḥ* discrimination.

What is discrimination between the Eternal and the transcient?

The Eternal is only One, which is Brahman; everything else is impermanent. This is discrimination between the Real and the unreal.

Anityam

The universe, our earth and all its beauty, our own bodies which we love so dearly, our mind, our brilliance—all are *anitya,* impermanent. They are not absolutely 'not there', like the hare's horn; they are relatively true. But they are not permanent. They are superimpositions, *adhyāsa,* on Reality. They are false creations, *vivarta*. They are false, *mithyā*. That which is impermanent or false or superimposition is also *asatya* or unreal. So we should seek the Real. *Naiṣkarmya Siddhi* (66) by Sureśvarācārya, a disciple of Śankara, says: 'This illusion is baseless and is opposed to all logic. It cannot endure inquiry even as darkness cannot endure the sun.'

The Eternal, *nitya,* cannot be seen by the telescope or any other instrument. It is beyond the intellect and mind. It is beyond words. It is a matter of innermost experience.

Brahman

Commenting on *Brahma Sūtras* (1.1.1), Śankara says that Brahman is to be cogitated upon because the aphorism says that Brahman is to be known. Why should we discuss Brahman, asks Śankara, and answers: 'There is a conflict about Its distinctive nature. Ordinary people as well as the materialists recognize the body alone to be the Self. Some say it is *śūnya*. Some say that the mind is the Self. Some others say that the soul is the experiencer and enjoyer of the fruits of its action. In order to clear such a confusion, Brahman is to be deliberated upon.'

The Truth which is everywhere, which is beyond internal or external divisions; which is One only, is called Brahman. In fact, we cannot name It. It is beyond name and form. Yet for convenience we give it a name. This Brahman is called *sat,* Existence Itself. It is called *cit*, Being Itself, and *ānanda,* Bliss Itself. This is the conception of Reality that Upaniṣads, the *Brahma Sūtras,* and the *Bhagavad Gītā* give us.

Reality and Unreality

How did this Reality become this universe we live in? How did we come into being? This is the eternal question that has bothered pundits and Vedantists. The illumined soul, the *brahmajñāni,* will say: 'Which universe are you speaking about?

I don't see any!' The Advaitins say, therefore, that the universe and ourselves are a superimposition on Brahman. How did this superimposition take place? To the realized soul there is no superimposition at all. But for us who see only this universe and not Brahman, there should be some explanation. *Brahmajñānis* will, in order to bring us out of this dream, say that the dream we are seeing is a concoction of ignorance (*ajñāna*). But we should add the phrase "as it were" in all places here.

Brahman and *Ajñāna*

Vedantins explain this universe to us, calling it 'a universe for practical purposes' (*vyāvahārika sattā*). To explain the dream we are in, and to make us get out of it, they say this dream is true for practical purposes. Brahman or Reality is called the absolute state (*pāramārthika sattā*). For all practical purposes, we have this universe of ours. It remains until we know we are Brahman.

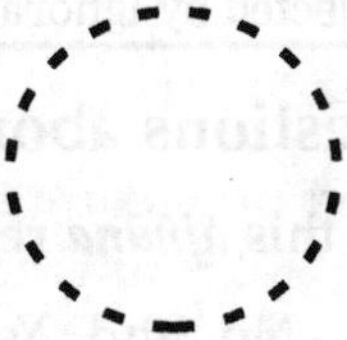

The Fourth State
The Absolute Truth State, the supreme Fourth (*turīya*). Brahman alone exists.

How did this 'real for practical purposes', the universe, come into being? The second aphorism of *Brahma Sūtras* (1.1.2) says that Brahman is the originator, [preserver, and destroyer] of the universe. We have said it is only a superimposition on Brahman. This superimposition is owing to ignorance. However, *jñānis* explain the universe to us in concrete forms. This is how they do it.

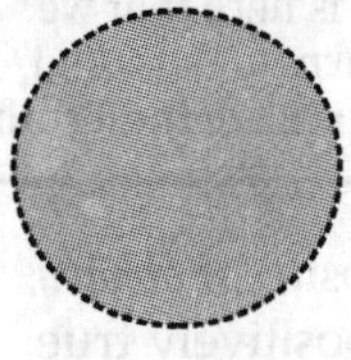

The Third State. Brahman is, as it were, enveloped by ignorance (Ajñāna). Brahman + ignorance is called **Īśvara**. This is the **causal** state

In the states shown in the diagrams, the first, second, and third, are from our viewpoint.

The Second State. Ignorance envelops as well as projects. This is the **Subtle** or Mental universe, called ***Hiraṇyagarbha,*** projected by ignorance.

We imagine a universe in which I and You, This and That, etc are present. For us there's the gross physical universe, the subtle universe, and the causal universe. This superimposition on the Reality of this three-fold universe is called *adhyāropa* by Vedantins. What is *adhyāropa* ? It is superimposing something on something else—like we keep one book on another.

Questions about *Ajñāna*

1. Is this *ajñāna* real?

No and Yes. If there was something real called *ajñāna*, the universe would become real. Then there would be two realities: Brahman and *ajñāna*. That, of course, cannot happen. So there is only One. If we deny *ajñāna*, how to explain this universe? So Vedantists say *ajñāna* is neither present or absent. It is *bhāva-rūpam yat kincit*, something that is between existence and non-existence. How is that? *Bhāva* is the opposite of *abhāva*, absence. Therefore ignorance is neither positively true, nor negatively untrue. As long as we see duality and multiplicity, there is this ignorance. When we attain that absolute state, there is no ignorance. This is the decision of the Vedantins.

The First State. The **gross** physical universe, called **Virāṭ**. The waking state. It is here that we learn, understand, and realize the Truth.

2. How does *ajñāna* create the universe?

First of all we should remember that this universe we experience is a false superimposition on Reality.

Yet, for the sake of the ignorant, Vedantins explain 'creation' as follows, basing their ideas on the Vedas.

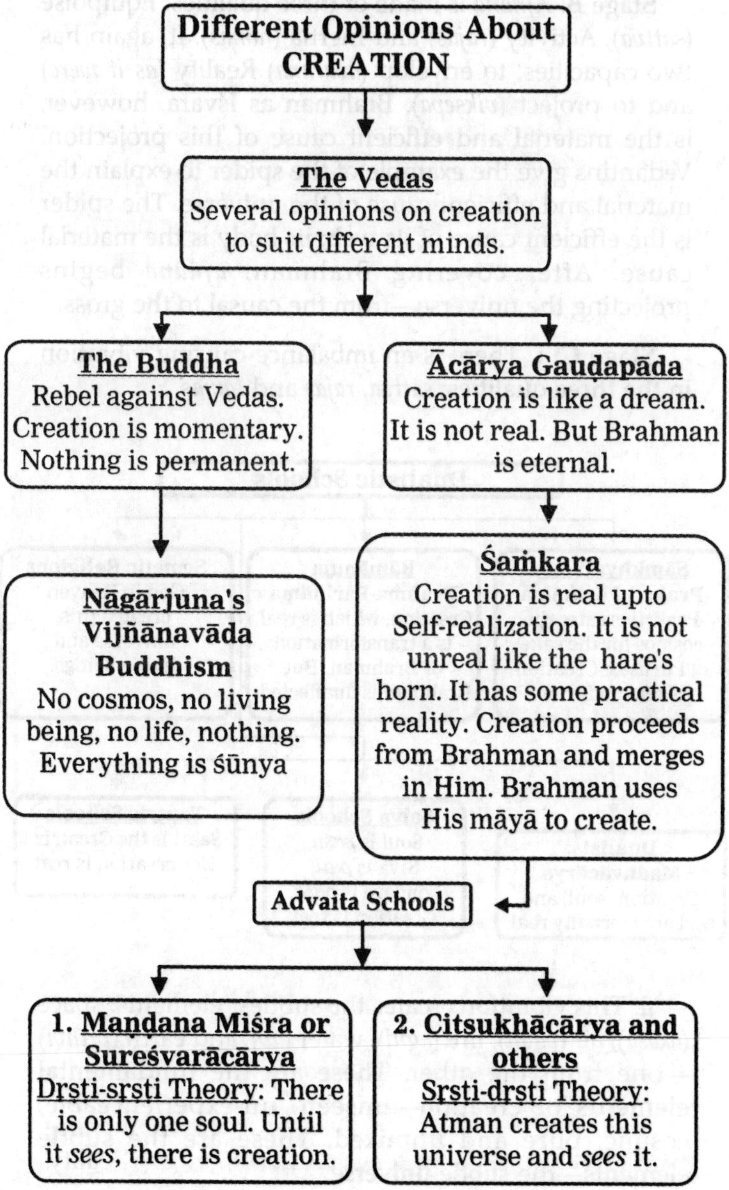
Different Opinions About CREATION
The Vedas
Several opinions on creation to suit different minds.
The Buddha
Rebel against Vedas. Creation is momentary. Nothing is permanent.
Ācārya Gauḍapāda
Creation is like a dream. It is not real. But Brahman is eternal.
Nāgārjuna's Vijñānavāda Buddhism
No cosmos, no living being, no life, nothing. Everything is śūnya
Śaṁkara
Creation is real upto Self-realization. It is not unreal like the hare's horn. It has some practical reality. Creation proceeds from Brahman and merges in Him. Brahman uses His māyā to create.
Advaita Schools
1. Maṇḍana Miśra or Sureśvarācārya
Dṛṣṭi-sṛṣṭi Theory: There is only one soul. Until it *sees*, there is creation.
2. Citsukhācārya and others
Sṛṣṭi-dṛṣṭi Theory: Atman creates this universe and *sees* it.

Stage A: Brahman is (as it were) covered by *ajñāna.* This state is called the state of Īśvara.

Stage B: *Ajñāna* is made of three qualities: Equipoise (*sattva*), Activity (*rajas*) and Inertia (*tamas*). It, again has two capacities: to envelop (*āvaraṇa*) Reality (*as it were*) and to project (*vikṣepa*). Brahman as Īśvara, however, is the material and efficient cause of this projection. Vedantins give the example of the spider to explain the material and efficient cause of the universe. The spider is the efficient cause of its web; its body is the material cause. After covering Brahman, *ajñāna* begins projecting the universe—from the causal to the gross.

Stage C: i. There is an imbalance causing vibration in the three qualities: *sattva, rajas* and *tamas*.

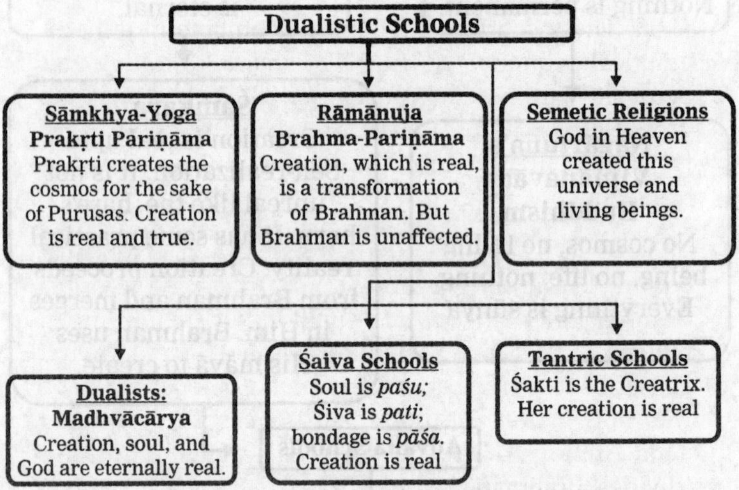
Dualistic Schools
Sāmkhya-Yoga
Prakṛti Pariṇāma
Prakṛti creates the cosmos for the sake of Purusas. Creation is real and true.
Rāmānuja
Brahma-Pariṇāma
Creation, which is real, is a transformation of Brahman. But Brahman is unaffected.
Semetic Religions
God in Heaven created this universe and living beings.
Dualists:
Madhvācārya
Creation, soul, and God are eternally real.
Śaiva Schools
Soul is paśu; Śiva is pati; bondage is pāśa. Creation is real
Tantric Schools
Śakti is the Creatrix. Her creation is real

ii. This vibration creates the subtlest elements: space (*ākāśa*), air (*vāyu*), fire (*agni*), water (*ap*) and earth (*pṛthvī*) —one from the other. These are the fundamental elements of creation—unseen, un-experienceable, cosmic, pure and unmixed. These are the subtle elements—the subtle universe.

The Supreme Harmonizer

Sri Ramakrishna

Advaita, Viśiṣṭādvaita, and Dvaita are true at different states of mind. Accept all. When we are experiencing the Absolute, it is Advaita. When we come down, Viśiṣṭādvaita is true. Still down, it is Dvaita. Again, Brahman and Śakti are non-different. When creation, etc, goes on, it is Śakti at work. When it is One only, it is Brahman. When the jñāni comes down from the highest state he sees the universe, true; but as Brahman. This is the Vijñāni state, a state after Advaita experience.

iii. These subtle elements inter-combine in a mathematical sequence called *pañcīkaraṇa,* (and this will be dealt with in detail in Chapter 38). This creates the gross elements: space (*ākāśa*), air (*vāyu*), fire (*tejas*), water (*ap*), and matter (*pṛthvī*). This is how our cosmos comes into being.

v. What about living beings? When ignorance covers Brahman initially, it (*as it were*!) 'divides' Brahman into smaller bits—millions of them! Rather, billions of Selves put together is Īśvara. These are *our* causal bodies. That is, we are trichotomous: we have this body, then the mind, and the soul or Atman. This Atman is what is "created" when ignorance 'divides' Brahman (*as it were!*).

vi. While on the one hand cosmic creation goes on from the causal state to the gross, the individual creation too goes on in a similar fashion. The individual then is deluded to believe that he is *not* Brahman or Atman. He thinks he is the body, that he is the doer and enjoyer. So the attachment to land, house, relatives, property.

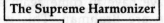

vii. Death will not end the confusion. Owing to our past actions, we have to come again and again till we know we are Brahman. This is the scheme of creation (*as it were*) according to Advaita Vedanta.

viii. There are several schools of Advaita Vedanta, and these differ in concepts of (a) creation; (b) individuality; (c) nature of Truth; (d) nature of God, and so on. We shall deal with this aspect later on.

Recapitulation:

- Cosmic Creation: Brahman alone is real, all else is illusory. This illusory universe is manufactured by ignorance (*ajñāna*). It covers Brahman as it were and projects the causal, the subtle and the gross universes.

- Individual Creation: Again, it, as it were, creates millions of souls by dividing Brahman and itself, and thus living beings are formed, having the Soul, the mind and the body.

- The knowledge of the so-called illusory creation from Brahman to the gross physical is called *adhyāropa*.

- The knowledge of the so-called reverse process—creation from gross physical to Brahman—is called *apavāda*.

In spite of all the variety and wonder in creation, it is just an illusion—a mirage—essentially. The wise do not attach themselves to it, but the ignorant like us become attached and suffer. When *ajñāna* goes, there is knowledge like the brilliant sun. So the sum and substance of the whole thing is that we should never be attached. For attachment to go, we should constantly discriminate. This is *viveka.*

Sri Ramakrishna says: 'There are two ways. One is the path of discrimination; the other is that of love. Discrimination means to know the distinction between the Real and the unreal. God alone is the real and permanent

Substance; all else is illusory and impermanent. The magician is real; his magic is illusory. This is discrimination.'[2]

Suggested Reading:

1. 'The Absolute and Manifestation' by Swami Vivekananda (*Complete Works*, Vol. 2, p. 130).

2. The Chapter on Right Knowledge ('*Saṁyag-mati Prakaraṇam'* in Śaṁkara's *Upadeśa Sāhasrī* (translation in English, published by Ramakrishna Math, Mylapore, Chennai).

3. Sureśvara's *Naiṣkarmya Siddhi,* English translation, Chapter II.

References

1. Gospel, p. 859.

2. Gospel, p. 179.

Chapter 6

DISPASSION

The Child Sage

'Dogen! O Dogen!...' No answer. 'Where is Dogen? Have you seen the boy?' 'No, I haven't. But where has he gone?' 'Dogen....! Ah! You sit here!' The caretaker wept even as she held little Dogen. 'I can imagine your suffering, my child! It was only six months back that you lost your mother. And today...!' The boy sat silently, looking downwards.

The caretaker said again: 'Why don't you speak, my child? At least cry! See there, so many relatives have arrived in the palace. Come on, all are searching for you. Come on, let's go.' Dogen was silent. Seeing his silence, the caretaker was worried. 'Why are you silent, my child? If you don't cry, the hurt will remain inside. After your mother's death you were so attached to your father. He too is gone now....'

Dogen, a boy of five, opened his mouth now: '*Sabbam Duḥkam*...The world is sorrow and suffering.'

The caretaker sat stunned. She never expected this boy to quote from Pāli, and at such a juncture.

'I know you are well-read for your age. But we must go to where your father lies. Come on, my child. People are searching for you....' Nothing moved Dogen.

Days passed. This orphan lived with the caretaker. He became indrawn. The same boy had wept bitterly when his mother had passed on. Now he was indrawn. After some days, when the caretaker saw the little boy in ochre, she was shocked: 'Your parents wanted you to become the Fujiwara minister. Why such robes? For fun?' 'No, I am leaving home for good. Life is sorrow. Relatives, friends, all are *sanghāta*, as the Buddha said. Let me go away. I shall seek *Sambodhi*. ...'

The caretaker pleaded again and again. Everyone pressed him. But Dogen was firm. And so the young monk walked away from everything. Decades later, after years of hardship, when Dogen brought Soto Zen to Japan, he had indeed fulfilled his parents' desire. He became the spiritual king of Japan.

The Quality of Dispassion

'Deny yourself, take up your cross, and follow Jesus.'[1] Once we know what is lasting and what is not, once we understand what is true and what is not, why should we engage our minds with the false and the impermanent? So saints and seers teach us dispassion or *vairāgya*. *Rāga* means attachment. *Virāga* means its opposite. All our attachments are vain. All our so-called love are vain. All our struggle to please the world is vain.

Sri Ramakrishna gives the example of the sages of old: 'The rishis of old attained the knowledge of Brahman. One cannot have this so long as there is the slightest trace of worldliness. How hard the rishis laboured! Early in the morning they would go away from the hermitage and would spend the whole day in solitude, meditating on Brahman. At night they would return to the hermitage and eat a little fruit or roots. They kept their minds aloof from the objects of sight, hearing, touch, and other things of worldly nature. Only thus did they realize Brahman as their own inner consciousness. ... The jñāni gives up identification with worldly things, discriminating "Not this, not this." Only then can he realize Brahman.'[2]

The *Imitation of Christ* glorifies the Desert Fathers: 'Oh, how strict and mortified a life did the holy Fathers lead in the desert! What long and grevious temptation did they endure! ... They renounced all riches, dignities, honours, friends and kindred; they desired to have nothing of this world;

they scarcely allowed themselves the necessities of life; the serving of the body, even in necessity, grieved them.'[3]

Holy Mother Sri Sarada Devi says that the entire life of Sri Ramakrishna was a living demonstration of renunciation. And everyone who has read her life knows that Holy Mother's own life was one of intense dispassion, though she lived like an ordinary householder.

Renunciation and dispassion are not meant only for monks and nuns. It is for all. Some renounce externally, while others renounce mentally. It is such absolute renunciation of all which is false that is required to attain the knowledge of Brahman.

The present verse says this:

विरागः कः ?

इह स्वर्गभोगेषु च इच्छा–राहित्यम्।

Viragaḥ kaḥ ?
Iha svarga-bhogeṣu ca icchā-rāhityam.

Kaḥ ? what is; viragaḥ renunciation. *Iha svarga-bhogeṣu ca* in this-worldly and heavenly pleasures; *icchā-rāhityam* desirelessness.

What is detachment?

Absolute disinterestedness in the pleasures of this world as well as of heaven, etc.

Virāga

The day the Buddha understood that all the pleasures of his palace could not answer the existential questions he was having, he renounced them. Jesus Christ said: 'Lay not up for yourselves treasures upon earth, where moth and rust doth corrupt, and where thieves break through and steal; for where your treasure is, there will your heart be also. ... No man can serve two masters. ... Ye cannot serve God and mammon. Therefore I say unto you, take no thought for your life, what ye shall eat, or what ye shall drink; nor yet for your body, what ye shall put on. … But seek ye first the kingdom of God, and his righteousness, and all these things shall be added unto you.'[4]

Svarga

According to yogis the world brings only misery and nothing else. For a person of discrimination, this world is nothing but sorrow. So the only way to attain true happiness is to seek the Truth. The Sāmkhyans, one of the earliest philosophers of India, have said that there is threefold misery in this world. Ordinary means of overcoming them are there, but those remedies are temporary. Try otherworldly means, like performing sacrifices, acquiring merit, and going to heaven, and so on. That too is not everlasting. So they say that the only remedy is to know the Self.

In order to know the Truth, we should renounce what is not the Truth firmly. Amongst those things which are not the Truth, heavenly pleasures are included. Almost all scriptures of the world speak of heaven and so there must be some such place. But that is not lasting. When our virtues born of good deeds are exhausted, we shall have to come down to the world once again. 'One who has fallen into the stream of births and deaths cannot save oneself by anything except knowledge,' says the great book, *Upadeśa Sāhasrī*.[5] The *Viveka Cūḍāmaṇī* goes a step further: 'Sense objects are more fearful than the poison of the cobra, which is fatal only when taken; but these—on mere sight—can cause death. Only he who is free from the entanglement of these strings of objects of senses—hard to avoid—is fit for liberation; none else, even if he knows the six philosophies and all scriptures.'[6]

Tyāga

Tyāga is renunciation. Yes, we have to attain supreme knowledge because it is our true nature. But why should we renounce the world and the pleasures of higher worlds? Swami Vivekananda answers: 'It is very well to say: Be contented with the things of the present. The cows and the dogs are, and so are all animals; and that is what makes them animals.'[7]

Vairāgya or renunciation is a fundamental quality expected of an Advaita seeker. Advaita, as a tradition, was meant chiefly for sannyāsins. This system is considered a superior system, and not for all. Most of the Advaitins were monks, though there were exceptions, as in the case of Vācaspati Miśra. So sannyāsa, though covetable for an Advaitin because he sees everything as impermanent, is not the only way to follow the path.

In sannyāsa there are several types and orders. Śrī Śankara organized the free-flowing system of mendicancy into ten orders of monks, called the *daśanāmī* order. He founded four *maṭhas* or monasteries in the four corners of India for the propagation of the highest Truth. These monasteries have done immense work for the good of Hinduism, and for the propagation of Advaita.

Sannyāsins, as a whole, have been released from all obligations in Hinduism so that they may devote themselves to prayer, worship, *vicāra* or deep thinking and discussion on various philosophical truths, and sadhana. These sannyāsins have remained a blessing to humanity. Their renunciation inspires the ordinary to awaken to the truth that life is transitory. Sannyāsins are the role models of humanity. Sannyāsins may be realized souls (*vidvāmsa*) or seekers of Truth (*vividiṣu*). Though *vidvat sannyāsa* is coveted by all, *vividiṣā* is also the way. Then there is *ātura sannyāsa,* renouncing before imminent death. Women were also allowed to be sannyāsinis in ancient times, but social security was a problem. Hence they were generally discouraged from taking the vows of sannyāsa. With the advent of Swami Vivekananda, a grand monastic order for women has been started.

Swami Vivekananda said that there will be no liberation without sannyāsa, reiterating Śankara's words. Holding on to the little house and at the same time thinking of liberation will not do—this is the idea. One must give up lower truths for the sake of higher. So an Advaitin should by all means give up everything.

Of the four stages of life (to be discussed later) in Hinduism, sannyāsa is the fourth, and the supreme ideal. It is a very high ideal when nothing of the world is coveted, nothing sought, nothing cared for, and heat, cold, misery, poverty, hunger, and so on are looked on with equipoise.

Recaptitulation

1. Vedanta is ultimate knowledge. **Advaita** is the ultimate Truth. Experience is the method of knowing It.

2. Brahman is the only Reality. This universe is a false superimposition on It.

3. The Goal of life is to know what we really are. In order to do that, we need some qualifications.

4. *Viveka, Vairāgya, Mumukṣutvam,* and the six sadhanas are the qualifications of an aspirant.

5. Renunciation(*Vairāgya*) is the most fundamental virtue. Without giving up what is false, we can never hope of attaining what is true.

Further Reading

1. 'One Existence Appearing As Many' by Swami Vivekananda (*Complete Works*, Vol. 3, p. 19).

2. Bhartṛhari's *Vairāgya Śatakam,* '100 Verses on Dispassion'.

3. Śrī Śaṁkara's *Moha-mudgara-Stotram,* a Hymn on Dispassion.

References

1. *St Matthew,* 16.24

2. Gospel, p. 193.

3. Imitation of Christ, Book 1, chapter 18.

4. *St Matthew,* 6.19,20, 25, 33

5. Śankara, *Upadeśa Sāhasrī,* 15.52.

6. Śankara,*Viveka cūḍāmaṇī,* 77,78.

7. Complete Works, Vol. 2, p. 3.

Chapter 7

THE SIX SADHANAS

Introductory

Knowing about higher life is the first necessity. This is done with the help of books and teachers. Striving to seek that higher truth is the next necessity. In that striving there are several steps, of which the first is to know what is true and what is not. This is called *viveka*. The second step is to firmly resolve to give up what is not real and, hence, is becoming an obstacle to our knowing the Truth. This is called *vairāgya*. The next step is sixfold. The author has mentioned this before. He discusses these in detail now as these are the fundamental sadhanas of Advaita. These spiritual practices are both to be practised and, when perfected, to be considered treasures.

The Six Treasures

The great Advaita treatise, *Vivekacūḍāmaṇī*, discusses false appearance and the Reality in a beautiful way. It says that having heard from elders, and having read in books that Brahman is Real and all else is illusory, if one still gets attached to falsehood, he or she will be in pain and misery for all time to come.[1]

How can we overcome our desire for sense objects? All saints are one voice in saying that practice is the method. The *Bhagavad Gītā* answer is *abhyāsa* and *vairāgya*. The *Gītā* uses the phrase 'Yoga of Practice' (*abhyāsa yoga*). Sri Ramakrishna also repeatedly stresses effort. The 'six treasures' of an Advaita aspirant suggest only that. The moment we stop seeking external things, our minds become cheerful and pure, asserts Śaṁkara in *Vivekacūḍāmaṇī*. Cheerful, controlled, quiet, and free from ambitions and desires, full of the power of endurance—it is for such that the doors of Truth will open, says the great teacher.

Controlling the mind is not that easy. In his *Bhagavad Gītā* commentary, Śaṁkara says that 'man becomes repeatedly deluded under the influence of a totally opposite perception. And forgetting the truth that has been heard again and again, he repeatedly raises false issues and questions! And, therefore, observing that the subject is difficult to understand, the Lord gives His answer again and again.'[2] Swami Brahmananda says: 'Repeated failure is inevitable in the beginning. But keep your faith and redouble your efforts.' The *Gheraṇḍa Saṁhitā* says: 'नास्ति मायासमः पाशो नास्ति योगसमं बलम। *Nāsti māyāsamaḥ pāśo nāsti yogasamaṁ balam.* There is no bondage worse than *māyā*, even as there is no power greater than yoga.' Here, the yoga of effort also is meant. Through the yoga of effort, the aspirant attains yoga or union with the Infinite.

The author of *Tattvabodha* mentions the six sadhanas now.

शमादि–साधन–सम्पत्तिः कः ?
शमो दमः उपरतिः तितिक्षा श्रद्धा समाधानं च इति ॥

Śamādi sadhana-sampattiḥ kaḥ?
Śamo damaḥ uparatiḥ titikṣā śraddhā samādhānaṁ ceti.

Kaḥ what are; śamādi mental control and the other six; *sadhana* spiritual practices; *sampattiḥ* which are like treasures? *Śamaḥ* mind control; *damaḥ* control of the senses; *uparatiḥ* mental equanimity; *titikṣā* endurance of all kinds; *śraddhā* potential faith; *ca* and *samādhānaṁ* concentrating on Brahman *iti*.

What are the six spiritual treasures of an aspirant? Mind control, sense control, mental tranquility, endurance, concentration, and potential faith are the six treasures.

Each one of these six treasures will be discussed individually by the author of this work. So we do not go into particulars now. These six sadhanas have been termed 'treasures' because they help remove our age-long bondage and bring lasting peace to us. The six have been so well arranged that, beginning with the control of the sense organs, through the control of the mind, the system takes us to the threshold of the Self.

We have discussed the six treasures already. Though *śama* is mentioned first, *dama* comes first—from outside in. *Dama* is sense control. *Śama* means mind control. Next is *uparati*. The controlled mind needs some object to think of. The only 'object', rather, 'subject', for contemplation is the Self. So the controlled mind is placed on the threshold of the Atman again and again. We have to again and again bring the mind back to the Self or Atman, which, our sages say, exists in the citadel of the heart. 'God resides in the heart of all beings (as the Self)', says Kṛṣṇa in the *Bhagavad Gītā*.[3] In the *Brahma Sūtras* (1.3.14), it is said: 'दहर उत्तरेभ्यः, *dahara uttarebhyaḥ*, the small space (in the heart), the *dahara ākāśa*, is Brahman.'

So we should bring the mind back to the 'source' repeatedly. This bringing back is *uparati*. In this way we gain the capacity to endure pain and pleasure without difficulty.

As this effort intensifies, the mind naturally runs to the Source. When the world fails to tempt us in any way (though there may be lapses at times due to past tendencies), the mind begins to earnestly think of the Atman. This is *samādhāna*. Due to such progress, there comes tremendous faith in the things spiritual—which was until now somewhat unclear—and the soul pants for the realization of its goal. We have translated *śraddhā* as 'potential faith' or 'active faith' because it is not merely faith but a tremendous force which breaks through all bonds to take the soul to the truth which it believes in.

This is the six-fold scheme of sadhana of the seeker of Advaita knowledge. Each of the six will be discussed in the next chapter.

Swami Vivekananda says:

> Only the fools rush after sense-enjoyments. It is easy to live in the senses. It is easier to run in the old groove, eating and drinking; but what these modern philosophers want to tell you is to take these comfortable ideas and put the stamp of religion on them. Such a doctrine is dangerous. Death lies in the senses. Life on the plane of the Spirit is the only life, life on any other plane is mere death; the whole of this life can be only described as a gymnasium. We must go beyond it to enjoy real life.[4]

Suggested Reading:

1. Swami Budhananda, *Mind and Its Control* (Kolkata: Advaita Ashrama).
2. Swami Vivekananda, Introductory lectures in his *Raja Yoga*

References

1. see *Vivekacūḍāmaṇī* , 331-360

2. see Swami Gambhirananda, tr., *Bhagavadgītā* with Śankara's Commentary (Calcutta: Advaita Ashrama, 1991) ,4.18.

3. *Bhagavad Gītā*, 18.61

4. Complete Works, Vol. 5, p. 286.

Chapter 8

MASTERING ONESELF

Introductory

The author of *Tattvabodha* now takes up the six sadhanas one by one. He begins with *śama*. In *The Imitation of Christ,* these great words have been put into Christ's mouth: 'The perfect victory is to triumph over oneself. For he who keeps himself in subjection, so that sensuality obeys reason, and reason in all things is obedient to me, he is indeed a conqueror of himself, and lord of the world. If you long to climb this hill, you must begin resolutely, and set the axe to the root, in order to root out and destroy secret and inordinate inclination to yourself and to every private and material good. From this vice, by which a man inordinately loves himself, derives all that which is to be rooted out and overcome; which being vanquished and brought under, a great peace and tranquillity will immediately ensue.'[1]

Śama

'The story is told that once while in a small town on the banks of a river in America, Swami Vivekananda chanced to meet a party of young men who were shooting vainly from a bridge at eggshells bobbing on the current of a small stream. These shells were loosely strung together with a string, at one end of which was a small stone that served as an anchor. The Swami watched them, smiling at their failure. One of the young men noticed this and challenged him to try his hand at the game, assuring him that it was not so easy as it looked. Then the Swami took a gun and successively hit about a dozen shells! They were astonished and thought he must be a practised hand. But he assured them he had never handled a gun before and explained that the secret of his success lay in the concentration of the mind.' We have quoted from the *Life of Swami Vivekananda* (Vol. 2, p. 529). When the mind comes under control a person can achieve anything.

Another incident showing Swamiji's concentration power is wonderful:

> One day he [Vivekananda] went for a walk with Hollister on Mr. Leggett's private and well-kept ninehole golf course. Seeing a small flag at a distance, Swamiji, not knowing the game, asked, "Why that flag flutters there?" Hollister explained the procedure and went to get a club and ball in order to demonstrate it. Returning, he told Swamiji that par for that particular hole was four, and seven or eight for beginners.
>
> Swamiji smiled. "I will make you a bet," he said. "I shall put the ball in the hole with one stroke." Hollister produced fifty cents, Swamiji took a dollar from his pocket. At this point Mr. Leggett appeared and asked what these two were plotting. Being told, he informed Swamiji that what he proposed was an impossibility even for good players. "What is your bet?" Swamiji said. Mr. Leggett took a ten dollar bill from his wallet, and the bet was made. Swamiji told Hollister to stand by the hole — not too close. Hollister took his position, Swamiji pulled up the sleeves of his robe, looked intently at the flag, and swung at the ball. It entered the hole.
>
> When Mr. Leggett was able to speak, he said, "Has your yoga got something to do with it, Swami?"
>
> "I don't use yoga for so trifling a thing," Swamiji replied. "What I did I will tell you in two sentences. First, I measured the distance by sight, and I know the strength of my biceps. Second, I told my mind that I would be richer by ten dollars and a half. And then I swung."'

Mind is at the root of all troubles. Sri Ramakrishna used to say that one becomes either bound or liberated through the mind only. One who has controlled the mind has controlled the senses and has become a victor.

शमः कः ? मनोनिग्रहः ।

Śamaḥ kaḥ ? Mano-nigrahaḥ.

Kaḥ what is; *Śamaḥ* mind control? *Mano-nigrahaḥ* (It is) restraining the mind.

What is mind control?

It is restraining the mind (from going towards sense objects).

Swami Vivekananda writes about *śama*: 'When I close my eyes and begin to think, the organs are active, but not the instruments. Without the activity of these organs, there will be no thought. You will find that none of you can think without some symbol. In the case of the blind man, he has also to think through some figure. The organs of sight and hearing are generally very active. You must bear in mind that by the word "organ" is meant the nerve centre in the brain. The eyes and ears are only the instruments of seeing and hearing, and the organs are inside. If the organs are destroyed by any means, even if the eyes or the ears be there, we shall not see or hear. So in order to control the mind, we must first be able to control these organs. To restrain the mind from wandering outward or inward, and keep the organs in their respective centres, is what is meant by the words Shama and Dama. Shama consists in not allowing the mind to externalise, and Dama, in checking the external instruments.'[3]

Dama

दमः कः? चक्षुरादि–बाह्येन्द्रिय–निग्रहः ॥

Damaḥ kaḥ ? Cakṣurādi-bāhyendriya-nigrahaḥ ||

Kaḥ what is; *damaḥ* sense control; *nigrahaḥ* (It is) the control of; *cakṣurādi* eyes and other; *bāhyendriya* external organs.

What is sense control? It is the control of eyes and other external organs.

'If we were perfectly dead to ourselves, and in no way entangled in worldly things; then we could be able to relish divine things, and experience something of heavenly contemplation,' comments *The Imitation of Christ*.

There are five sense organs: the eyes, ears, nose, skin, and tongue. These organs are not situated in the physical body. The gross physical body is only an instrument of the subtle body. The sense organs are situated in the subtle body. When a person dies, only the external instrument falls but the subtle body along with the causal goes out and takes another body. Along with the subtle body go all the sense organs and organs of action.

From the beginning of creation up to dissolution, a personality goes from body to body and suffers endlessly because the sense organs experience the world repeatedly and bring desires to the mind.

Our senses are the doors to destruction. They lead (rather, mislead) us to their respective objects, convincing us that the objects—like smell, taste, touch, sight, and sound—are eternal and pleasure-producing. But we are deceived.

The yogi who sits in meditation closes the eyes. The moment eyes are closed, half of the problem is solved because the yogi cuts himself off from the world altogether. If he can similarly master 'closing' the ears, skin, tongue and nose—restraining them, he has mastered the sense organs. Swami Turiyananda, a disciple of Sri Ramakrishna, underwent surgery without receiving anaesthesia. He told the doctors to wait for a moment, pulled his mind from the skin or sense of touch, and said, 'Proceed.' The surgery went off painlessly.

The wise ones control their senses and bring them back towards the Truth. Such a control is called *dama*. In the *Bhagavad*

Gītā Śrī Kṛṣṇa gives the example of a tortoise in danger: it sucks its limbs inside. So does the yogi control all his senses and mind. Without *dama* one cannot hope of controlling the mind. The first stage is control of the senses and then comes controlling the inner sense organ, the mind.

Uparati

उपरतिः कः ? स्वधर्मानुष्ठानमेव ।

Uparatiḥ kaḥ ? Svadharma–anuṣṭhānam-eva.

kaḥ what is *uparatiḥ* mental restraint? (It is) *anuṣṭhānam-eva* the following of; *svadharma* one's natural duties.

What is mental equipoise? It is the following of one's natural duties.

This is a novel definition of *uparati*. Generally, *uparati* is defined as giving up actions, or to formally accept the vows of *sannyāsa*. The other definition of *uparati* is that we should place the restrained mind in the Self. Here, the author says that *uparati* means to follow one's natural duties.

Though a person may receive the formal vows of *sannyāsa*, his mind needs to be controlled. So mere external acceptance is not all. One has to accept the vows mentally too. For this, one has to perform all his duties—worship, prayer, daily obligatory works—with dedication, and must not expect anything in return. This is what is meant here. By doing daily duties (*nitya karma*) without ambitions in mind, one becomes pure in heart. And *uparati* precisely means purifying the heart.

Through the faculty called *dama* we restrain our senses. Through the faculty called *śama* we control our mind. When these two 'controlled' organs are left for themselves, they once again go outwards. Hence the third, *uparati*, comes to our help. *Uparati* is placing the controlled mind and senses on some inward object—engaging them. The best object is the Self. This is our *svadharma*. Our natural duty is to think of and realize the Self. Why is this so? Human birth is the most precious gift of God to us. As Swamiji says, 'This human body is the greatest body in the universe, and a human being the greatest being. Man is higher than all animals, than all angels; none is greater than man. Even the Devas (gods) will have to come down again and attain to salvation through a human body. Man alone attains to perfection, not even the Devas. According to the Jews and Mohammedans, God created man after creating the angels and everything else, and after creating man He asked the angels to come and salute him, and all did so except Iblis; so God cursed him and he became Satan. Behind this allegory is the great truth that this human birth is the greatest birth we can have.'[4]

Our human birth is the greatest because we can master ourselves and attain the Truth. Our lives will be in vain if we do not do this. The Upaniṣads repeatedly say that those who die without realizing their true nature are worthless. Sri Ramakrishna says that the only goal of humankind is to know God or the Self. Everything else is secondary, or, a help towards that end.

Swami Vivekananda comments on *uparati*:

> Now comes Uparati which consists in not thinking of things of the senses. Most of our time is spent in thinking about sense-objects, things which we have seen, or we have heard, which we shall see or shall hear, things which we have eaten, or are eating, or shall eat, places where we have lived, and so on. We think of them or talk of them most of our time. One who wishes to be a Vedantin must give up this habit.[5]

Titīkṣā

Swami Vivekananda in the West: New Discoveries writes: 'In Boston, [his] money was fast disappearing, the weather, even in August, seemed to him like winter, and his clothes were not only inadequate against the early autumn chill but could incite violence in the streets. The story of one such occasion he told long afterward: "I landed [in Boston] once, [he said] a stranger in a strange land. My coat was like this red one and I wore my turban. I was proceeding up a street in the busy part of the town when I became aware that I was followed by a great number of men and boys. I hastened my pace and they did too. Then something struck my shoulder and I began to run, dashing around a corner, and up a dark passage, just before the mob in full pursuit swept past—and I was safe!" But just a few days before that, the same Swamiji had received this compliment: '...a superbly well-qualified delegate, one "who is more learned than all our learned professors put together" and who is like the sun, with no need of credentials in order to shine....'[6]

During his wandering days, Swamiji had to go without food for days at a stretch. He had to live with the poorest of the poor, and kings would be his hosts occasionally. Rain, sun, cold, heat—he had to endure everything. His life had been at stake on several occasions. He even escaped death miraculously, by divine intervention. All his life, Swamiji had to witness betrayals and faithful service, desertions and absolute dedication, rejection and acceptance, love and hate. Yet, Swamiji was the same. This is forbearance.

The story is told of Haridāsa, Śrī Caitanya's companion. Haridāsa was born in a Brahmin family, but since his parents died while he was still a baby, a pious Muslim couple brought him up. When they tried to train him in Persian literature, Haridāsa wanted to read only the *Bhāgavata.* When they tried to arrange for his marriage, Haridāsa left home. The name of 'Kṛṣṇa' was his only refuge. The sky was his roof and Mother Earth his bed. When the local Muslim king was complained that Haridāsa was not following Muslim customs but was repeating the names of Hari, the king ignored the complaint. But when the complainers persisted, he had Haridāsa brought, enquired, and punished him with death by beating.

People saw Haridāsa being dragged and beaten by the police. Haridāsa's body was all torn and bleeding. Yet he was smiling all the time, and repeating the Lord's names. Unable to kill him, the police threw him into the river, and by God's grace he was saved.

Tattvabodha deals with this rare quality of forbearance now:

तितिक्षा का ?
शीतोष्णसुखदुःखादि द्वन्द्व सहिष्णुत्वम् ।

Titīkṣā kā ? Śītoṣṇa-sukha-duḥkhādi dvandva-sahiṣṇutvam.

Kā what is; *titikṣā* forbearance? *Śitoṣna* heat and cold; *sukha-duḥkhādi* happiness and misery, etc; *dvandva* dualities; *sahiṣṇutvam* tolerating with equanimity.

What is forbearance?

To tolerate with equanimity the dualities like heat and cold, happiness and misery, etc.

Forbearance is a great quality. The ordinary get affected at the slightest touch of problems. Whenever there is a difficulty, we ordinary people suffer immensely. We cannot withstand ordeals even to the slightest extent. This is because we are too body-conscious. Then there are the touchy souls, who are so sensitive that even a grave look seems to bring suffering to them. They cannot stand a stare. And they become overjoyed even at the slightest touch of happiness. So they become weathercocks—every change in weather telling upon their person.

Can such people be happy, let alone their being spiritual aspirants? Therefore one of the six qualities mentioned as imperative for a *mumukṣu* is forbearance.

While the extremely body-conscious become veritable thermometers, the extremely spiritual become like a huge rock. They care not what happens to their bodies and minds, yet they possess soft hearts. They know fully well that these are but passing phases. Here, one should be cautious to exclude the brutish personalities who are too dull even to understand what is happening. While the brute is unaware of what is happening, the saint is aware of what is happening but is so controlled as not to react at all.

Why does the saint or the *mumukṣu* not react? This world is transitory, its experiences are transitory, and our moods too are transitory. There is no point in getting excited at every step. So they do not react. A few words from *The Imitation of Christ* will make things clearer:

> He is not truly a patient man who wants to suffer no more than he thinks good and only from whom it pleases him. The truly patient man does not mind by whom he is exercised, whether by his superior, or by one of his equals, or by an inferior; whether by a good and holy man, or by a perverse and unworthy person. But to any creature whatsoever and how much and how often soever any adversity happens to him, he is indifferent to it; he receives all from the hand of God, with gratitiude, and esteems it a great gain. Because nothing, how little it may be, which is suffered for God's sake, can pass without merit before God. Be you, therefore, prepared to fight, if you want to gain the victory. Without fighting you cannot obtain the crown of patience. If you will not suffer, you refuse to be crowned; but if you desire to be crowned, fight bravely and endure with patience.[7]

Śraddhā

Regarding faith in God and guru, Sri Ramakrishna has numerous wonderful things to say. He says, for instance: 'You must have heard about the tremendous power of faith. It is said in the purana that Rama, who was God Himself—the embodiment of Absolute Brahman—had to build a bridge to cross the sea to Ceylon. But Hanuman, trusting in Rama's name, cleared the sea in one jump and reached the other side. He had no need of a bridge.' Further, Sri Ramakrishna narrates a story and tells what happens to sinners who have faith:

Once a man was about to cross the sea. Vibhishana wrote Rama's name on a leaf, tied it in a corner of the man's wearing-cloth, and said to him: 'Don't be afraid. Have faith and walk on the water. But look here —the moment you lose faith you will be drowned.' The man was walking easily on the water. Suddenly he had an intense desire to see what was tied in his cloth. He opened it and found only a leaf with the name of Rama written on it. 'What is this?' he thought. 'Just the name of Rama!' As soon as doubt entered his mind he sank under the water.

If a man has faith in God, then even if he has committed the most heinous sins—such as killing a cow, a brahmin, or a woman—he will certainly be saved through his faith. Let him only say to God, 'O Lord, I will not repeat such an action', and he need not be afraid of anything.[8]

The author of *Tattvabodha* defines faith now:

श्रद्धा कीदृशी ?

गुरु-वेदान्त-वाक्येषु विश्वासः श्रद्धा ।

Śraddhā kīdṛśī?
Guru-vedānta-vākyeṣu viśvāsaḥ śraddhā|

Kīdṛśī of what nature is *śraddhā* active faith? *Guru-vedānta-vākyeṣu* in the teacher and Vedantic statements; *viśvāsaḥ* active faith (is) *śraddhā* .

Of what nature is *śraddhā* ?

***Śraddhā* is faith in the words of the guru and the Vedanta.**

To have absolute faith in the guru's words and in the teachings of the scriptures has been called *śraddhā*. As we mentioned earlier, Swami Vivekananda said he could not translate this wonderful word into English. *Śraddhā* is not mere faith but *active* faith. It is potential faith. Sri Ramakrishna gives the example of a robber who comes to know there is gold hidden behind the wall. Will he ever keep quiet? He will strive his utmost to get it. This is active faith.

All the spiritual books of the world speak of faith. The 'rational' people can never have faith. They keep on criticizing the spiritual people. Bertrand Russell spoke on 'Why I am not a Christian?' in the 1930s. That was considered a classic piece of rational literature. Yet there are several questions that appear silly from the Vedantic point of view. One could answer all of them from the Vedantic viewpoint because Vedanta is as clear as science itself.

Samādhāna

Samādhāna has been called concentration in this book. Concentration comes through practice. The oldest and most-sought-after method of practice of concentration is contemplation or meditation, *dhyāna*. Meditation is undoubtedly Indian contribution to the world.

What is meditation? According to Śankara, Rāmānuja, and other world-teachers, meditation is the continuous flow of the mind towards one object or subject; it is like oil being poured uninterruptedly from one container to another (*taila-dhārā-vat*). Through consistant practice, the restless mind is brought under control, and it flows towards one single object. What is a restless mind? A restless mind is one in which countless modifications (*vṛttis*) keep rising and falling constantly. All of us are suffering from this energy-dissipating restlessness of the mind. The mind is restless because of the desires in the mind. Desires are born of past experiences, and they in turn are born of ignorance. So ignorance or *avidyā* is at the root of mental modifications.

Meditation in Indian Thought

Yoga and Vedanta teach us that we must control this restlessness of the mind by controlling the *vṛttis*. For this, they suggest meditation. But before that, all schools ask us to prepare ourselves. While the eight-limbed Yoga has several steps like *yama, niyama, āsana,* etc, others have moral virtues to be cultivated. After all this comes meditation.

In the Indian tradition, meditation has become a household word. Almost all the schools invariably discuss meditation. Yoga is becoming popular nowadays—for health reasons, as well as for spiritual benefit.

There are several techniques of meditation in the Indian tradition. Generally, however, meditating on some form of God which appeals to our minds is advised. We are told to concentrate on the deity as sitting in the heart region. This, says the *Gītā* and other scriptures, is the best place for meditation. Formless meditation too is taught by Advaita. But meditation on God with form (who is also formless according to Sri Ramakrishna) is preferred by all.

There are two forms of meditation in a very broad generalization. One is object meditation, where mind is made to think and re-think of an object that is outside or inside the body. The second is subject meditation, in which the mind is made to think of the Self or Atman. Through all such struggles and repeated practices, our minds become concentrated and calm. A desire-less mind is a pure mind. A *vṛtti*-less mind is a concentrated mind. Such a mind can achieve anything easily. Water flowing in a hundred streams can do little. But water flowing in a single stream can bore a hole in the rock also.

A time comes, promise yogis, when there will be only one thought rising and falling. To retain this single thought for as long as possible is the ideal. This they call the *savikalpa samādhi* state. This is a supreme state, attained by perfected yogis. When that thought too stops, it is *nirvikalpa samādhi.* This is the highest state attainable.

From countless thoughts rising and falling, to no thought at all for some time—this is the journey of the soul. This is spirituality. Spiritual teachers tell us time and again that the joy experienced in such states is beyond description.

Tattvabodha now defines *samādhāna:*

समाधानं किम् ? चित्तैकाग्रता ॥

Samādhānaṁ kim ? Cittaikāgratā .

Kim what is *samādhānam* concentration? *Cittaikāgratā* (It is) making the mind one-pointed.

What is concentration?

It is making the mind one-pointed [on the Atman].

When Sri Ramakrishna used to meditate in the Pañcavaṭī birds used to peck on his head, and sit on his shoulders. He would have no consciousness at all of his surroundings.

Such is the perfection of concentration. Holy Mother says: 'Regardless of whether you get into water willingly or are pushed, your clothes will be soaked. Practise meditation regularly, for your mind is still unripe. After prolonged practice of meditation your mind will become steady. And you should constantly discriminate between the real and the unreal. Know the worldly objects to which the mind is drawn to be unreal and surrender your mind to God. A man was angling in a pond all by himself when a bridegroom's procession with its music passed by. But his eyes remained fixed on the float.'[9]

Concentration is 'resting' the mind—calming the mind finally—after ages of turbulence. When the mind is running towards the world, it is restless and fickle. When it runs towards its source—the Self, it is calm and composed. When that is achieved, there is no more desire for worldliness; but the purer the mind, the greater its urge to know the Truth. Thus the mind, which was hankering after worldly objects before, will seek the Truth with intensity. There is intense hankering for the Self. This is the next quality of the seeker.

Mumukṣutvam

मुमुक्षुत्वम किम?

मोक्षो मे भूयात् इति इच्छा ॥

Mumukṣutvaṁ kim ?
Mokṣo me bhūyāt iti icchā.

Kim what is *mumukṣutvaṁ* Mumukṣutva? *Icchā* (It is) the desire; *mokṣo me bhūyāt iti* 'May I be liberated.'

What is *mumukṣutvam*?

It is the intense desire (which says), 'May I be liberated.'

According to the scriptures of Vedanta, *mukti* or liberation means the destruction of *avidyā* or ignorance and all its creations and the knowledge that Brahman and Atman are one reality. When all desires are removed, the individual soul becomes immortal and free. Sri Ramakrishna says that the desire for liberation is not a desire.

It is after years of struggle with the senses, the mind, and the past tendencies that the individual becomes a victor and enters the realm of the Supreme Spirit. Once he or she understands that liberation alone will bring true and unconditioned happiness, the seeker will pant for liberation. 'Liberation means entire freedom—freedom from the bondage of good, as well as from the bondage of evil. A golden chain is as much a chain as an iron one,' says Swamiji. This state has been called *mumukṣtvam*. It has been explained as a state similar to the one where a person whose head has caught fire runs to find water. Such is the aspiration of the seeker.

Why should a seeker be so eager for liberation? Truth has evaded us since time immemorial. We have been in delusion for so long. At last the truth is at hand. At last we are going to be free. When we truly understand freedom and bondage, the desire to be free becomes so strong that none can stop us from that. *Upadeśa Sāhasrī* (231, 232) says: 'One does not try to attain anything in which one has lost interest. No one likes to eat poison even if pressed by hunger.'

The worth and glory of liberation becomes evident when we read Swamiji. He says:

> Those who do good works in this world and help others, but with an eye to reward, hoping to reach heaven or to get the praise of their fellow-men, must when they die, reap the benefit of those good works—they become these gods. But that is not salvation; salvation never will come through hope of reward. Whatever man desires the Lord gives him. Men desire power, they desire prestige, they desire enjoyments as gods, and they get these desires fulfilled, but no effect of work can be eternal. The effect will be exhausted after a certain length of time; it may be aeons, but after that it will be gone, and these gods must come down again and become men and get another chance for liberation.[10]

He also says: 'As the tortoise tucks its feet and head inside the shell, and you may kill it and break it in pieces, and yet it will not come out, even so the character of that man who has control over his motives and organs is unchangeably established. He controls his own inner forces, and nothing can draw them out against his will. By this continuous reflex of good thoughts, good impressions moving over the surface of the mind, the tendency for doing good becomes strong, and as the result we feel able to control the Indriyas (the sense-organs, the nerve-centres). Thus alone will character be established, then alone a man gets to truth. Such a man is safe for ever; he cannot do any evil. You may place him in any company, there will be no danger for him. There is a still higher state than having this good tendency, and that is the desire for liberation.'[11]

The *Vivekacūḍāmaṇī* (361) says: 'As gold, purified by thorough heating on the fire, gives up its impurities and attains to its own brilliance, so the mind, through meditation, gives up the impurities and attains to the reality of Brahman.'

एतत् साधन–चतुष्टयम्, ततः तत्त्वविवेकस्य
अधिकारिणो भवन्ति ॥

Etat sadhana-catuṣṭayam, tataḥ tattva-vivekasya
adhikāriṇo bhavanti.

Etat This is *sadhana-catuṣtayam* the four-fold spiritual practice. *Tataḥ* after (practising these) *tattva-vivekasya* of Self-knowledge *bhavanti* (they) become *adhikāriṇaḥ* fit aspirants.

This is the fourfold spiritual practice. After practising these they [i.e., the aspirants] will be called fit aspirants to attain Self-knowledge.

In this way, we have studied the characteristics of a spiritual aspirant who is fit for the path of knowledge. He practises the fourfold injunctions, which we have discussed before. These injunctions are: (a) discrimination between the eternal and the ephemeral; (b) dispassion for enjoyments here or elsewhere; (c) sense-control, mind-control, concentration, forbearance, Self-awareness, and faith in the teacher and scriptures; and (d) hankering for liberation.

When a person has all these qualities, he becomes a fit aspirant, an competent *adhikarī*, to know Brahman. The gist of the whole thing is this: One who wishes to know the Truth should be qualified for it. To be qualified for it means to be pure. To be pure, one has to follow some prescriptions. Following them, the aspirant becomes freed from the dirt accumulated through many lives. This makes him ready for knowledge. One word from the able teacher about the Truth, and he becomes illumined.

Swami Vivekananda remarks: 'Only the path of Jnana is of quick fruition and the rationale of all other creeds; hence it is equally esteemed in all countries and all ages. But even in the path of discrimination there is the chance of the mind getting stuck in the interminable net of vain argumentation.

Therefore along with it, meditation should be practiced. By means of discrimination and meditation, the goal or Brahman has to be reached. One is sure to reach the goal by practising in this way.'[12]

Recapitulation

1. Here is a person of the world. He does not know why he is suffering, even though he seeks joy. Pain, misery, disease, death, and so on pester him. He wants to escape from them.

2. Some one tells him about religion. This person thinks that he would follow it. He reads books concerning religion.

3. He comes to know that he has to become pure first. For this, he has to perform good deeds, avoid bad deeds, control his senses and mind, meditate on God, pray, worship, and endure everything.

4. He does all this for years and, gradually, is unable to remain the way he is. His heart pants for something higher. Thus he has become a seeker of liberation.

References:

1. *Imitation of Christ*, Book III, Chapter 53.
2. Marie Louise Burke, *Swami Vivekananda in the West: New Discoveries*, Vol. 3, p. 79
3. Complete Works, Vol. 1, p. 414
4. Complete Works, Vol. 1, p. 142
5. Complete Works, Vol. 1, p. 406
6. New Discoveries, Vol. 1, p. 20
7. *Imitation of Christ*, Book 3, Chapter 19
8. Gospel, p. 87
9. Gospel of Holy Mother, pp. 214-5
10. Complete Works: Vol. 2, p. 243-4
11. Complete Works, Vol. 1, p. 69
12. Complete Works, Vol. 7, p. 198

Chapter 9

SELF KNOWLEDGE

The Trouble Maker

There is a beautiful incident in the *Gospel of Sri Ramakrishna.* Pratap Chandra Hazra was a vainglorious person, who was from Sri Ramakrishna's native village. He was an antithesis to Sri Ramakrishna's life. Out of campassion, Sri Ramakrishna made him stay in Dakshineswar Temple. This fellow would sit at Sri Ramakrishna's door, and pretend to be a great scholar and devotee. He would dissuade people from meeting Sri Ramakrishna, and would have his own teachings ready at hand to give to people. Here is one such teaching of his.

Hazra began to explain *tattvajnana.*

Hazra: 'The meaning of *tattvajnana* is the knowledge of the existence of the twenty-four *tattvas,* or cosmic principles.'

He was wrong about the meaning of the word.

A devotee: 'What are they?'

Hazra: 'The five elements, the six passions, the five organs of perception, the five organs of action, and so forth.'

M. *(to the Master, smiling)*: 'He says that the six passions are included in the twenty-four cosmic principles.'

MASTER *(smiling)*: 'Listen to him! Notice how he explains *tattvajnana!* The word really means 'knowledge of Self'. The word *'tat'* means the Supreme

Self, and the word *'tvam'*, the embodied soul. One attains Supreme Knowledge, *tattvajnana,* by realizing the identity of the embodied soul and the Supreme Self.'

After a few minutes Hazra left the room and sat on the porch.

MASTER *(to M. and the others)*: 'He [meaning Hazra] only argues. This moment perhaps he understands, but the next moment he is his old self again.[1]

What is *Tattva–Viveka*?

Tattvabodha begins with an invocation. It then mentions that any book should pass four tests:

(a) Who is it meant for? What should be the qualifications of the aspirant who reads this book and wishes to know the Truth?

(b) What is its theme? What is the theme of Vedanta?

(c) What is the connection between its theme and the seeker? What does the seeker want when he reads this book, and what does the book give? What does the book give, and what connection does that have with the theme of Vedanta? and

(d) What is the use of reading it?

In the last few chapters, the book discussed the fit aspirant who wishes to know the Truth. It now deals with the theme of the book, and of Vedanta. And that theme is knowing the Self.

'With the mind controlled in *samādhi,* see the Atman of infinite glory. Cut off your bondage, strengthened by the impressions of previous births, and carefully attain the consummation of your human birth,' says the *Vivekacūḍāmaṇī* (411).

Sri Ramakrishna says: 'I learnt Vedanta from Nangta: "Brahman alone is real; the world is illusory." The magician performs his magic. He produces a mango-tree which even bears mangoes. But this is all sleight of hand. The magician alone is real.'[2]

Having brought us upto the threshold of *mumukṣutvam*, the author of *Tattvabodha* presents the ideal now. The aspirant has practised the fourfold sadhana and has grown tremendous dispassion, discrimination, right knowledge, and concentration, and is the possessor of the six treasures. He will be ready to know what he is truly seeking.

तत्त्वविवेकः कः ?

आत्मा सत्यः तदन्यत्सर्वम् मिथ्या इति ॥

Tattva-vivekaḥ kaḥ?
Ātmā satyaḥ,
tadanyat sarvaṁ mithyā iti.

Kaḥ what is; *tattva-vivekaḥ* true knowledge? *Ātmā* the Self *satyaḥ* is true, *tadanyat sarvaṁ* all the rest *mithyā (are)* false *iti.*

What is true knowledge?

The Self alone is True and everything else is false—this is true knowledge.

Ātmā Satyaḥ

Upadeśa Sāhasrī (18.25-26) declares: 'Everything such as agency—superimposed on the Self by the ego—is negated along with the ego on the basis of the scriptural injunction, "Not this, not this." Then we know the Self to be Self-effulgent, Innermost Existence, free from actions, true, and the Self of all.'

Knowing the Self

Sri Ramakrishna says: "One ultimately discovers God by trying to know who this 'I' is. Is this 'I' the flesh, the bones, the blood, or the marrow? Is it the mind or the buddhi? Analysing thus, you realize at last that you are none of these. This is called the process of 'Neti, neti', 'Not this, not this'. One can neither comprehend nor touch the Atman. It is without qualities or attributes."[3]

There is a beautiful verse in the *Upadeśa Sāhasrī* (11.6): 'I am Brahman, of the nature of Pure Consciousness, without qualities, free from ignorance, free from the three states of waking, dream, and deep sleep. I am the Witness, free from defects. I am in everyone.'

Swami Vivekananda says: 'If we have known the Atman as It is, if we have known that there is nothing else but this Atman, that everything else is but a dream, with no existence in reality, then this world with its poverties, its miseries, its wickedness, and its goodness will cease to disturb us. If they do not exist, for whom and for what shall we take trouble? This is what the Jnana-Yogis teach. Therefore, dare to be free, dare to go as far as your thought leads, and dare to carry that out in your life.'[4]

Vivekacūḍāmaṇī (412) says that the seeker should meditate on the Atman, which is devoid of all limitations, which is of the nature of Being-Consciousness-Bliss Absolute, and which is one without a second. By doing so he or she will not be born in this world of suffering again.

About Tattva-Vivekins

Are there enlightened souls who have succeeded in their efforts, and also recorded their experiences? Of course yes. The number of those who have succeeded in attaining the Self or Truth down the ages is numerous. Though the *Gītā* says that of the thousands who strive to attain the Self only a few succeed, those few are a huge number.

In the *Taittirīya Upaniṣad* (1.10) there is a wonderful mantra, an exclamation from a sage immediately after attaining the Truth. Sage Triśanku, immediately after realization, said: 'I am like the topmost twig of the tallest tree. My fame has spread far and wide. I am everywhere. I am pure from top to bottom. I am victorious. I am immortal.'

Even in modern times we have the experiences of all the direct disciples of Sri Ramakrishna, of Holy Mother, and of Sri Ramakrishna himself. Sri Ramakrishna said towards the end of his physical existence: 'Nowadays I do not see Your form. Now I see You both inside me and outside. I see that it is You who have become the universe, all living beings, the twenty-four cosmic principles, and everything else. You alone have become mind, intelligence, everything. ...Now I see that I and the Mother have become one.'[5]

Swamiji remarks: 'He is with me, the Beloved, He was when I was in America, in England, when I was roaming about unknown from place to place in India. What do I care about what they talk — the babies, they do not know any better. What! I, who have realised the Spirit and the vanity of all earthly nonsense, to be swerved from my path by babies' prattle! Do I look like that?'[6]

The Nature of the Self

The Atman is beyond thought and word. It cannot be expressed. Yet some expressions have been given to make us, ignorant people, understand It at least intellectually, so that we may know It. Knowing, in the strict sense, is not possible because the Atman cannot be known. It is knowledge itself. By 'knowing' removal of the veil of ignorance is meant. If knowledge is acquired, it may go away also because that which is born will die. Not so with *tattva viveka.* So the Atman is revealed when ignorance is removed.

The Atman is described in some words so that we may understand its existence. It is, for instance, called *sat-cit-ānanda.* The *Kaṭha Upaniṣad* (1.3.2-8) gives the example of the charioteer to express the nature of the Self. It finally says (2.3.17) that the Self or Atman is the size of the thumb, and is ever present in the hearts of living beings. It has to be carefully and with great patience separated from the body-mind complex. Then alone can a person become immortal. All the Upaniṣads give similar glorious explanations of the Atman. The next chapter will discuss the Atman further. Now, what is the use of such discussion if the Atman is not comprehended by the intellect?

Vedantins say that *vicāra* or thinking and cogitating about the Truth is a good exercise. According to Advaitins, there are three ways of knowing the Truth; rather, the sadhana of the path of knowledge is threefold: (a) *vicāra*; (b) *dhyāna* on the formless; and (c) listening, thinking and meditating on the Vedantic truths like 'You are That.' The first, *vicāra* is generally about the temporality and non-eternality of things. What is permanent in this changing universe? This is the fundamental question of the student. He either questions himself as to who he is, or follows the negative method of rejecting everything that is not the real "I" by the method of '*neti, neti*'. This *vicāra* purifies the mind, makes the intellect sharp, and brings in dispassion for the non-eternal things.

Anyat Sarvam Mithyā

'Everything else is unreal.' *Mithyā* is unreality, but this unreality connotes impermanence. The Truth that there is only one Reality, called Brahman by Advaita, and that the world is a superimposition on that, is the spiritual viewpoint—the *pāramārthika* viewpoint. From the secular viewpoint—the *vyavahāra,* creation becomes a changing reality. Yet this creation, including our body and mind, are impermanent. 'When the pure, effulgent Atman is covered by *tamas,* being deluded, the fool takes the body to be the Self. From this confusion comes all other negative qualities. Thus there is bondage,' declares the *Vivekacūḍāmaṇī* (140).

From our scriptures, we can gather the process of the soul's evolution in brief: The living being first of all is in a state of ignorance where he understands that the world alone is real and everything else is false. As his intelligence grows, he begins to understand that there is some higher reality. But that reality is vague and is somewhere in heaven. Further still, the individual understands that the Reality or God is within all beings, and is hidden. When he does sadhana and finally reaches a stage where he sees the Self or God alone, he understands that God alone is real and everything else—the body, the world—is unreal like a dream.

Sri Ramakrishna goes further. He says:

> But for my part I accept everything: ... I accept all—Brahman and also *māyā* , the universe, and its living beings. If I accepted less I should not get the full weight.
>
> A devotee asks him: 'The full weight? How is that?'
>
> Sri Ramakrishna: 'Brahman is qualified by the universe and its living beings. At the beginning, while following the method of "Not this, not this", one has to eliminate the universe and its living beings. But as long as 'I-consciousness' remains, one cannot but feel that it is God Himself who has become everything. He alone has become the twenty-four cosmic principles.'[7]

This state is called *vijñāna* by Sri Ramakrishna. This state, according to pundits, has not been recorded in the scriptures. Sri Ramakrishna himself has declared that his experiences have gone beyond the Vedas and the Vedanta.

Sri Ramakrishna and *Vijñāna*

For the Advaitin, *tattva viveka* ends when knowledge of the Atman is revealed. But Sri Ramakrishna goes beyond. Sri Ramakrishna says: '... a man cannot preserve his body after attaining Brahmajnana. The body drops off in twenty-one days. ... He is like those who retain their bodies, even after attaining Brahmajnana, in order to teach others. Divine Incarnations belong to this class.'[8] He speaks of the next higher state called *vijñāna.* What is *vijñāna* according to Ramakrishna? One may conjecture that *vijñāna* is a state after *jnāna*. The usual questions are: (a) What happens to a *brahmajnāni* after he attains knowledge? (b) How does he live in the world? (c) How does he look at the world? (d) How does he behave here in this world until he has *videha-mukti*? Though these ideas are taken up towards the end of this book by Śankara, we shall mention Sri Ramakrishna's ideas here. These questions are answered by Sri Ramakrishna's *vijñāna*.

Ramakrishna says that *vijñāna* is (a) a special type of knowledge; (b) going beyond the three gunas; (c) seeing the universe as the manifestation of Brahman; (d) realizing God; (e) talking intimately to God; (f) to know God as one's own relative. In all, there are about 8 entries on *vijñāna* in the *Gospel of Sri Ramakrishna* and we provide them here.

> The jnāni gives up his identification with worldly things, discriminating, 'Not this, not this.' Only then can he realize Brahman. ... But the vijnāni, who is more intimately acquainted with Brahman, realizes something more. He realizes that the steps are made of the same materials as the roof: bricks, lime, and brick-dust. ...The vijnâni sees that the Reality which is Nirguna, without attributes, is also saguna, with attributes. ... Those who realize Brahman in samâdhi come down also and find that it is Brahman that has become the universe and its living beings. .... The vijñāni further sees that what is Brahman is the Bhagavān, the personal God.[9]
>
> 'But there is a stage beyond even Brahmajnana. After jnāna comes *vijñāna*. ... What is *vijñāna*? It is knowing God in a special way. The awareness and conviction that fire exists in wood is jnāna, knowledge. But to cook rice on that fire, eat the rice, and get nourishment from it is *Vijñāna*. ... The realization that God alone has become the universe and all living beings is *vijñāna*.[10]
>
> 'What is *vijñāna*? It is to know God distinctly by realizing His existence through an intuitive experience and to speak to Him intimately. That is why Sri Krishna said to Arjuna: 'Go beyond the three gunas.' 'In order to attain *vijñāna* one has to accept the help of vidyāmāyā. Vidyāmāyā includes discrimination... and dispassion, and also chanting God's name and glories, meditation, the company of holy persons, prayer and so forth.[11]

'...In other words (the jīva) removes the thorn of ajñāna, ignorance, by means of the thorn of jñāna, knowledge. But on attaining *vijñāna,* he discards both thorns, knowledge and ignorance. Then he talks intimately with God day and night. It is no more vision of God.[12]

'Jñāna is the realization of Self through the process of 'Neti, neti', 'not this, not this'. ...But *vijñāna* means knowledge with a greater fullness. ...After having the vision of God one talks to Him as if He were an intimate relative. That is *vijñāna.*[13]

'The jnâni says "This world is a framework of illusion." But he who is beyond both knowledge and ignorance describes it as a "mansion of mirth". He sees that it is God Himself who has become the universe, all living beings, and the twenty-four cosmic principles.[14]

'To know many things is ignorance. To know that God dwells in all beings is knowledge. And what is *vijñāna*? It is to know God in a special manner, to converse with Him and feel Him to be one's own relative.[15]

'To know many things is *ajñâna,* ignorance. To know only one thing is *jñāna,* Knowledge—the realization that God alone is real and that. He dwells in all. And to talk to Him is *vijñāna,* a fuller Knowledge. To love God in different ways, after realizing Him, is *vijñāna.*[16]

Swami Vivekananda uses *vijñāna* in a slightly different sense. For him, jñāna is intellectual knowledge, and *vijñāna* is realization. There are only three instances where he uses *vijñāna* in *Complete Works*. He says: 'There are two words: one is Jnana, the other Vijnana. Jnana may be translated as science—this means intellectual [knowledge] only—and Vijnana as realization. God cannot be perceived by intellectual knowledge. He who has realized [the Self] by that supreme knowledge—what will become of that man?'[17] 'There are two ends or aims of human life, real knowing (Vijnana) and bliss.'[18] 'According to Vedanta, the three fundamental factors of consciousness are, I exist, I know, and I am blessed.... That knowledge itself is Vijnana, neither intuition, nor reason nor instinct. The nearest expression for it is all-knowingness.'[19]

In our scriptures, the word *vijñāna* has not been used in the sense in which Sri Ramakrishna uses it. By this term, our Upaniṣads mean special knowledge, that is all. But there is the idea of the *jīvanmukta,* the *paramahamsa,* or the *avadhūta.* These illumined souls live in this world after their Self-realization. What they do, how they live, and so on are mentioned in *Bhāgavata* and other scriptures.

Suggested Reading

1. About the Atman:

a. *Upadeśa Sāhasrī,* Chapters 3 and 9.

b. *Bhagavadgitā,* Chapter 2.

c. *Kaṭha Upaniṣad,* Chapter 1.3.

2. About *Vijñāna* of Sri Ramakrishna:

'Sri Ramakrishna as the Spiritual Teacher' in *Sri Ramakrishna the Great Master.*

References

1. Gospel, p. 591
2. Gospel,p. 297
3. Gospel, p. 180
4. Complete Works, Vol. 3, p. 11
5. Gospel, p. 440, 942

6. Complete Works, Vol. 5, p. 136
7. Gospel, p. 652
8. *Gospel,* p. 354
9. *Gospel,* p. 104
10. *Gospel,* pp. 287-88
11. *Gospel,* p. 781
12. *Gospel,* p. 404.
13. *Gospel* p. 417
14. *Gospel,* p. 523
15. *Gospel,* p. 911
16. *Gospel,* pp. 598-9
17. Complete Works, Vol. 9, p. 239
18. Complete Works, Vol. 8, p. 23
19. Complete Works, Vol. 2, p. 462-3

Chapter 10

THE ATMAN

The Glory of the Atman

Little Bhṛgu, a boy of five or six, came to his father Varuṇa. The father asked his son what he wanted. Bhṛgu said that he wanted to know Brahman. If a modern father hears this he will either laugh at his son, scold him, or beat him. Varuṇa did none of this. That was the spirit of ancient India. He told his son: 'Your question is indeed virtuous, my son. What I would suggest is, strive to know the Truth yourself!' If the father, who was a knower of Brahman, had told his son what Brahman was, the son might not have understood it. Preparations were needed. So the father showed him the way.

Thus began the wonderful *tapas* of Bhṛgu. He would spend days and months in deep thought and contemplation, and he would discover something; some truth would become clear to him. He would rush to his father and say: 'I have known Brahman.' The father would understand with a single glance that the boy had not yet reached the highest. So he would only say again and again: 'Know Brahman by striving.'

Bhṛgu first discovered that food was Brahman and had reasons for it. Then he thought *Prāṇa* or life force was Brahman. Then he discovered mind was Brahman. Then he said *vijñāna* was Brahman. He was almost at the doorstep of Truth, thought Varuṇa, and sent him back for the final discovery. When Bhṛgu came back at last, his face said he had achieved it. His final discovery was that bliss was Brahman. This is the wonderful method taught in the *Taittirīya Upaniṣad* (*Bhṛguvallī*).

Atman in the Upaniṣads

In the *Bṛhadāraṇyaka Upaniṣad* (4.4.20), it is said: 'विरजः पर आकाशादज आत्मा महान्ध्रुवः ॥ The Atman is purer than space and is for ever true.' The Upaniṣad says in the next mantra that by thinking and meditating on that alone do sages attain fulfilment. This Atman is eternal.

Describing the Atman in glorious terms, this Upaniṣad says (4.4.22) that the Atman is 'the source of all, the end of all, the Lord of all, the heart of all. It never increases by good deeds nor decreases by bad ones. It or He is the supreme Source of all. He is the Liberator. In order to attain Him, sages perform sacrifices, give alms, and perform severe austerities. After attaining It, they become *munis,* enlightened sages. It is for the sake of this Atman that mendicants renounce the world and wander everywhere. It is for the sake of the Atman that men give up everything, thinking that wealth, progeny, heavenly pleasures, and everything else is worthless; they thus take to begging. They give up all desires for the sake of the Atman.' Such is the glory of the Atman.

The *Śvetāśvatara Upaniṣad* (3.19,20) says that the Self is fastest though without legs, grasps though without hands, sees everything though without eyes, and hears everything though without ears. He knows the knower and there is no one who can know It. It is smaller than the smallest atom and bigger than the biggest. It is in the citadel of the heart of all beings. He who sees It overcomes sorrow and bondages.

The Upaniṣads never tire of declaring that the Atman alone is real, eternal, source of bliss, and strength. Truth is eternality. Untruth is temporality. The body perishes and so does the mind. The world is constantly changing. There is something that is unchanging in this scenario of change. That is the Self. According to Śri Śaṁkara, the Upaniṣads exhaust themselves in describing the Self. The *Īśāvāsya Upaniṣad* (4) speaks about the nature of the Self in this manner: 'It moves, it moves not; It is near; it is far; It is within everything and everyone; it is outside everything and everyone.'

Was the Self Created?

Our scriptures do not leave anything to chance. They take all aspects of everything into consideration, and give satisfying answers based on experience. There could be a question that, since everything is created, Brahman too could have been created. To this, the *Brahma Sūtras* (2.3.9) says: 'असम्भवस्तु सतोऽनुपपत्तेः, *asaṁbhavastu sato'nupapatteḥ*, the origin of Brahman is impossible on account of illogicality.' The illogicality here is, how can everything and everlasting Truth come out of nothing, since It is the source of everything? 'असद्वा इदमग्र आसीत्, ततो वै सदजायत, *asadvā idamagra āsīt, tato vai sadajāyata,* in the beginning there was non-being; from this came out being,' declares the *Taittirīya Upaniṣad* (2.7.1). The next question is about the Atman. Did the Atman originate? Vedanta asserts that the Atman, which is nothing but Brahman, is never born, and never dies. *Brahma Sūtras* (2.3.17) declare: 'The individual soul has no origin because the Upaniṣads do not mention this. Moreover, it is eternal.' In the *Bṛhadāraṇyaka Upaniṣad* (4.4.25), the Vedas declare: 'This birthless Self is unchanging, immortal, without death, fearless, and is Brahman.' The *Kaṭha Upaniṣad* (1.2.18) says: 'The Self is neither born nor dies. It is birthless, eternal, and unchanging.'

The Struggle for the Atman

The question asked in the previous chapter was, what is *tattva-viveka* or the knowledge of the Truth? The answer given was that knowing the Atman is knowledge. We quoted from scriptures and authorities about what Truth is and how it is known. In this chapter, the author discusses the Atman, which was mentioned in the previous chapter.

What we see is not real; what we do not see is real. This is a puzzling situation. The sages of India strove immensely to pierce through the thick veil of ignorance and discover the Atman. Totapuri, for example, said that he had taken 40 long years to know the Truth, and expressed intense surprise when

Sri Ramakrishna entered *nirvikalpa samādhi* in just three days. If Totapuri took so long, what to speak of our ancient masters! We should therefore be ever grateful to those ancient masters who gave us this knowledge. The Upaniṣads are a repository of such glorious knowledge.

Swami Vivekananda tells us the way the Self was reached: 'We know how in old times, in all the ancient scriptures, this power, this manifestation of power, was thought to be a bright substance having the form of this body, and which remained even after this body fell. Later on, however, we find a higher idea coming—that this bright body did not represent the force. Whatsoever has form must be the result of combinations of particles and requires something else behind it to move it. If this body requires something which is not the body to manipulate it, the bright body, by the same necessity, will also require something other than itself to manipulate it. So, that something was called the soul, the Atman in Sanskrit. It was the Atman which through the bright body, as it were, worked on the gross body outside. The bright body is considered as the receptacle of the mind, and the Atman is beyond that. It is not the mind even; it works the mind, and through the mind the body.'[1]

Different Views about the Atman

There were different views about this Atman, though by and large there was agreement that it is beyond the body and mind. Some said the Atmans are many, some said it is one.

Some thought that the body is the Self. Such people are there even today. The Cārvākas were a school of philosophy in India. They had various opinions about the Self. One group thought that the son was the Self of the father. Still others were there, who thought that the senses were the Self. There were some other Cārvākas who said that the life force, *prāṇa* was the Atman. One more group went a little further still, and said that the mind was the Self.

The Buddhists come next. They do not believe that there is any permanent element behind the transitory. They therefore say that the intellect, *buddhi,* is the Atman.

Even amongst those who followed the Vedic religion, there was some confusion about the Self. The Pūrva Mīmāsakas, the followers of the sacrificial portion of the Vedas,

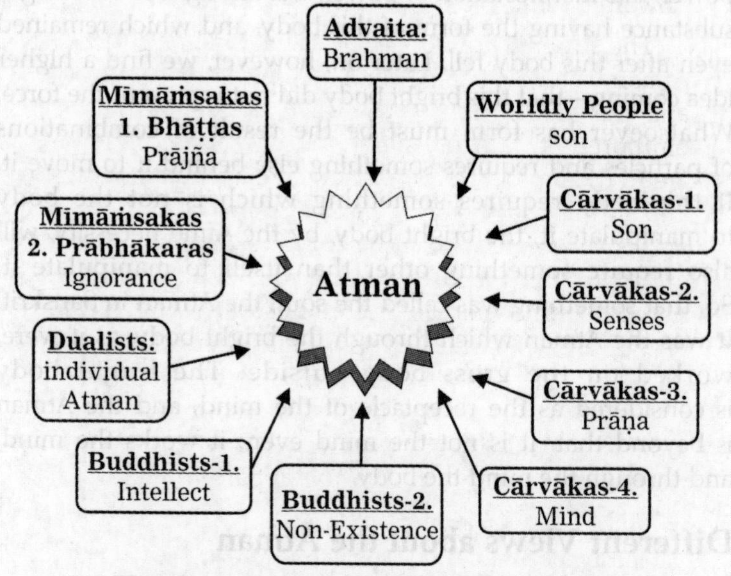

Different Opinions about the Atman

said that the causal body is the Self. They had two schools. One was headed by Prabhākara Miśra, and the other by Kumārila Bhaṭṭa. Prabhākara said that ignorance (*ajñāna*) is the Self. The Bhāṭṭas too said that the Self, enveloped by *māyā*, is the Self. The Buddhists of the Void School (*Śūnyavādi*), originated by Nāgārjuna, said that 'Nothing' is the Self. The Christian idea of the soul is that it is the mind. The Islamic concept of the soul too is that it is the mind. The Jains consider the soul to be that which is freed from all *pudgala* or dust, and that it is of the same size as that of the body. The Atmans, according to them, are countless.

Thus we see that there have been different conceptions about the Atman. Even amongst the Vedantists there are varied ideas about the Self. The Viśiṣṭādvaitins, the Rāmānujites, say that the Atman is of the size of an atom. This Atman is a quality of Brahman. The dualists say that the Self is separate and God is separate.

Swamiji said:

> The different philosophies seem to agree that this Atman, whatever it be, has neither form nor shape, and that which has neither form nor shape must be omnipresent.... Time, space and causation, therefore, are in the mind, and as this Atman is beyond the mind and formless, it must be beyond time, beyond space, and beyond causation. Now, if it is beyond time, space, and causation, it must be infinite. Then comes the highest speculation in our philosophy. The infinite cannot be two. If the soul be infinite, there can be only one Soul, and all ideas of various souls—you having one soul, and I having another and so forth—are not real. The Real Man, therefore, is one and infinite, the omnipresent Spirit. And the apparent man is only a limitation of that Real Man.[2]

Tattavabodha defines the Atman now.

आत्मा कः?

स्थूल-सूक्ष्म-कारण शरीराद्-व्यतिरिक्तः,
पञ्चकोशातीतः सन् अवस्थात्रय-साक्षी
सच्चिदानन्द-स्वरूपः सन् यस्तिष्ठति स आत्मा ॥

Ātmā kaḥ?
Sthūla-sūkṣma-kāraṇa śarīrād-vyatiriktaḥ, pañca-kośātītaḥ san avasthā-traya-sākśī
saccidānanda-svarūpaḥ san yaḥ tiṣṭhati sa ātmā.

Kaḥ who is *Ātmā* the Self? [That which is] *vyatiriktaḥ* different [from] *sthūla* gross; *sūkṣma* subtle; [and] *kāraṇa* causal; *śarīrād* bodies; *pañca-kośātītaḥ* beyond the five sheaths; *sākṣī* the witness; [of the] *avasthā-traya* three states of being; *svarūpaḥ* of the nature of; *saccidānanda* Being, Consciousness and Bliss; *yaḥ* he who *tiṣṭhati* remains; *saḥ* that is; *ātmā* is the Atman or Self.

Who is the Self?

Who or what is this Self? That which is different from the gross, subtle and causal bodies, that which is beyond the five sheaths, that which is the witness of all the three states of existence, and that which is of the nature of Being, Consciousness and Bliss, is the Self.

In this section, several terms have been used: gross (*sthūla*), subtle (*sūkṣma),* and causal (*kāraṇa*) bodies (*śarīras*); the five sheaths (*pañca-kośāḥ*); and the three states of being (*avasthā-traya*). The author of this book will take up each topic in the subsequent chapters.

The Atman: Its Nature

Swamiji says: 'According to our Indian system, there are two existences: nature on the one side and the Self, the Atman, on the other. By the word nature is meant not only all this external world, but also our bodies, the mind, the will, even down to what says "I". Beyond all that is the infinite life and light of the soul—the Self, the Atman. According to this philosophy the Self is entirely separate from nature, always was and always will be. There never was a time when the spirit could be identified even with the mind.'[3]

The Self or Atman is the only reality. It is the eternal principle behind the transcient phenomena. The goal of every individual is to know the Self or Atman. Swami Vivekananda says: 'The Advaitists here have a theory which they call Vivarta Vada or apparent manifestation. According to the dualists and the Sankhyas, the whole of this universe is the evolution of primal nature. According to some of the Advaitists and some of the dualists, the whole of this universe is evolved from God. And according to the Advaitists proper, the followers of Shankaracharya, the whole universe is the *apparent* evolution of God.'[4]

The sage of *Upadeśa Sāhasrī* expresses the glory of the Atman in numerous beautiful verses. We quote two of their translations: 'That person who sees the Atman as non-agent of actions and as having absolutely no connection with anything pertaining to lower ego, is the person of knowledge (14.22). If the Atman was subject to changes, it would become limited like any other object of the world. But it is beyond change and changelessness, and is all-pervasive (15.17).'

Tattvabodha began its discussion with salutations to the teacher. It then told us who a fit aspirant is to know the Truth. The book went on to explain the theme of the text, its connection with the philosophy as well as the seeker's desire to know, and the use of this knowledge. Tattvabodha then begins discussing the Self, and then the gross body.

References:

1. Complete Works, Vol. 2, p. 77.
2. Complete Works, Vol. 2, p. 78
3. Complete Works, Vol. 1, p. 470-1
4. Complete Works, Vol. 1, p. 372

Chapter 11

THE PHYSICAL BODY

The Vedanta View

Vivekacūḍāmaṇi (117) gives a beautiful description of the body: 'This body of ours is the product of food and comprises the material sheath; it lives on food and dies without it; it is a mass of skin, flesh, blood, bones and filth, and can never be the eternally self-existent Atman.' Continuing, the scripture adds (296): 'Therefore give up the identification with this lump of flesh.'

The body is the source of all trouble for us spiritual aspirants. Its upkeep, fulfilling its whims and so on, takes all our time. The more we indulge in it, the more are its demands. It is an unending chain reaction. It would have been good if this indulgence had brought us something positive. The body brings us nothing but suffering—a little thinking will tell us this fact. So all that we are doing for the body, except for the minimum, is a waste. And we keep on busying ourselves with our bodies—decorating, painting and fattening them—life after life.

Why this Body?

The body is not meant for enjoyment even as the pen is not meant for biting it. The body is an instrument in the hands of the subtle body. This body should be used only for liberating the Self or Atman from bondage and misery; for it is misery to imprison Bliss in a filthy cage. This is why we get suitable bodies. Our scriptures and saints are never tired of warning us not to indulge in bodily pleasures, but to make the body a fit instrument to cross over the ocean of worldliness. But we become attached to our bodies.

How did we get these bodies of ours? Our bodies are born of our past actions. Our bondage and suffering have been caused by the fruits of our past deeds, called *karmaphala*. We not only work out these *karmaphalas*, but add newer ones with each birth. This leads to newer birth, suffering, and death. The cycle goes on. In order to overcome this suffering, we should perform desireless, noble actions and dedicate all their fruits to God, say the teachers. Thus the *karmaphalas* will be reduced, and our spiritual practices like meditation, prayer, and so forth will further purify the mind, and then there is illumination. Once we know the Truth, the functions of the body will come to an end.

The Greatness of Human Birth

Of all the bodies, the human body is the greatest. It is through this body that we derive the maximum benefit. It is through this body that we can think of God and realize Him.

Śrī Śaṁkara says in his *Vivekacūḍāmaṇī* (4): 'The individual who, having attained the human birth and a male body, does not strive to attain the Truth is really a suicide. This is because he clings to the unreal.' Human birth is considered a great good fortune to get rid of the bondage of *samsāra* by all religions—ancient or modern. Hinduism, Buddhism, Jainism, Sikhism, even Christianity and Sufiism consider human birth as an opportunity to overcome bondages.

The human birth is great. Further, the male body has been eulogized from the ancient Indian viewpoint, because the woman was deprived of several social advantages and privileges, freedom of movement, and, not infrequently, education. This situation has changed now. In the Vedic age there were numerous women sages. In subsequent times, alien invasions and other causes made women prisoners, though there were exceptions always.

Anyway, the human birth is valuable. The human body is the greatest achievement of a person, because, as we said, it is our karma that leads to either bondage or release.

In this chapter, Śrī Śaṁkara speaks of the physical body:

स्थूल–शरीरं किम्?
पञ्चीकृत–पञ्चमहाभूतैः कृतम्
सत्कर्म–जन्यम् सुख–दुःखादि–भोगायतनम् शरीरम्,
अस्ति, जायते, वर्धते, विपरिणमते, अपक्षीयते,
विनश्यतीति षड्विकारवत् एतत् स्थूल–शरीरम् ॥

Sthūla-śarīraṁ kim?
Pañcīkṛta-pañca-mahā-bhūtaiḥ kṛtaṁ
satkarma-janyaṁ sukha-duḥkhādi-bhogāyatanaṁ śarīraṁ,
asti, jāyate, vardhate, vipariṇamate, apakṣīyate,
vinaśyati iti ṣaḍ-vikāravat etat sthūla-śarīram.

Kim what is *sthūla* gross physical *śarīraṁ* body? *Pañcīkṛta* [that which has undergone] the process of *pañcīkaraṇa; pañca* five, *mahā-bhūtaiḥ* of the five supreme elements; *kṛtaṁ* done; *satkarma-janyaṁ* born of good actions; *sukha* happiness; *duḥkhādi* misery etc; *bhogāyatanam* the experiencing instrument; [is] *śarīraṁ* the body. [It undergoes the following transformations:] *asti* is there; *jāyate* takes birth; *vardhate* grows up; *vipariṇamate* undergoes change; *apakṣīyate* decays; *vinaśyati* dies; *iti ṣaḍ-vikāravat* such six transformations; *etat* this *sthūla-śarīram* gross body.

What is this gross physical body?

That which is constituted of the gross elements and is made of the permutation of the five supreme elements;

and that which is called the experiencer of happiness or misery born of past good or bad actions is called the physical body. The body undergoes the following six transformations: it is born, it lives, it grows, it undergoes change, it decays, and it dies. This is the gross body.

Introductory

Tattvabodha began with the adoration of the guru. It then spoke about the four fundamental questions about the necessity of such a book: the aspirant, the subject-matter, the connection, and the use of such works. In discussing the fit aspirant, the qualifications of the aspirant for Brahman knowledge was discussed. The book next took up the subject-matter: knowledge of the Self or Brahman. It then discussed the Self. While discussing the Self, it mentioned that the Self is beyond the three bodies. It takes up those bodies one by one. First comes the physical body.

Pañcīkaraṇa

The term *pañcīkaraṇa* needs a small introduction. This subject will be dealt with fully in a separate chapter. Here we shall only introduce the topic. *Pañca* means 'five' and *karaṇa* means 'to do' or 'organs'. This means that the subject is related to something with 'five'. There are five elements: earth, fire, water, air, and space. These elements are in two forms: gross and subtle. Their subtle form is called *tanmātra*—'they alone'. That is, in their subtle form, each of these five elements is in a pristine pure state, unmixed with anything else. So they are neither experienced nor seen. When they become gross they are seen and experienced. To become gross, they are to be mixed with something else. Since there is nothing but the five elements only, they are mixed with one another. Thus, in air, there are water, earth, fire, and space. In fire, there is air, water, space, and earth also. This mixing follows a rule. If everything was mixed with one another in equal proportions, there would be only one element instead of five. So there is a method. This method is *pañcīkaraṇa*.

The system followed is, half of one element is mixed with one-fifth of the others. The major portion will contribute the characteristic. In air, half is air, while others are one-fifth each. In water, half is water, and the others contribute one-fifth each. This is *pañcīkaraṇa,* and thus we have the gross elements. This will be taken up later (see chapter 38).

In gross state, nothing is pure. Everything is mixed with one another.

Formation of the Subtle and Gross Bodies

We have seen now that (a) Brahman is enveloped by ignorance; (b) ignorance projects the five subtle elements; (c) the subtle elements undergo a transformation called *pañcīkaraṇa* to become gross elements. And thus from the supreme Fourth state, through the causal and subtle, there is the gross state. So Brahman, owing to *māyā,* becomes the causal, subtle, and then gross universe, as it were.

How are we individual beings—with bodies, minds, and souls — formed in this system? Our so-called individuality is unreal. This is the fundamental point of Śaṁkara. The moment we think 'I am separate', 'You are separate', etc, there is suffering. Our real individuality comes only

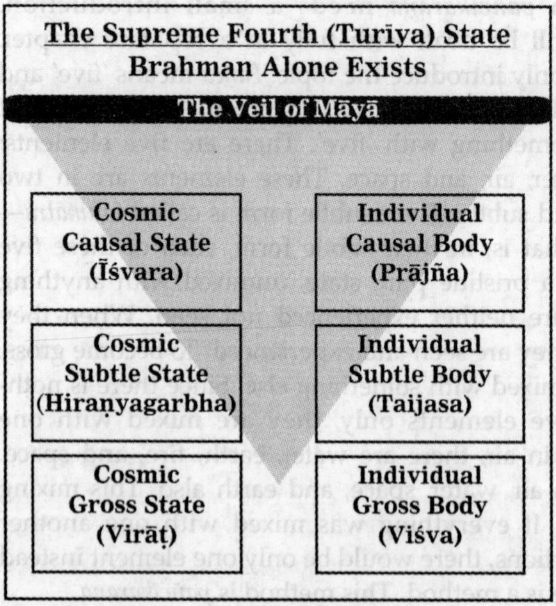

when we attain Oneness. Yet we are in ignorance now and our state needs explanation. So Vedanta has an answer to this question also.

When *māyā* envelops Brahman and thus consciousness plus ignorance becomes Īśvara, something more happens. This consciousness or Brahman enveloped by ignorance is, as it were, divided into a billion pieces—one in many and many in one. Just as the processing of the total Īśvara takes place, the processing of the individual too takes place. Īśvara, therefore, is nothing but a conglemoration of billions of tiny Īśvaras, called *prājñas*—a name for *our* causal personality. When the subtle elements are projected by *māyā* which has enveloped Brahman and made It Īśvara, these subtle elements give a subtle body to each little bit of Īśvara, called *taijasa.* This subtle body is interesting. While our causal body is nothing but Brahman plus ignorance, the subtle body is a coming together of 19 different things: 5 sense organs, 5 organs of action, 5 life forces called *prāṇas,* and 4 states of mind—mind, intellect, memory and ego. All these are created by the five subtle elements.

After *pañcīkaraṇa,* the five gross elements combine to create the gross body. The gross body of living beings are born of egg, seed, or by other means. The chart (on p.120) shows us the relative development from the Fourth state to the gross in the individual as well as the collective.

Initially, *māyā* covers Brahman (*āvaraṇa*) and 'divides' Brahman into trillions of parts, each representing a living being. Each living being is Brahman plus *māyā*. But Brahman can never be divided into parts. When we think of separateness, we are told that this 'separateness' is because of *māyā*.

Bhoga-āyatanam

Āyatana means the body. *Bhoga* means enjoyment. This body is created for the enjoyment of the fruits of our past actions. It is therefore called *satkarma-janyam* born of good actions. It is also called *sukha-duḥkhādi bhogāyatanam* the instrument experiencing happiness and misery.

Holy Mother Sri Sarada Devi says that this world is nothing but misery. In his Yoga commentary, Vyāsa says: 'सर्वम् दुःखं विवेकिनः, *sarvaṁ duḥkham vivekinaḥ,* for the wise, everything here is suffering only.' One such wise one was the Buddha. What we call enjoyment is only misery. Yet, we have birth, life, and death only on account of our past deeds. The body is there only for working out our past and realizing our true nature. Yet we get entangled and involve ourselves in newer karmas again.

When the soul suffers agony in this world endlessly, and finds no means of overcoming it, it turns to spiritual life. Slowly and steadily, it strives to know the cause of suffering and misery. Then it understands that the source of trouble is within, not outside. That troublemaker is ignorance. Through steady effort, the soul realizes its true identity, and thus ignorance goes. All the creation, if we may call it so, from Brahmā down to the individual physical body is to make us realize we are the Self.

From what has been said about the physical body, there may be a doubt about the Atman's relation with the three bodies, especially the gross. Is the body essential for the Atman? Or can Atman exist independently of the physical body? Some go to the extent of saying that since the Atman depends on the physical body for its expression, without the physical body it has no existence at all! In *Brahma Sūtras* (3.3.53), this very question of the doubters has been mentioned: 'एकः आत्मनः शरीरे भावात्, *ekaḥ ātmanaḥ śarire bhāvāt;* Since the soul depends on the body for its existence, the Self is no more when the body dies.' In the next *sūtra*, the answer is given: 'व्यतिरेकस्तद्भावाभावित्वान्न तूपलब्धिवत्, *vyatirekas-tadbhāvābhāvitvāt na tūpalabdhivat;* This cannot be. The body and soul are different because consciousness may not exist even if the body exists, as it is in the case of perception.'

Ṣaḍ-Vikāras

The six changes of the physical body. The six changes are: it is born (*jāyate*), it lives (*asti*), it grows (*vardhate*), it ages (*vipariṇamate*), it decays (*apakṣīyate*), and it dies (*naśyati*). These are the six changes of the body.

A. The Body Takes Birth (*jāyate*):

Living beings get their bodies in one of the four ways according to scriptures: through the womb, egg, moisture, and soil. Higher beings are born of the womb (*jarāyuja*); lower beings from the egg (*aṇḍaja*); still lower from moisture (*svedaja*); and the lowest from the soil (*udbhija*). The third division is evidently unscientific, since whether moisture or soil, the seed is needed. However, modern scientific methods are tallying with the words of the scriptures: we clone, we graft plant cuttings; we layer branches.

Some schools of thought in the world think that the body comes and goes and there ends the matter. Hindus too thought so once upon a time. They too believed that one-life theory is the correct theory. But nothing could be explained if this theory was adapted. A baby blind at birth, or lame at birth cannot be explained away as genetic or hereditary. Something else should be there. So the theory of karma was adapted after experience and deep thought. The soul takes up newer physical bodies endlessly, until it awakens to the truth that Truth is One.

Sri Ramakrishna says:

> He [Keshab Chandra Sen] asked me, 'Sir, is there an after-life?' I didn't commit myself either way. I said that the potters put their pots in the sun to bake. Among them you see both baked and soft pots. Sometimes cattle trample over them. When the baked pots are broken, the potters throw them away; but when the soft ones are broken they keep them. They mix

them with water and put the clay on the wheel and make new pots. They don't throw away the unbaked pots. So I said to Keshab: 'The Potter won't let you go as long as you are unbaked. He will put you on the wheel of the world as long as you have not attained Knowledge, as long as you have not realized Him. He won't let you go. You will have to return to the earth again and again; there is no escape. You will be liberated only when you realize God. Then alone will the Potter let you go. It is because then you won't serve any purpose in this world of maya.' The jnani has gone beyond maya. What will he do in this world of maya?

But God keeps some jnanis in the world of māyā to be teachers of men. In order to teach others the jnani lives in the world with the help of vidyamaya. It is God Himself who keeps the jnani in the world for His work. Such was the case with Sukadeva and Shankaracharya.[1]

B. The Body Lives (*asti*), It Grows (*vardhate*), It Ages (*viparinamate*):

After birth, the next problem is upkeep. For the upkeep of our bodies, we need food. Our scriptures have considered all angles of life. Though ignorant people blame our religion as otherworldly, it considers all issues—from birth to death and liberation—in detail. Regarding food, our sages have done a lot of thinking. They had to live in the forests and eat what little they got. They had to struggle to keep their bodies alive till they achieved the goal. So they knew the problem.

Scriptures declare that good and nourishing food, not necessarily vegetarian, should be taken for the body to help the aspirant in his meditation. Though purity of food is a different topic altogether, we may mention

Bhagavad Gītā (17.8-10), which says that that food which brings health, mental peace, strength, longevity, happiness, love, and other noble qualities is pious food. Bitter, salty, very hot or pungent, dry or burnt food produces pain, sorrow, and disease. So such food is better avoided. Food which is not properly cooked, putrid, stale, eaten by others, and so on is to be discarded altogether. So our scriptures are careful in such things. The *Taittirīya Upaniṣad* (2.2) says that human beings are born and they live through food. Food is Brahman, it declares. The Upaniṣad (3.2-6) also gives four important and practical norms regarding food: (a) Never waste food; (b) Increase food production by every means; (c) Never turn away someone seeking food in your house; treat guests well; and (d) Do not neglect food.

There are rare occasions when life has to be preserved by some means. At such times, one need not think about the purity of food, declare our compassion-ate scriptures. In the *Chāndogya Upaniṣad* (1.10.11), there is a remarkable story. Uśasti, a Brahmin by birth, is extremely poor. He and his wife have nothing to eat. So he goes to a *māhut*, an elephant keeper, definitely of a lower birth in those days, and begs food. That man has some beans (*kulāṁśa*), meant for the elephant, perhaps. Uśasti brings that home. He eats, but his wife does not. She gives it to him and asks him to go to the king to beg for food. Here, the scripture says that we can eat any food when our lives are in danger.

We read these words in the Bible: 'There is nothing from without a man that entering him can defile him but the things which come out of him, those are they that defile him.'[2] When our lives are in danger, our scriptures permit us to eat anything at hand—the purity or impurity of food need not be considered then. In *Brahma Sūtras* (3.4.28), we have this injunction: 'सर्वान्नानुमतिश्च प्राणात्यये तद्दर्शनात्, *sarvān–nānumatiśca prāṇātyaye tad-darśanāt*, One can eat all kinds of food when life is in danger.'

Sri Ramakrishna's opinion about food is best stated through this conversation he had with Narendra, which was Swami Vivekananda's pre-monastic name.

> Narendra: 'As regards food, one should take whatever comes.'
>
> Sri Ramakrishna: 'What you say applies only to a particular state of the aspirant's mind. No food can harm a jnani. According to the *Gita*, the jnani himself does not eat; his eating is an offering to the Kundalini. But that does not apply to a bhakta. The present state of my mind is such that I cannot eat any food unless it is first offered to God by a brahmin priest. Formerly my state of mind was such that I would enjoy inhaling the smell of burning corpses, carried by the wind from the other side of the Ganges. It tasted very sweet to me. But nowadays I cannot eat food touched by anybody and everybody. No, I cannot. But once in a while I do. *(To Narendra)* With you it is all right. You are in 'this' as well as in 'that'. You can eat everything now. *(To the devotees)* Blessed is he who feels longing for God, though he eats pork. But shame on him whose mind dwells on 'woman and gold', though he eats the purest food — boiled vegetables, rice, and ghee.[3]

Yogic practices can prolong life and keep away diseases. But for how long? There is always the problem of ageing. In spite of all our efforts, we can never make our bodies immortal. We have this concept of immortality because our Self is immortal. So we wish to keep the body immortal. This cannot be. Disease is always knocking at our doors. Our past actions have decided our lifespan and death. We do not know when death will come. So do all saints say that we should be up and doing. Death may come any moment. If this life is lost, God knows what our next birth would be like.

C. The Body Decays (*apakṣīyate*), and Dies (*naśyati*)

Death has puzzled human beings since time immemorial. The pre-historic peoples had their own ways of defining death and afterlife. Paintings, crude as they are, have been discovered, which show their conception of death and dying. Then there were the Egyptians who had terrible paintings done to scare away their enemies. The Egyptians, under Asurbanipal, are said to have painted men and women being slaughtered and murdered so as to scare their enemies. That was their way of looking at death. The Phoenician, early Judaic, Homeric, Epicurean, and Stoic Sumero-Akkadian peoples, says the *Encyclopedia*, didn't have much knowledge of afterlife. Whereas the ancient Egyptian, Zoroastrian, Orphic, Platonic, Christian, and Islamic civilizations have a concrete, "physical" notion of afterlife in which the soul (*nous*, mind), plays a vital role.

Afterlife gripped the imagination of almost all races to such an extent that the dead were 'preserved' and /or 'sent' with wonderful arrangements so that they might live peacefully hereafter. Egyptian mummies are an example of how well the ancient people thought about afterlife and how elaborate their arrangements were. Servants, chariots, army, priests, food, drink—the arrangements were simply astounding. They would embalm the body using bitumen and other costly ingredients. Removing the entrails, sucking out the brain from the nostrils, flushing out the inner stuff, filling the stomach and other organs with bitumen—it was a science in itself. The process of embalming and mummification was so elaborate that it would take seventy to eighty days to complete the preservation of one body. Truly enough, such an effort on the part of the Egyptian doctors has not gone in vain. Several thousand years later, we of the modern age are re-discovering those bodies, still intact, and are trying to take out cells from such bodies for cloning.

If such brilliant scientific thinking become realities, the efforts of our ancients could become fruitful indirectly, to some extent at least.

The ancient Greeks preserved the bodies of their heroes very well. For instance, their greatest hero, Alexander, was carried from Babylon, where he died, to Macedonia, in a casket filled with honey. Alexander the Great, we should remember, died only when he was 33 years old—a young and most successful ruler the world has ever produced. It was worthwhile that his body should have been preserved for posterity.

The Chinese too have had their own techniques of preserving the dead; and, recently, a woman's body has been unearthed, which is said to be at least 3,000 years old. The Christian and the Muslim have almost similar beliefs regarding death and afterlife, where the soul is taken for the Last Judgement. A 'good death' is what is expected of every Christian soul, and so extreme unction is given to the departing.

Holy Mother on Death and Afterlife

Why such troubles at preserving the body? The desire was that through this the person may become immortal. A devotee asked Holy Mother Sri Sarada Devi regarding death and rebirth. She gave wonderful answers to them. It is perhaps for the first time in world's history that the Divine Mother Herself answers vital questions of the human race. We have used the dialogue method to mention Holy Mother's answers here. Some questions were framed by us while most of them were by the questioner.

Why are we reborn?

Holy Mother: 'As long as a man has desires, there is no end to his transmigration. ... It is like taking the soul from one pillowcase and putting it into another; only one or two out of many men can be found who are free from all desires. Though one gets a new body on account of desires, yet one does not completely lose spiritual consciousness if one has to one's credit merits from previous births.'[4] '... One must live very carefully. Every action produces its results. It is not good to harass others or use harsh words towards others.'[5] 'The human being—today he is, tomorrow he is not. No one will accompany a person after his death. Only his actions—good or bad—follow him even after death.'[6]

You mentioned that some dead souls do not lose their consciousness. Is there any example for not losing one's awareness?

Holy Mother: 'A priest in the temple of Govinda in Brindavan used to feed his mistress with the food-offerings of the Deity. As a result of this sin, he got the body of a ghoul after his death. But he had served God in the temple. As a result of this merit, he one day appeared before all in his own physical body. It was possible for him to do so on account of his past good actions. He told people the cause of his inferior birth and said to them further, "Please arrange a religious festival and music for the redemption of my soul from this state. That will free me."'[7]

Is it possible to be freed from such states through religious festivals and music?

Holy Mother: 'Yes; that is enough for the Vaishnavas. They do not perform such obsequies as Śrāddha and so forth.'[8]

You just referred to the dead souls attaining to a divine state. Do they go there by themselves or does someone lead them there?

Holy Mother: 'No, they go by themselves. The subtle body is like a body made of air.'

We hear of ghosts and spooks. Are they the attendants of Siva or simply spirits? Or are they the spirits of dead people?

Holy Mother: 'They are the spirits of the dead. The spirit attendants of Siva belong to a special group.'[9]

Should we suffer for our bad actions then? Or is there a way out of this?

Holy Mother: 'No one will suffer for all time. No one will spend all his or her days on this earth in suffering. Every action brings its own result, and one gets one's opportunities accordingly.'[10]

What other way is there for sinners?

Holy Mother: 'If one surrenders himself totally at His feet, then the Master will see that everything is set right. One must bear with everything, because everything is determined by actions. Again, our present actions can counteract the effect of past actions.'[11]

Can action ever cancel action?

Holy Mother: 'Why not? If you do a good action, that will counteract your past evil action. Past sins can be counteracted by meditation, japa, and spiritual thought.'

What happens after one dies?

Holy Mother: 'All people, excepting highly evolved souls, live in the spirit body for a year. After that, food and water are offered in Gayā for the satisfaction of the departed souls and religious festivals are arranged. By these means the souls of the departed are released from their spirit body. They go to other planes of existence and experience pleasure or pain, and in course of time, are born again in human forms according to their desire. Others attain salvation from those planes. But if a person has some meritorious action to his credit in this life, he does not lose spiritual consciousness altogether in his spirit body'[12]. ...Deities and angels, whoever they be, are born again on this earth. They do not eat or talk in their subtle bodies. Hence they cannot stay in those planes for long.[13]

If they neither eat nor talk, how do they spend their days then?

Holy Mother: 'Immersed in meditation, they remain like wooden images where they are for ages! Like the images of the kings I saw in Rameswaram, standing there dressed in royal robes.'[14]

Then what is the necessity of spiritual practices?

Holy Mother: 'These dead souls, no doubt, attain to a higher state and live there for some time. But afterwards they are again born in this world according to their past desires. After their birth in a human body some of them obtain salvation in this life, whereas others take inferior births to reap the results of their karma. The world is moving around like a wheel. That indeed is the last birth in which one gets rid of all desire completely.'[15] ... 'It is the body alone that changes, the Atman always remains the same.'[16]

Is it possible to attain salvation by performing śrāddha in Gayā?

Holy Mother:' Yes, that is true.'

What is the proof of this?

Here, Holy Mother *shows* a tangible proof. That proof is in the form of a remarkable incident. The book says: 'The Holy Mother was in Banaras. I [i.e., Brahmachari Rasbehari, the author] had left a day or two before for Gaya to perform the Shraddha ceremony for my dead ancestors. I had said to the Holy Mother before my departure. "Mother, please give your blessings that my ancestors may attain heaven." On the very night of the day I offered food and drink in Gaya for the gratification of my departed ancestors, Bhudev, the Mother's nephew, who had accompanied her to Banaras, saw Holy Mother in a dream, engaged in Japa, with a crowd of people around her, saying, "Please give me salvation! Please give me salvation!" The mother sprinkled over them the holy water kept in a jar and said, "Go away, you are saved." Then they departed in great happiness. Then another man appeared. The mother said to him, "I cannot continue like this any longer." He begged of her a long time and at last received her grace. The next day Bhudev narrated this dream to the Holy Mother and she said in reply: "Rasbehari has gone to Gaya to perform the Sraddha ceremony of his ancestors. Therefore all these people have obtained their salvation." In fact, while offering oblations for my departed ancestors with great sincerity, I had also offered food and drink for the salvation of all those persons whose names I could remember at that time. I had prayed for the salvation of all of them.'[17]

Now, what happens to those for whom no śrāddha ceremony is performed in Gayā?

Holy Mother: They live in the spirit body until some fortunate ones born in their family perform the śrāddha ceremony in Gaya or some other forms of obsequies.

Is it not correct to eat śrāddha food?

Holy Mother: 'One should not eat food given at funeral obsequies (*śrāddha* ceremony). It does harm to devotional life.'[18]

Mother, we are householders. What shall we do at the Shraddha ceremony of our relatives?

Holy Mother: 'Supervise the ceremony and give help to your relatives so that they may not be offended. But try somehow to avoid taking meals on that day. If you cannot do that, on that day of the śrāddha ceremony eat what is offered to Viṣṇu or other gods. The devotees can partake of the food of the śrāddha ceremony if it is offered to God.'[19]

Will all those who see Lord Jagannātha during the Car Festival attain liberation?

Holy Mother: 'Once I visited the image of Jagannātha at Puri at the time of the Car Festival. I wept for sheer joy to see so many people having a view of the image of the deity. "Ah," I said to myself, "It is good. They will all be saved." But later on I realized that it was not so. Only one or two who were absolutely free from desires could attain liberation. When I narrated the incident to Yogin-Ma, she corroborated this by saying, "Yes, Mother, only people who are free from desires attain liberation (Mukti)."'[20]

Conclusion about *Ṣaḍ-Vikāras*

The body dies. True. But what about our sense organs, mind, and so on? What *we* call eye, ear, nose, and so on are only physical apertures or apparatus. The true eye, ear, and other sense organs are within us, in the subtle body. The subtle body is created just once. It goes on and on and on, in numerous bodies, until the Self realizes the Truth. So what changes with each birth is only the outer covering, called physical body. Nothing else changes. The same personality can take birth once as the human being, and another time as a tree—all due to the sins and virtuous acts committed in life. So our actions are extremely important. Noble actions—service to others, prayer, worship, meditation, selflessness—lead to higher realms while ignoble actions take us down. And this procession of birth and death goes on.

Swami Vivekananda says: 'We always forget that this world is a means to an end, and not an end itself. If this were the end we should be immortal here in our physical body;

we should never die. But we see people every moment dying around us, and yet, foolishly, we think we shall never die; and from that conviction we come to think that this life is the goal. That is the case with ninety-nine per cent of us. This notion should be given up at once. This world is good so far as it is a means to perfect ourselves; and as soon as it has ceased to be so, it is evil. So wife, husband, children, money and learning, are good so long as they help us forward; but as soon as they cease to do that, they are nothing but evil. If the wife help us to attain God, she is a good wife; so with a husband or a child. If money help a man to do good to others, it is of some value; but if not, it is simply a mass of evil, and the sooner it is got rid of, the better.'[21]

Thus, though the physical body is imperative to practise spiritual disciplines and to attain knowledge, it is not of any other value after one attains knowledge. It is definitely not meant for worldly enjoyments. As Sri Ramakrishna says: 'There is no harm in giving up one's body.... After attaining Knowledge some people give up their bodies. After the gold image has been cast in the clay mould, you may either preserve the mould or break it.'[22]

So the causal body is the doer, the subtle body is the agent, and the gross body is the instrument. The Self, which is even beyond the causal body, is beyond everything.

The Sheath Theory

Vedanta has several ways of approaching the same Reality. Once it is decided on explaining this superimposition called the cosmos as a relative reality to aid the ignorant, it divides this cosmos into three states: the causal, subtle, and gross. The individual too is divided similarly.

The second way of dividing the three states is in the form of five sheaths, called *kośas* in Sanskrit. The 'sheath' idea came to Vedantists perhaps because many of them were of the warrior class and had used the sword frequently. The five sheaths have been given five different names according to their essential nature.

This gross body is called the food (*annamaya*) sheath, since it is made up of food (*anna*). The other names will be mentioned as we pass on to those subjects.

In the case of the three states here, *māyā* or *avidyā* acts as the outer covering or sheath. Inside it is the Atman. *Brahma Sūtras* (2.3.16) says: 'चराचरव्यपाश्रयस्तु स्यात्तद्व्यपदेशो भाक्तस्तत्भावभावित्वात्, *caracara-vyapāśrayastu syāttadvyapadeśo bhāktastat bhāvabhāvitvāt*. Birth and death are in relation to the moving and the

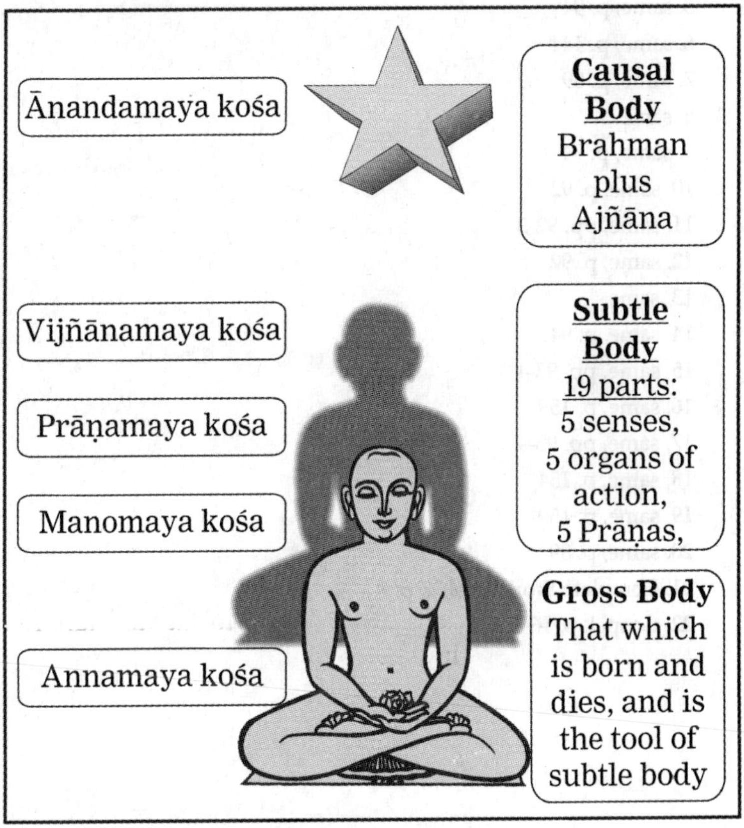

non-moving. With respect to the soul it must be taken in the secondary sense because only when the body is there do such things become valid.'

Tattvabodha has discussed the gross body here. It will next take up the subtle body.

References

1. Gospel, p. 669
2. *St Mark* (7.15)
3. Gospel, p. 564
4. Gospel of Holy Mother, p.89
5. same, p. 94
6. same, p. 144
7. same, p. 89
8. same
9. same, p. 94
10. same, p. 92
11. same, pp. 92-3
12. same, p. 92
13. same.
14. same, p. 94
15. same, pp. 93-4
16. same, p. 159
17. same, pp. 93-4
18. same, p. 154
19. same, p. 159
20. same, p. 89
21. Complete Works, Vol. 4, p. 8
22. Gospel, p. 164

Chapter 12

THE SUBTLE BODY

The Vision

In the *Gospel of Sri Ramakrishna,* we observe an interesting conversation. It is regarding Sri Ramakrishna.[1]

> In the mean time Vijay had become engaged in conversation with the other devotees.
>
> Vijay [Krishna Goswami]: "I feel as if someone were always moving with me. He shows me what is happening even at a distance."
>
> Narendra: "Like a guardian angel"
>
> Vijay: "I have seen him [meaning the Master] in Dacca. I even touched his body."
>
> Master [Sri Ramakrishna] *(with a smile):* "It must have been someone else."
>
> Narendra: "I too have seen him many a time. *(To Vijay)* How can I say I do not believe your words?"
>
> Vijay *(to Sri Ramakrikshna, with folded hands):* "I have now realized who you are. You don't have to tell me."
>
> Sri Ramakrishna *(in a state of ecstasy):* "If so, then so be it!"
>
> Saying, "Yes, I have understood", Vijay fell prostrate before the Master.

Living in this physical body and identifying ourselves with it, we human beings tend to forget the powers that are hidden within each one of us. We therefore reject any little thing that goes beyond our physical grasp and give such phenomena the name 'miracles'. Anything that happens beyond the pale of our comprehension is a miracle for us.

The human being is not merely the physical body. He has a subtle body, a causal body, and then the universal Spirit. What happens in the subtle and causal worlds is beyond our imagination. The incident we quoted above was related to the avatar, who, at his sweet will, can make anything happen. But even ordinary individuals can accomplish so-called supernatural feats, and it is all normal. How can that be done? In *vibhūtipāda*, Patanjali has given a big list of all that can happen when the mind is concentrated on some particular spots and things. According to yoga, the yogi can create newer physical bodies—exact replicas of himself if need be—to work out his past karma. Everything is science. 'Do this, and you will achieve this,' is the challenge. We do not strive, we do not want to strive, and therefore limit ourselves to the dumb, dead, physical body and say we are rational. A knowledge of the subtle world is imperative to live meaningfully. Further, by knowing the workings of our subtle bodies in detail, we can rise higher, assures Vedanta.

Swamiji says: 'Man is man so long as he is struggling to rise above nature, and this nature is both internal and external. Not only does it comprise the laws that govern the particles of matter outside us and in our bodies, but also the more subtle nature within, which is, in fact, the motive power governing the external. It is good and very grand to conquer external nature, but grander still to conquer our internal nature.'[2]

Tattvabodha takes up the subtle body now:

सूक्ष्म–शरीरं किम् ?

अपञ्चीकृत–पञ्चमहाभूतैः कृतम् सत्, कर्मजन्यम्
सुख–दुःखादि–भोग–साधनम् पञ्चज्ञानेन्द्रियाणि,
पञ्चकर्मेन्द्रियाणि, पञ्चप्राणादयः, मनश्चैकं,

बुद्धिश्चैका, एवम् सप्तदश–कलाभिः सह यस्तिष्ठति
तत्सूक्ष्म–शरीरम्।

Sūkṣma śarīraṁ kim?
Apañcīkṛta-pañca-mahābhūtaiḥ kṛtaṁ sat, karma-janyaṁ sukha-duḥkādi-bhoga sādhanaṁ pañca-jñānendriyāṇi, pañca-karmendriyāṇi, pañca-prāṇādayaḥ, manaścaikaṁ, buddhiścaikā, evaṁ saptadaśa-kalābhiḥ saha yastiṣṭhati tat-sūkṣma-śarīram.

Sūkṣma śarīraṁ kim What is the subtle body? *Apañcīkṛta-pañca-mahābhūtaiḥ* from the natural (unmixed) five supreme elements; *kṛtaṁ sat* those which are formed, *karma-janyaṁ* born of past actions; *sukha-duḥkādi-bhoga sādhanaṁ* the instruments of experience of pleasure and pain; *pañca-jñānendriyāṇi* the five organs of knowledge; *pañca-karmendriyāṇi* the five organs of action; *pañca-prāṇādayaḥ* the five vital forces; *manaścaikam* the mind; *buddhiścaikā* the intellect; *evam* in this manner; *saptadaśa-kalābhiḥ saha* with the seventeen elements; *yastiṣṭhati* that which is *tat-sūkṣma-śarīram* is called subtle body.

What is the subtle body?

Those organs that are formed from the unmixed five supreme elements, which are born due to past actions, and which are the instruments of pleasure and pain [are collectively called the subtle body. Its constituents are] the five organs of knowledge, the five organs of action, the five vital forces, the mind, and the intellect—these seventeen organs constitute the subtle body.

Sūkṣma śarīram

Sūkṣma śarīra means the subtle body. It is subtle because it cannot be seen by the eye or comprehended in any way. Yet it is there because our gross bodies are their expressions. As we said in the previous chapter, the gross physical body is only the external covering—a 'pillow case', as Sri Ramakrishna was fond of calling it. The gross body has several apertures using which the subtle body functions.

Swamiji gives a comprehensive view of the importance of the subtle body in a beautiful way. He says: 'According to this [Advaitic] theory, we have a body, of course, and behind the body there is what they call a fine body. This fine body is also made of matter, only very fine. It is the receptacle of all our Karma, of all our actions and impressions, which are ready to spring up into visible forms. Every thought that we think, every deed that we do, after a certain time becomes fine, goes into seed form, so to speak, and lives in the fine body in a potential form, and after a time it emerges again and bears its results. These results condition the life of man.

'Thus he moulds his own life. Man is not bound by any other laws excepting those which he makes for himself. Our thoughts, our words and deeds are the threads of the net which we throw round ourselves, for good or for evil. Once we set in motion a certain power, we have to take the full consequences of it. This is the law of Karma.

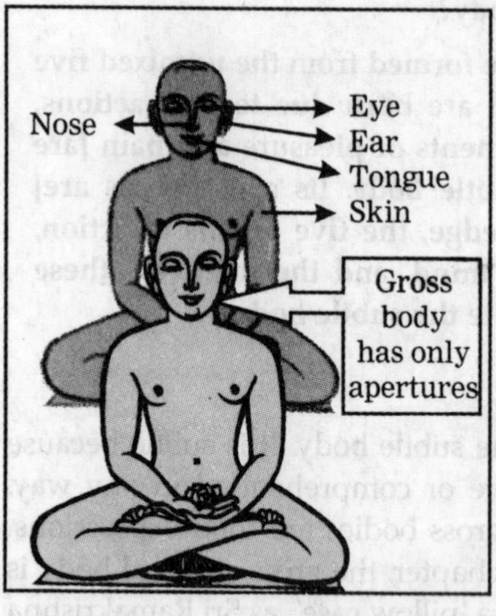

'Behind the subtle body lives Jiva or the individual soul of man. There are various discussions about the form and the size of this individual soul. According to some, it is very small like an atom; according to others, it is not so small as that; according to others, it is very big, and so on. This Jiva is a part of that universal substance, and it is also eternal; without beginning it is existing, and without end it will exist. It is passing through all these forms in order to manifest its real nature which is purity. Every action that retards this manifestation is called an evil action; so with thoughts. And every action and every thought that helps the Jiva to expand, to maniest its real nature, is good.'[3]

Swamiji has thus explained why the subtle or fine body is needed, what its activities are, and so on.

Karma-janyaṁ sukha-duḥkādi-bhoga sādhanam

'Born of actions and the instrument of enjoying or suffering.'

The human being, like all other beings, is trichotomous: we have a gross body, a subtle body, and the Self. Of itself, the gross body cannot do anything: it is made of dead matter, and it is totally dependent on the subtle body. The subtle body too is matter alone; yet it is finer. This subtle body runs the gross body. The light of the Atman falls on the subtle body and it is thus illuminated. This makes the subtle body active. The next section will tell us what the constituents of the subtle body are.

Saptadaśa-kalāḥ

The subtle body consists of seventeen constituents. These have been listed by the author of *Tattvabodha* as the following:

❋ Five Sense Organs (*Pañca-jñānendriyas*): eye, ear, nose, tongue and skin;

❋ Five Energies (*pañca-prāṇāḥ*): *prāṇa, apāna, vyāna, udāna,* and *samāna;*

❋ Five Organs of Action (*pañca-karmendriyas*): hands, legs, speech, organ of excretion, and organ of generation;

❋ *Manas* or the mind; and

❋ *Buddhi* or the intellect.

These are the seventeen elements forming the subtle body. The ego (*aham*) and the faculty of memory (*citta*) are included, respectively, in *manas* and *buddhi*. Therefore they are not mentioned separately. In all, thus, there are 19 elements.

The subtle body enters the gross body along with the causal body, and makes the gross body function. We confuse the gross body to be the true Self and try life after life to satisfy its needs. But its needs will never end. Whatever is done is done by the subtle body. The gross is only an instrument.

How is the individual subtle body created?

At the outset, scriptures say that unlike the gross the subtle body is manufactured once and for all. At the beginning of creation we get this subtle body, and it remains with us till we attain illumination. Its creation happens in this way: We have mentioned the five fundamental elements: earth, fire, water, air and space. In their essentially unmixed and pure state these five are called 'They Alone', *tanmātras*. These are formed from *māyā* or prakṛti. Prakṛti consists of the three qualities or *guṇas*. So these five *tanmātras* too are formed of the three *guṇas*. These five elements create the 17 constituents of the subtle body of the individual.

Combining all the subtle bodies on the cosmos, we get the supreme Subtle Body, the Hiraṇyagarbha, also called the cosmic Egg or the Source of the gross physical universe. Because Hiraṇyagarbha is the collective subtle body, it has intellect. This supreme intelligence a combination of all the intellects of all the beings put together, must be enormous. Hence that supreme intelligence is called *mahat*. This cosmic intelligence or Hiraṇyagarbha becomes the source of the physical cosmos and our own individual physical bodies.

The next part discusses the different parts of the subtle body.

References

1. Gospel, p. 885
2. Complete Works, Vol. 2, pp. 64-5
3. Complete Works, Vol. 2, p. 348

Chapter 13

THE ORGANS OF KNOWLEDGE

Introduction

Vedantic scholars have discussed every aspect of life and afterlife in detail. Their thoroughness is worth noticing. These scholars, who were persons of experience, have left no place for confusion. Thus in their explanation of the practical reality or *vyāvahārika sattā,* there are minute details of all the constituents of the subtle body, how they are formed, who governs them, and so on.

To go back a little: the aspirant comes to know about higher life and strives to purify his mind. He thus becomes a *mumukṣu.* This seeker after liberation should first of all know (a) what he actually is, (b) what this cosmos is, and (c) what Truth is. This book initially took up (a). It discussed the physical body. It has now begun discussing the subtle body. Having introduced the subtle body in the previous chapter, its constituents are considered one by one now. The first set is the sense organs.

श्रोत्रं त्वक् चक्षुः रसना घ्राणमिति पञ्च ज्ञानेन्द्रियाणि।
श्रोत्रस्य दिग्देवता, त्वचो वायुः, चक्षुषः सूर्यः,
रसनाया वरुणः, घ्राणस्य अश्विनौ इति ज्ञानेन्द्रिय-
देवताः ॥

श्रोत्रस्य विषयः शब्द-ग्रहणम्, त्वचो विषयः
स्पर्शग्रहणम्, चक्षुषो विषयः रूपग्रहणम्, रसनाया
विषयो रसग्रहणम्, घ्राणस्य विषयो गन्ध-ग्रहणमिति ॥

Śrotram tvak cakṣūḥ rasanā ghrāṇam iti pañca-jñānendriyāṇi. Śrotrasya dig-devatā, tvaco vāyuḥ, cakṣuṣaḥ sūryaḥ, rasanāyā varuṇaḥ, ghrāṇasya aśvinau iti jñānendriya-devatāḥ. Śrotrasya viṣayaḥ śabda-grahaṇam, tvaco viṣayaḥ sparśa-grahaṇam, cakṣuṣo viṣayaḥ rūpa-grahaṇam, rasanāyāḥ viṣayaḥ rasa- grahaṇam; ghrāṇasya viṣayaḥ gandha-grahaṇamiti.

Śrotram the ear; *tvak* the skin; *cakṣūḥ* the eyes; *rasanā* the tongue; *ghrāṇam* the nose; *iti pañca-jñānendriyāṇi* these are the five instruments of knowledge. *Śrotrasya* of the ear; *dig-devatā* [the presiding deity is] direction; *tvaco* of the skin, *vāyuḥ* air; *cakṣuṣaḥ* of the eyes *sūryaḥ* the sun; *rasanāyā* of the tongue *varuṇaḥ* the water-god Varuṇa; *ghrāṇasya* of the nose *aśvinau* the Aśvins; *iti jñānendriya-devatāḥ* these are the deities of the organs of knowledge. *Śrotrasya* of the ears, *viṣayaḥ* the object is *śabda-grahaṇam* sensing sound; *tvaco* of the skin *viṣayaḥ* object is *sparśa-grahaṇam* sensing touch; *cakṣuṣo* of the eyes *viṣayaḥ* the object is *rūpa-grahaṇam* sensing form; *rasanāyāḥ* of the tongue *viṣayaḥ* the object is *rasa- grahaṇam* sensing taste; *ghrāṇasya* of the nose *viṣayaḥ* the object is *gandha-grahaṇamiti* sensing smell.

The ear, the skin, the eyes, the tongue and the nose—these are the five instruments of knowledge. Of the ear, the presiding deity is direction. Of the skin, it is air. Of the eyes, it is the sun. of the tongue, it is Varuṇa. Of the nose, it is the Aśvins. These are the deities of the organs of knowledge. The function of the ear is sensing sound. Of the skin it is sensing feeling or touch. Of the eyes it is sensing form. Of the tongue it is sensing taste. And of the nose it is sensing smell.

Jñānendriyāṇi

'Organs of knowledge'. It may appear a bit surprising that Vedantins, who are so rational, should become a bit emotional at times and say that there are gods ruling over our sense organs. But this is the traditional view, which these Vedantins have adapted. Vedanta is nothing but the Vedas, and the Vedas have numerous gods and goddesses, which are expressions of that one supreme Being. These gods and goddesses are like officers looking after different quarters. In the *Brahma Sūtras* (1.3.25-33), there is a discussion about the gods. The discussion is whether the gods too can attain knowledge. Bādarāyaṇa, the author of the *Brahma Sūtras*, upholds the view that the gods can indeed attain knowledge, though other schools oppose this. So there are gods, and they have their responsibilities. There could be some scientific basis in saying, for instance, that the sun rules over the eye, etc. Who knows?

'Jñāna', knowledge; *'indriyāṇi'*, the sense organs. There are five sense organs which link us to the outer world. The external world, as we saw earlier, is made up of the five elements. The internal world, our subtle body, is made of the five elements. So it is all the play of the five elements alone. Distilling things further, it is all the play of Prakṛti alone.

Suppose there was no contact with the outer world at all. What would have happened? We would have remained sealed within our bodies like in a capsule. This is what is happening in the case of lower types of bodies—the tree for instance. It is unable to express itself. Similarly, we would have remained where we are, and would neither evolve to attain knowledge, nor evolve to enjoy the world. We would be like the dead body inside a coffin. In order to attain liberation, we should know we are bound and that we can attain liberation by study and meditation. If there were no sense organs to keep us in touch with the outer world, we would be like stocks and stones, with 'darkness hidden in darkness'—not knowing that we are in ignorance at all.

Consider a deaf, mute, and blind person who is insensitive to touch and cannot distinguish smell. All the doors of his to perception are closed. The first doubt is, are there no sense organs in this person? Oh yes, they are there. The outer apertures, in the physical body, are closed, that is all. When this person takes a new body, the latent sense organs begin to function, if the apertures are there.

The second doubt regarding such a person is, how is he or her to know that there is bondage and that liberation is possible? How can this person contact a teacher and acquire knowledge? How can this person meditate, and on what?

Therefore, just as the physical body is imperative to knowing the Truth, the physical world too is imperative, and our contact with the physical world too is necessary. So, says the *Kaṭha Upaniṣad,* that the Lord Himself created the senses as outgoing. The sense organs go out, and bring back knowledge of the external world. It is only after the sense organs reveal the external world that our organs of action begin to act. So the sense organs are vital.

2. The Process of Knowing: How do we know? How do sense organs function? According to Yoga and Vedanta, all knowledge—everything we know—is born of the modification of the mind. Mental modification is called *vṛtti.* When we see something, hear something or think of something, the mind becomes that thing seen, thought, or heard of for the moment. This becoming is called *vṛtti.* All knowledge we get, either internal through memory or dreams, or external through experiences, is *vṛtti* knowledge.

Of all the ways of knowing, to see, hear, smell, taste, and touch are the best and *direct* means of perception. Then there is the *inference*. The sound comes and you understand that someone has started the car. You read from the sacred books and learn the truth about God. This is another sort of perception. Thus there are six ways of knowing according to Indian thought, especially Advaita (see p.150). For all these, however, the sense organs are needed. The way the sense organs function has been shown in the figures on page 147.

Whatever we know must be known by the mind's going out, taking the form of the object, and returning to the

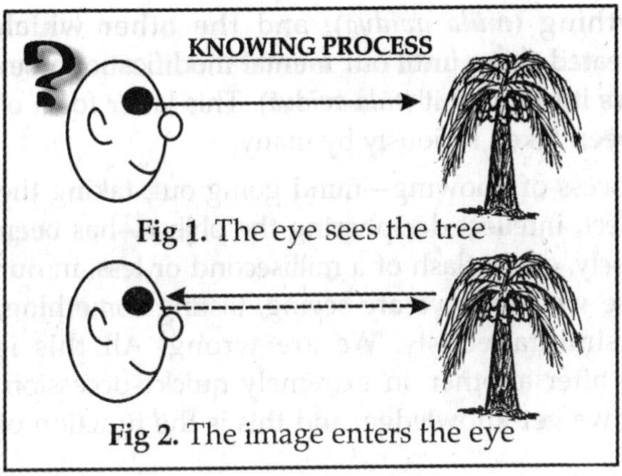

Fig 1. The eye sees the tree

Fig 2. The image enters the eye

brain centre. *Antaḥkaraṇa* means 'inner organ'. The mind, intellect, ego, and memory are inner organs while the life-forces, organs of knowledge, and organs of action are external organs, *bahihkarana.* The mind is generally confused. It cannot say what is what clearly. It refers the thing to the intellect. The intellect is the decisive factor of the *antaḥkaraṇas* or inner organs.

Before saying that something that was seen is a tree, for instance, it will refer to the storehouse of memory, called *citta.* This memory is not only one's own memory of millions of past lives but also the collective memory of the sum total of all souls. The answer comes from here that the thing seen was the tree. Thus there is knowledge. Yet it is not complete. The ego should identify itself with the thing seen. This is complete knowledge. There is a school of Advaita which speaks of two types of ignorance—that which envelops and

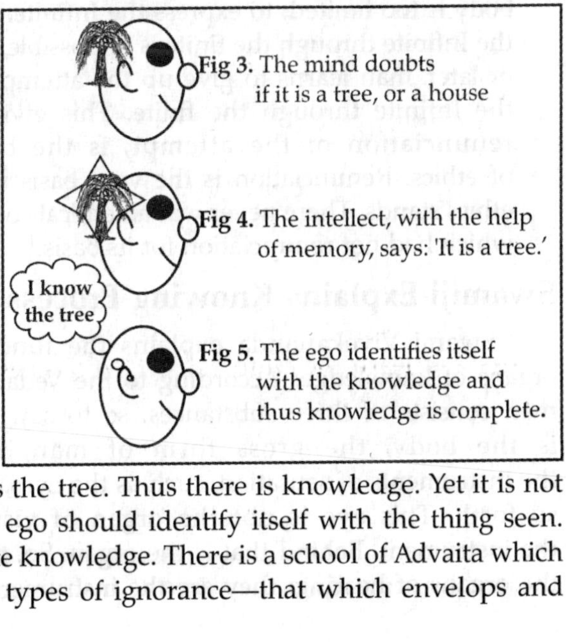

Fig 3. The mind doubts if it is a tree, or a house

Fig 4. The intellect, with the help of memory, says: 'It is a tree.'

Fig 5. The ego identifies itself with the knowledge and thus knowledge is complete.

projects everything (*mūla avidyā*), and the other which envelops the created thing until our mental modification goes out and destroys it to know it (*tūla avidyā*). This latter form of *avidyā* has not been taken seriously by many.

Such a process of knowing—mind going out, taking the form of the object, intellect deciphering the object—has been going on endlessly, every flash of a millisecond or less, in our system. Suppose we think we are seeing, tasting something, and listening simultaneously. We are wrong. All this is happening one after another, in extremely quick succession. This is the way we get knowledge, and this is the function of the senses.

Yet, in spite of all that the sense organs can show us, they are terribly limited. Swami Vivekananda says:

> But a few quickly discover that although they are struggling for infinite power, it is not through the senses that it can be reached. They find out very soon that that infinite pleasure is not to be got through the senses, or, in other words, the senses are too limited, and the body is too limited, to express the Infinite. To manifest the Infinite through the finite is impossible, and sooner or later, man learns to give up the attempt to express the Infinite through the finite. This giving up, this renunciation of the attempt, is the background of ethics. Renunciation is the very basis upon which ethics stands. There never was an ethical code preached which had not renunciation for its basis.[1]

Swamiji Explains Knowing Process

Swami Vivekananda explains the functioning of the organs of knowledge: 'According to the Vedanta philosophy, man consists of three substances, so to say. The outermost is the body, the gross form of man, in which are the instruments of sensation, such as the eyes, nose, ears, and so forth. This eye is not the organ of vision; it is only the instrument. Behind that is the organ. So, the ears are not the organs of hearing; they are the instruments, and behind them is the organ, or what, in modern physiology, is called the centre. The organs are called Indriyas in Sanskrit. If the centre which governs the eyes be destroyed, the eyes will not see; so with all our senses. The organs, again, cannot sense anything by themselves, until there be something else attached to them. That something is the mind.

'Many times you have observed that you were deeply engaged in a certain thought, and the clock struck and you did not hear it. Why? The ear was there; vibrations entered it and were carried into the brain, yet you did not hear, because the mind was not joined to the organ. The impressions of external objects are carried to the organs, and when the mind is attached to them, it takes the impressions and gives them, as it were, a colouring, which is called egoism, "I".[2]

'Take the case of a mosquito biting me on the finger when I am engaged in some work. I do not feel it, because my mind is joined to something else. Later, when my mind is joined to the impression conveyed to the Indriyas, a reaction comes. With this reaction I become conscious of the mosquito. So even the mind joined itself to the organs is not sufficient; there must come the reaction in the form of will. This faculty from which the reaction comes, the faculty of knowledge or intellect, is called "Buddhi". First, there must be the external instrument, next the organ, next the mind must join itself to the organ, then must come the reaction of the intellect, and when all these things are complete, there immediately flashes the idea, "I and the external object" and there is a perception, a concept, knowledge.'[3]

Six Ways of Knowing

We saw that the senses are like doorkeepers which bring knowledge of the outer world to the mind. Not all things in this universe are grasped straightaway by the five senses—of touch, smell, taste, hearing, and sight. There are so many things which we know indirectly, without the direct aid of the senses. Hindu sages have classified all such

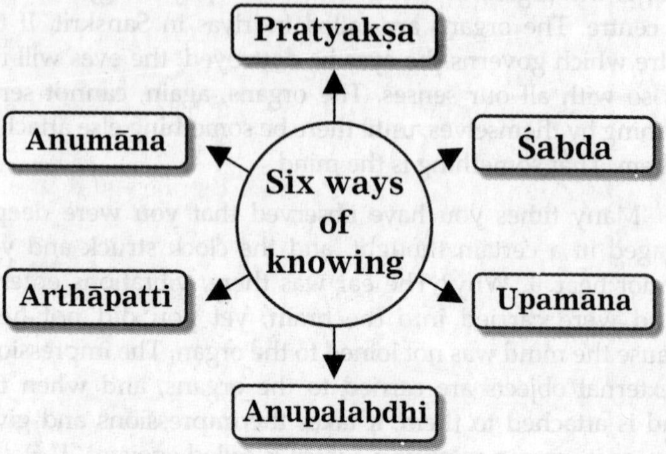

means of valid knowledge into six broad groups. These are called *pramāṇas. Pramāṇas* are valid means of knowledge. The knowledge that we gain through all these means should be foolproof. These six means of knowing are: (a) Direct Perception by Sense Contact (*Pratyakṣa*); (b) Inference by Previous Experience (*Anumāna*); (c) Verbal Testimony of the Vedas (*Śabda*); (d) Knowing by Example (*Upamāna*); (e) Conjecture from Insignificant Information (Arthāpatti); and (f) Absence of a Thing (Anupalabdhi).

a. Direct Perception by Sense Contact (*Pratyakṣa*):

I see, hear, smell, taste, and feel. Through these I come to know about the objects of the world. This is called *pratyakṣa.* If the object is not subtle, distant, very near, in darkness, or covered; or unless our eyes are defective, we can all see the thing clearly and know it.

b. Inference by Previous Experience (*Anumāna*):

There is smoke on the yonder hill. There must be fire over there. We have seen on countless occasions that where there is smoke there is fire. So we infer that

No.	The School of Philosophy	Number	The Ways of Knowing they Accept
1.	The Worldly Cārvākas	1	Only Direct Perception (Pratyakṣa)
2.	Buddhists	2	Perception and Inference (Anumāna)
3.	Dualists (Madhvācārya)	2	Perception and Verbal Testimony
4.	Vaiśeṣikas	2	Perception and Inference
5.	Jains	3	Perception, Inference, and Verbal Testimony (Śabda)
6.	Qualified Non-Dualists of Rāmānuja	3	Perception, Inference, and Verbal Testimony
7.	Sāṁkhyans	3	Perception, Inference, and Verbal Testimony
8.	Nyāya People	5	Perception, Inference, Verbal Testimony, and Knowing by Example (Upamāna)
9.	Pūrva Mīmāṁsākas of Prabhākara Miśra	5	Perception, Inference, Verbal Testimony, Example, Conjecture (Arthāpatti)
10.	Pūrva Mīmāṁsākas of Kumārila Bhaṭṭa	6	Perception, Inference, Verbal Testimony, Example, Conjecture, and Absence (Anupalabdhi)
11	Advaitins of Śaṁkara	6	Perception, Inference, Verbal Testimony, Example, Conjecture, and Absence.

there is fire on the hill. This is inference. Sense organs are needed here also, for unless we see smoke the other things will not follow.

c. Verbal Testimony of the Vedas (*Śabda*):

Regarding supernatural and divine things, there is only one source of knowledge—the words of the sages. Their words are compiled in the Vedas. The Vedas are infalliable. But even here we need the senses to either read or listen to the Vedas.

d. Knowing by Example (*Upamāna*):

'Have you seen Mars?' 'No, I haven't.' 'Have you not seen the pictures of Mars either?' 'No, I haven't. And I do not know what Mars is. What is Mars and how does it look like?' 'Ah! You know nothing then? Mars is a planet. It is like our earth.' 'Like the earth. Ah! I understand.'

This is knowing by visible examples.

e. Conjecture from Insignificant Information (Arthāpatti):

'Is Mr So-and-so home?' 'No, he is not.' 'Aha! Then he must be dead.'

Why should Mr So-and-so be dead just because he is not home? His not being at home means he is out; that he may return soon. Such conjecture using some information is called *arthāpatti*.

f. Absence of a Thing (Anupalabdhi):

'There is no car on this table. Therefore here is its absence.' Absence is not seen directly, but inferred.

So Advaitins and one group of Pūrva Mīmāṁsakas accept this as a means of knowledge.

These, then, are the six means of valid knowledge. Using them, we come into contact with the universe outside and know it.

Recapitulation:

Living beings are trichotomous: the gross, subtle, and causal are the three bodies we have. The gross body is made of food, and comes and goes. The subtle body is a complex thing with several items within it: 5 sense organs, 5 organs of action, 5 life forces, and 4 aspects of mind—mind, intellect, ego, and memory.

In this chapter, the senses, their functions, and so on were discussed. The six means of valid knowledge were also discussed.

Suggested Reading:

1. *Methods of Knowledge,* by Swami Satprakashananda

2. *Sāṁkhya Kārikā* by Īśvarakṛṣṇa with Vācaspati Miśra's, 'Sāṁkhya Tattva Kaumudī'. English translation by Swami Virupakshananda. See *Karikā* 4.

References

1. Complete Works, Vol. 2, p. 62.
2. Complete Works, Vol. 2, p. 66
3. Complete Works, ibid.

Chapter 14

THE ORGANS OF ACTION

'You are creating this bondage all the time. How? By putting in your share. We are all making our own beds, forging our own chains. . . . When the identifying ceases between this external object and myself, then I will be able to take my contribution off, and this thing will disappear.'

—**Swami Vivekananda**[1]

Seeing and Acting

Rāmāyaṇa has the story of Sītā who saw the golden deer. The deer attracted her. She said she wanted it. If Sītā had simply seen the deer, there would have been no problems. She not only saw it, she said she wanted it. That led to the story of *Rāmāyaṇa*.

Knowledge inspires will, and will inspires action. First we know, and then we act. That is, we see or hear, identify the sight or sound with our ego, and either like it or dislike it. If we like something we want it, and if we dislike it we want that to go. *Rāga* and *dveṣa* inspire the will to act. When we know there is an apple there and that it can end our hunger, we go for it.

The sense organs give us knowledge of the outer world. They tell us there are countless things in the world. When we know them, our ego begins to act. It either wants some of them or hates some of them. This leads us to use our organs of action. This is the beginning of our true involvement in the world. We can know a thousand things in a detached way.

But the moment we say we want them and begin to act, we are bound.

The *Bhagavad Gītā* (3.6-7) therefore forewarns aspirants that the main problem is the senses and the mind. The organs of action are helpless machines in the hands of the mind. But the organs of perception and the mind do all the mischief. Therefore, says the *Bhagavad Gītā,* he or she who engages in selfless action by controlling the organs and the mind, is a great one. But the other way round is bad. One who appears to be sitting quietly, controlling the organs of action, but is engaged mentally in numerous actions, is a hypocrite.

So the root of the problem, desire, born of ignorance, has to be rooted out if we are to restrain the mind, the senses, and the organs of action.

This section teaches us what the organs of action are, and how they function. As we saw in the previous chapter, here too there is mention of the gods who rule over the organs of action. This could have been the tradition which the Vedantins have followed.

वाक्-पाणि-पाद-पायू-उपस्थानि इति
पञ्च-कर्मेन्द्रियाणि।
वाचो देवता वह्निः, हस्तयोरिन्द्रः, पादयोः विष्णुः,
पायोर्मृत्युः उपस्थस्य प्रजापतिरिति कर्मेन्द्रिय-देवताः।

vāk-pāṇi-pāda-pāyu-upasthāni iti pañca-karmendriyāṇi. Vāco devatā vahniḥ, hastayoḥ indraḥ, pādayoḥ viṣṇuḥ, pāyoḥ mṛtyuḥ, upasthasya prajāpatiriti karmendriya-devatā.

Vāk the organ of speech, *pāṇi* hands, *pāda* feet, *pāyu* the generative organ, *upasthāni* the organ of excretion, *iti pañca-karmendriyāṇi* are the five organs of action. *Vāco* of speech *devatā* the presiding deity is *vahniḥ* fire; *hastayoḥ* of the hands, *indraḥ* [it is] Indra; *pādayoḥ* of the feet *viṣṇuḥ* Viṣṇu; *pāyoḥ* of the generative organs; *mṛtyuḥ* it is Death; *upasthasya* of the organ of excretion, *prajāpatiriti* it is Prajāpati; *karmendriya* of the organs of action *devatāḥ* these are the gods.

The organ of speech, hands, feet, the generative organ, the organ of excretion—these are the five organs of action. The presiding deities of these organs are: Fire presides over speech, Indra presides over hands, Viṣṇu presides over feet, Death (Yama) presides over the organ of excretion, and Prajāpati presides over the organs of generation.

वाचो विषयो भाषणं, पाण्योः विषयो वस्तु-ग्रहणम्,
पादयोर्विषयो गमनं, पायोर्विषयो मलत्यागः, उपस्थस्य
विषय आनन्द इति ॥

Vāco viṣayo bhāṣaṇaṁ, pāṇyoḥ viṣayo vastu-grahaṇaṁ,
pādayoḥ viṣayo gamanaṁ, pāyorviṣayo mala-tyāgaḥ,
upasthasya viṣaya ānanda iti.

Vāco of speech, *viṣayaḥ* the function, *bhāṣaṇaṁ* (is) talking, *pāṇyoḥ* of the hands, *viṣayaḥ* the function, *vastu-grahaṇaṁ* (is) grabbing things, *Pādayoḥ* of the feet, *Viṣayaḥ* the function, *gamanaṁ* (is) moving, *Pāyoḥ* of the organ of excretion, *viṣayaḥ* the function, *mala-tyāgaḥ* (is) to excrete, *upasthasya* of the organ of generation, *Viṣayaḥ* the function, *ānanda iti* (is) to enjoy.

The function of the organ of speech is talking; the function of the hands is grabbing things; the function of the feet is moving; the function of the organ of excretion is to excrete; the function of the organ of generation is to enjoy.

Karmendriyāṇi

The organs of action are five in number. These are, as stated above, the hands, the feet, the organ of generation, the organ of excretion, and the organ of speech.

Where are the organs of action located? In the physical body? No! Though it appears that we have our organs of action in the body, they are not the true organs of action. They are just openings. The true organs of action are within, in the subtle body. It may surprise us, but it is absolutely true. The outer physical covering is just a 'pillow case'—an inert support or instrument for the subtle body to act. Therefore if a man is dumb, his organ of speech is there within but is not functioning. Trees do not walk. But all the same their organ of action called feet are there within. They are latent, that is all.

How They are Created

The organs of action are created along with the creation of the organs of knowledge. They are created by using the *rajas* or activity part of the five supreme elements.

How They Function

The mind sees and knows some object. The ego identifies itself with it. And the hand begins its adventure. There is the effort. And when everything goes well, the object is obtained. The power to function comes from the *prāṇas* or life-forces. The desire to function comes from the mind.

Suppose I see a sweet. I desire it. I get it. The impression of the sweetness, the pleasant sensation of eating it, and so on will remain as a latent impression (*vāsanā*). The *vāsanā* part goads me to do the same action again and again, while the *samskāra* part keeps track of all the emotions and other things involved in that action, if I do it. These *samskāras* lead me to take new birth, suffer in a new body, and also decide my lifespan. So the organs of action are the great links in the chain of births.

After discussing the physical and subtle bodies, *Tattvabodha* now takes up the causal body.

References:

1. Complete Works, Vol. 4, p. 229

Chapter 15

THE CAUSAL BODY

Introduction

The gross body, the subtle body, and now the causal body—this is the method followed by the author of *Tattvabodha*.

The causal body is the 'combination' of the Atman and ignorance. Rather, it is the individual Self. When the idea of individuation comes, there is the causal body.

कारणशरीरं किम्?
अनिर्वाच्य–अनादि–अविद्या–रूपम् शरीरद्वयस्य कारण–
मात्रम् सत् स्वस्वरुपाज्ञानं निर्विकल्पक–रूपं यदस्ति
तत्कारण–शरीरम् ॥

Kāraṇa śarīraṁ kim ? Anirvācya-anādi-avidyā-rūpaṁ śarīra-dvayasya kāraṇa-mātraṁ sat sva-svarūpa-ajñānaṁ nirvikalpaka-rūpaṁ yadasti tat-kāraṇa ṣarīram.

Kim what is *kāraṇa* the causal *śarīraṁ* body? *Anirvācya* the indescribable *anādi* the beginningless *avidyā* ignorance *rūpaṁ* form *śarīra-dvayasya* of the two bodies *kāraṇa-mātraṁ* cause alone *sat* is *sva-svarūpa* of its own nature *ajñānaṁ* ignorance *nirvikalpaka* without modification *rūpaṁ* form *yadasti* that which is *tat-kāraṇa ṣarīram* is called the causal body.

What is meant by 'causal body'? That which is formed from the indescribable, beginningless ignorance; that which is the cause of the other two bodies;

that which is ignorant of its own nature; and that which does not undergo any modification is called the causal body.

Brahman, enveloped by ignorance, is the first development—the first stage of our so-called creation. This stage is called the stage of the causal body in the individual. All the causal bodies put together are collectively called Īśvara—the supreme Lord. Brahman to Īśvara—this, then, is the first ever change, owing to ignorance.

Ignorance has two powers: to envelop and to project. Ignorance envelops Brahman, as it were, and thus there is the causal body. It then projects the subtle and gross bodies. And it brings the idea in the causal body like 'I am the doer', 'I am the experiencer,' and so on.

The causal body is called the Blissful Sheath (*ānandamaya kośa*). It is blissful because Brahman, which is of the nature of Bliss, is the only Reality that has been enveloped by *māyā* here.

Swamiji on the Three Bodies

We shall quote at length from Swami Vivekananda's *Jnana Yoga* lectures since this clarifies everything about the three bodies:

> The external organ, which is only the instrument, is in the body, and behind that is the internal organ which is finer; then there is the mind, then the intellectual faculty, then egoism, which says, "I"—I see, I hear, and so forth. The whole process is carried on by certain forces; you may call them vital forces; in Sanskrit they are called Prana. This gross part of man, this body, in which are the external instruments, is called in Sanskrit, Sthula Sharira, the gross body; behind it comes the series, beginning with the organs, the mind, the intellect, the egoism. These and the vital forces form a compound which is called the fine body, the Sukshma

Sharira. These forces are composed of very fine elements, so fine that no amount of injury to this body can destroy them; they survive all the shocks given to this body.

The gross body we see is composed of gross material, and as such it is always being renewed, and changing continuously. But the internal organs, the mind, the intellect, and the egoism are composed of the finest material, so fine that they will endure for aeons and aeons. They are so fine that they cannot be resisted by anything; they can get through any obstruction. The gross body is non-intelligent, so is the fine body, being composed of fine matter. Although one part is called mind, another the intellect, and the third egoism, yet we see at a glance that no one of them can be the "Knower".

None of them can be the perceiver, the witness, the one for whom action is made, and who is the seer of the action. All these movements in the mind, or the faculty of intellection, or egoism, must be for some one else. These being composed of fine matter cannot be self-effulgent. Their luminosity cannot be in themselves....

Therefore there must be some one behind them all, who is the real manifester, the real seer, the real enjoyer and He in Sanskrit is called the Atman, the Soul of man, the real Self of man. He it is who really sees things. The external instruments and the organs catch the impressions and convey them to the mind, and the mind to the intellect, and the intellect reflects them as on a mirror, and back of it is the Soul that looks on them and gives His orders and His directions. He is the ruler of all these instruments, the master in the house, the enthroned king in the body. The faculty of egoism, the faculty of intellection, the faculty of cognition, the organs, the instruments, the body, all of them obey His commands. It is He who is manifesting all of these.

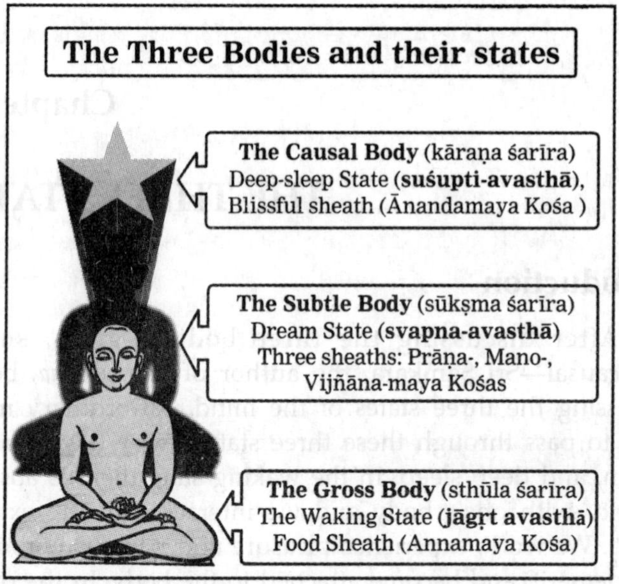

This is the Atman of man. Similarly, we can see that what is in a small part of the universe must also be in the whole universe. If conformity is the law of the universe, every part of the universe must have been built on the same plan as the whole. So we naturally think that behind the gross material form which we call this universe of ours, there must be universe of finer matter, which we call thought, and behind that there must be a Soul, which makes all this thought possible, which commands, which is the enthroned king of this universe. That soul which is behind each mind and each body is called Pratyagatman, the individual Atman, and that Soul which is behind the universe as its guide, ruler, and governor, is God.'[1]

References:

1. Complete Works, Vol. 2, pp. 427-9

Chapter 16

THE THREE STATES

Introduction

After discussing the three bodies—gross, subtle, and causal—Śrī Śaṁkara, the author of *Tattvabodha*, begins discussing the three states of the mind. All ordinary minds have to pass through these three states every day—waking, dream, and deep sleep. In the waking state there is absolute identity with one's body and we interact with the external world. We work, experience pleasure and pain, acquire merit and demerit, and become attached to the body. In the dream state we go to sleep and see dreams. There is no end to the variety and content of dreams. Hindu philosophers have given a suitable place to dreams. In the dream state, the physical body is for the time being forgotten and we are in a different world altogether. Yet that state is a shadow of the waking state. Finally, when we are in deep sleep, we are oblivious of our body and mind. We wake up and say 'I had a good sleep.'

These are the Three States

Swami Vivekananda says: 'To me it seems very natural that the glimpse of religion should come through dreams. The first idea of immortality man may well get through dreams. Is that not a most wonderful state? And we know that children and untutored minds find very little difference between dreaming and their awakened state. What can be more natural than that they find, as natural logic, that even during the sleep state when the body is apparently dead, the mind goes on with all its intricate workings? What wonder that men will at once come to the conclusion that when this body is dissolved for ever, the same working will go on? This, to my mind, would be a more natural explanation of the supernatural, and through this dream idea the human mind rises to higher and higher conceptions. Of course, in time, the vast majority of mankind found out that these dreams are not verified by their waking states, and that during the dream state it is not that man has a fresh existence, but simply that he recapitulates the experiences of the awakened state.'[1]

Swami Vivekananda says elsewhere: 'When a man goes into deep sleep, he enters a plane beneath consciousness. He works the body all the time, he breathes, he moves the body, perhaps, in his sleep, without any accompanying feeling of ego; he is unconscious, and when he returns from his sleep, he is the same man who went into it. The sum total of the knowledge which he had before he went into the sleep remains the same; it does not increase at all. No enlightenment comes. But when a man goes into Samadhi, if he goes into it a fool, he comes out a sage.'[2]

अवस्था–त्रयं किम्?
जाग्रत्–स्वप्न–सुषुप्ति–अवस्थाः।

Avasthā-trayaṁ kim?
Jāgrat-svapna-suṣupti-avasthāḥ.

Kim what are *trayam* the three *avasthāḥ* states? *Jāgrat* the waking *svapna* dream *suṣupti* deep sleep *avasthāḥ* [are the] three states.

What are the three states?

The waking, dream, and deep sleep are the three states of existence.

Avasthā

Avasthā means 'state of existence'. The root *sthā* ('to be') is the basis of this word. It means the state in which the mind remains at any given time.

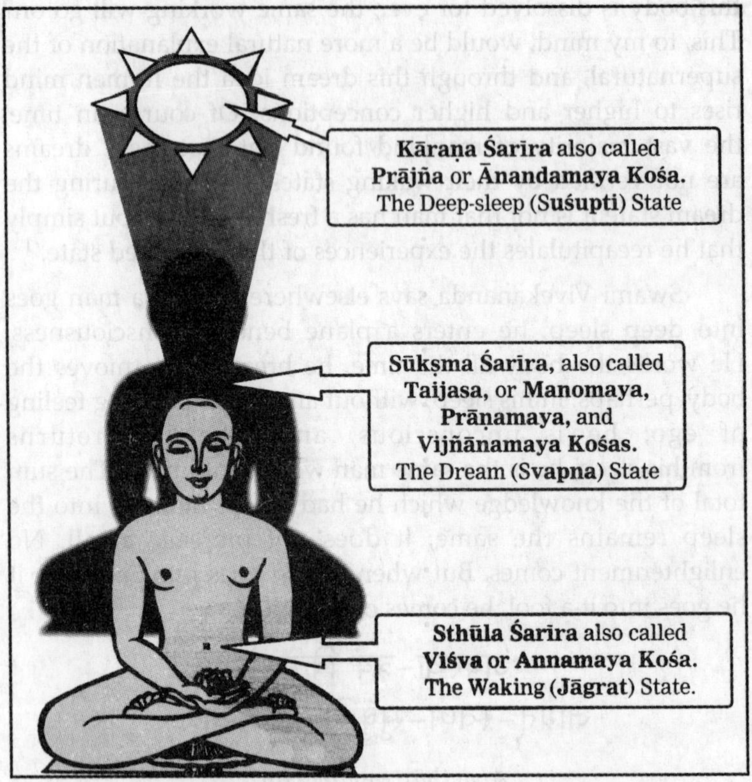

Jāgrat

'The Waking'. This state is the most important state of life. It is in this state that the soul can either get bound or be liberated. Whatever we do we should do consciously, they say. And it is in this state that we can do that.

Svapna

'Dream'. The cosmos itself is considered to be like a dream by the Advaitin. Yet, in this dream there is another dream when we see dreams in sleep.

Suṣupti

'Deep Sleep.' This is a state which is absolutely essential for every soul to enter into, if it needs refreshing itself. Deep sleep and samādhi are different.

All these three states will be discussed by *Tattvabodha* individually now.

References

1. Complete Works, Vol. 2, pp. 59-60
2. Complete Works, Vol. 1, p. 188

Chapter 17

THE WAKING STATE

Introduction

> To the jnanis the waking state is no more real than the dream state.
>
> —Sri Ramakrishna[1]

One of the most appealing calls of the Vedas is: 'उत्तिष्ठत, जाग्रत—Arise! Awake!' This call was re-echoed by Swami Vivekananda when he called upon the world to awaken to Reality.

We are sleeping, as it were. Though we are proud to say we are awake and alert, we are most of the time in a dream or unconscious state. Our activities—which are so limited though they appear varied—are done unconsciously, most of the time. We are half-dreaming and half-awake. The tiger sleeps, but is always alert. Its sleep has been termed 'alert tranquility'. Ours is just the opposite. Our waking state is 'sleeping alertness'. What is true awakening then? It is waking up to the Truth.

Why are we leading unconscious lives? There is very little consciousness in inert things, and the universe is inert. Our gross bodies are inert too. So our lives are by and large unconscious. Further, we are leading unconscious lives because routine work does not attract much of our attention. Moreover, our minds are restless and filled with worries and ambitions. Anxieties and sorrows crowd the mind and make us listless. We do not do things consciously, with full awareness. One more thing; the farther away we are from our true Self, the smaller our circles are. Moving within small circles, like the calf tied to a post with a long rope, is a routine affair. Eric Fromm says that our daily activities, weekly trips to the park or movie—everything is routine. This shows we are bound hand and foot.

A contemplative person is always alert and conscious. His or her actions are always meaningful. Such meaningful actions bring fruits in abundance too.

So waking is very important if we are to succeed in ordinary life. More so if we are to succeed in spiritual life, in knowing the Atman.

How is it so? In sleep we do not have control over our mind and body. Our senses may be functioning, but we are unconcerned about them. In unconscious states we are oblivious of our body. It is only in the conscious and waking state that we are fully aware we have a body and mind.

Our minds have to be controlled. But this cannot be done in the dream or deep sleep states, but only in the conscious state. To control the senses, to restrain the mental modifications, to meditate, to seek the spiritual teacher—everything is to be done in the waking state alone. So this is a very important state of being.

In this section, Śankara discusses the waking state:

जाग्रदावस्था का?

श्रोत्रादि-ज्ञानेन्द्रियैः शब्दादि-विषयैः च ज्ञायत इति यत्सा जाग्रदावस्था। ।

स्थूल-शरीराभिमानी आत्मा विश्व इति उच्यते ॥

Jāgratāvasthā kā?
Śrotrādi jñānendriyaiḥ śabdādi-viṣayaiḥ ca jñāyate iti yatsā jāgadāvasthā.
Sthūla-śarīrābhimānī ātmā viśva iti ucyate.

Kā what is *jāgratāvasthā* the waking state? *Śrotrādi* hearing and other *jñānendriyaiḥ* organs of perception *śabdādi* sound and other *viṣayaiḥ* objects; *ca jñāyate* will know *iti yat sā* that [state] in which *jāgadāvasthā* is called the waking state. *Sthūla-śarīrābhimānī ātmā* the Self identified with the gross physical body *iti ucyate* is called *viśva* viśva.

What is the waking state? The state of awareness in which the organs of perception like hearing come in touch with their respective objects like sound is called the waking state. The Self, identified with the gross physical body, is called *viśva.*

Creation would become meaningless had there not been the waking state. If *māyā* had enveloped Brahman and left it at that, there would have been no bondage or liberation. But she projects too. Thus we have the cosmic causal, subtle, and gross bodies as also the individual causal, subtle, and gross bodies. In the waking state we are aware that we are separate from others, that we have some identity, we have pleasure and pain, we must rise up in life, and so on. However, the truly awakened individual is the illumined soul alone, who is awake. The *Gītā* (2.69) says that that which is night for all beings is day for the illumined soul. Thus, though we ordinary people are not truly awake in this world, we think we are.

'According to Vedanta the waking state, too, is unreal,' says Sri Ramakrishna.[2] Why is that so? Because everything created is a false superimposition on the Self or Atman.

Whether or not the waking state is real is a matter of debate amongst the Buddhists. While one school says that what we see outside is but a projection of the mind, according to Nāgārjuna, the Vijñānavādin, everything is zero. It is all nothing. What is the reality behind? Nothing, he said. As a reaction to this 'false' proposition, Gaudapāda and others put forth the theory, based on the Vedas, that Brahman is the sole reality.

The Atman, identified with the gross body, is called *viśva*. The difference between the dead and the living is in the consciousness. The light of consciousness falls on the three bodies and makes them alive, as it were.

How important is the waking state? All that we experience through the five senses is insensate, *jaḍa*. And those that experience everything—our intellect, mind, senses, body—are also *jaḍa*. How do we derive happiness or sorrow from them? The experience of happiness or sorrow too is insensate or *jaḍa* in one sense. Joy or sorrow is in the mind. However, joy is nothing. Since Brahman pervades everything, we experience the little happiness we get. The same object, which might have produced joy two days ago, may bring sorrow now. So it is all within, in the mind.

Sage Yājñavalkya told his wife that in this world all love is for one's own sake. When ordinary people say they love others, they are loving their own little ego only. It is all selfishness pure and simple. Only the enlightened person can truly love others, because he or she sees the Atman everywhere and in everyone. Our love for other bodies and things are only selfish love of our egos. What is true happiness is not known to us. For that, we have to turn to consciousness.

Sri Ramakrishna remarks that the body is extremely dear to everyone. We identify ourselves with our bodies and say that we are big or small, fair or dark, and so on. Yet the body is not permanent, even as the waking state is. This lesson we could not have learnt either in the dream or deep-sleep state. So the waking state is a great teacher which teaches us that everything is vain and Truth alone triumphs.

Suggested Reading

Miracles of Mindfulness, by Thich Nhat Hanh

References:

1. Gospel, p. 236
2. Same, p. 417

Chapter 18

THE DREAM STATE

To me it seems very natural that the glimpse of religion should come through dreams. The first idea of immortality man may well get through dreams.

—Swami Vivekananda [1]

A Dream Come True

One day Kshudiram Chattopadhyay, Sri Ramakrishna's father, went to another village on business. On his way back he became tired and rested under a tree. He then had a dream in which he saw standing before him his chosen Ideal, Bhagavan Sri Ramachandra, in the guise of a divine boy. his body green like the tender blades of Dūrva grass. Pointing to a particular spot, the Boy said, 'I have been staying here for a long time without food and without anyone to take care of me. Take me to your house. I have a very strong desire that you should serve me.'

Kshudiram was overcome with emotion and said, paying homage to the Lord again and again: 'O Lord, I am without devotion and am very poor. Service befitting you is not possible in my hut, and I shall incur sin, should there be any flaw in it. So why do you make such a difficult request to me?' At this, the Boy Ramachandra comforted him and said graciously, 'Do not be afraid. I shall not take offence at any shortcoming. Take me with you.' Unable to control his feelings at the Lord's unexpected grace, Kshudiram burst into tears. Just then his dream came to an end.

When he woke up, Kshudiram wondered at the strangeness of his dream and thought, 'Ah! If only such a good fortune would be mine!' Then suddenly his eyes fell upon the paddy field close by, and at once he recognized it as the very place he had seen in the dream. Out of curiosity he approached the spot, where he saw a beautiful Salagrama stone and a snake with expanded hood guarding it. Eager to possess the stone, he hastened towards it. On reaching it, he found that the snake had disappeared and that the Salagrama was lying at the entrance to its hole. Seeing that the dream had come true, his heart leaped with joy, and he felt no fear of the snake, convinced, as he was that he had received God's command. Crying out, 'Glory to Raghuvir!' Kshudiram took the stone in his hands. He carefully examined the marks on it and, with his knowledge of the scriptures, found it to be a Raghuvir Śilā (*Sālagrāma*). Beside himself with joy and wonder, he turned home, performed the purificatory ceremony of the *sālagrāma* according to the scriptures, and installing it as the family deity, began worshipping it.

It is worshipped even today in Kamarpukur.

Study in dreams in Our times

Are dreams real then?

Since unknown times, dreams have been playing a significant part in our lives. Though whenever we see dreams most of us say they are false, imagination, or 'just dreams', some of us nevertheless give credence to them. Thus there are always two opinions about dreams. Some say dreams are important, while others say that dreams are to be ignored. There is a third group which says that dreams themselves are not true but the effect they produce is true. If I see a tiger in dream, even when I wake up my heart will be beating fast. According to saints and scriptures, dreams with spiritual content are real—in the sense that if one sees forms of Gods and Goddesses, they are visitations. Further, they say that owing to the impurities still remnant in the mind of the devotee, perhaps the Lord cannot answer his or her prayers straightaway. So He comes in dreams and blesses, guides, and saves His devotee. There is one more opinion current: not all religious dreams are truly visitations. Some may be dreams only. But the effect they leave on the mind—peace, happiness, desire for higher life—are real, and the devotee is advised to hold on to any support that may come in his or her way of spiritual progress. A sinking man holds on to anything he can lay hands on. Patañjali provides provision for meditation on dream objects also.

In the ancient world, dreams were both objects of awe and reverence. There are several papyri available even now about the ancient interpretations of dreams. Oneirocritica (critica = study of; Oneiros = dreams) by Artemidorus Daldianus (2nd century AD), is considered the best of the ancient dream literature. In Greece, as well as in the Middle Ages, dreams were mediums of healing the sick.

Psychoanalysis took up dreams as a significant factor in studying human nature. Initiated by Sigmund Freud in his famous *The Interpretation of Dreams*, dreams were considered an expression of the libido in the human being. In the waking state the libido cannot express itself fully because the ego censors ideas. In dream, however, there is a free expression. Thus, for Freud, dreams were expressions of hidden desires of living beings.

Carl Jung did not accept Freud's view that dreams were secret expressions of one's overt desires. He took a positive view and said that the personality cannot express itself fully in daytime. So it expresses its positive traits in dreams. He said that dreams should be studied with reference to archetypes—cultural history. Later psychoanalysts have developed several techniques to study dreams: when there is rapid eye movement (REM) in a sleeping person, he or she must be dreaming then. Such a state has been called D-Sleep state. In psychoanalysis, study of successive dreams, reported promptly without inhibitions or hiding, and their interpretation by competant psychoanalysts, may help to some extent in knowing the unconscious. For this, the analyst should be a deeply spiritual personality.

How do Western philosophers look at dreams? 'The English philosopher, Bertrand Russell (1872-1970), wrote, "It is obviously possible that what we call waking life may be only an unusual and persistent nightmare," and he further stated that "I do not believe that I am now dreaming but I cannot prove I am not."'[2]

The Hindu View

The Hindu view of dreams has been varied. From ignoring some as stupid to revering some as epoch-making revelations, ancient Hindu religious persons have diverse opinions about dreams. Dreams have been described both in the Vedas and the Upaniṣads. The *Bṛhadāraṇyaka Upaniṣad* (2.1.18) says that when the *jīva* sees the dream it may appear as if the living being is going places. But no, it moves about in its own body as it wishes. That is all; it does not go where it wishes.

Sage Yājñavalkya says that [see *Bṛhadāraṇyaka Upaniṣad* (4.3.9)] in dreams there will be no chariots, no animals to be fixed to them, nor roads to travel on. But all these are created by the individual soul. The dream state has been called the junction, *sāndhyaṁ sthānam*. There are quite a number of instances in the Vedas which discuss dreams. The *Brahma Sūtras* (3.2.3) says that dream is nothing but *māyā*, because it does not give a total picture of everything as seen in the waking state. *Vivekacūḍāmaṇī* (100) says: 'Dreams belong to the subtle body. They enjoy the subtle objects, and see what was seen in the waking state.' The *Upadeśa Sāhasrī* (14th chapter) feels that dreams are reconstructions of the waking-state experiences. The reason this scripture gives is this: objects seen in dreams resemble those of the waking state (14.1). The *Buddhi* is the material and efficient cause of dreams, because there are no materials or other intelligence in the dream state (14.8).

If dreams are the creation of ignorance, as our scriptures say, why should we give any importance to them at all? Why should we not ignore them as the workings of the mind in sleep? Human beings have tried to ignore dreams. But there are some which appear to have *some* connection with waking life. So our scriptures are compassionate enough to accept dream omens.

The scriptures say that dreams are 'सूचकश्च... *sūcakaśca...*, indicators also...' (*Brahma Sūtras,* 3.2.4). In the *Chāndogya Upaniṣad* (5.2.8) there is the injunction that if people see a woman in their dreams during the days when they are performing some important act, they should understand that the work will be successful. Such indicators are true, say the scriptures.

Such indications have come in the lives of none other than Sri Ramakrishna, Holy Mother, Swamiji, and the other illumined souls of the modern times. There are several incidents in the lives of Holy Mother, Sri Ramakrishna, and Swamiji, which go to show the importance of dreams. One such has a physical verification. 'One day, while Holy Mother was taking rest in the afternoon, she dreamt that Sri Ramakrishna had got up from bed and was on the floor. Sri Ramakrishna had passed away by then. Holy Mother used to worship his picture. Surprised at seeing the dream, she woke up, approached the shrine room where there was the Lord's bed, and saw the photograph covered with ants. Evidently the ants had come from the flowers, and her dream indicated that they disturbed the rest of him who was a living presence to her.[3]

Swamiji had a dream while he was travelling by sea about the Crete island. He immediately woke up and asked the captain of the ship where they were. They were near Crete. The Kālī Temple in Dakshineswar was built, based upon a dream that Rani Rasmani had.

In this way there are several schools, and several ways of interpreting the value of dreams. Some Hindu philosophers have viewed dreams as if they were mythological realities. Some have thought that dreams have a natural bearing on waking life. Some others feel that spiritual dreams are visitations. Some say that dreams are experiences which need not be counted at all. And the Advaitins, who feel that even the waking state is as good as a dream, consider dreams to be of no consequence at all, but as merely *māyā*. Yet, for us ordinary individuals, the effects that dreams leave should be real. Instead of harping much on dreams, saints advice us to pray and practise spiritual practices.

In this section, *Tattvabodha* defines dreams.

स्वप्नावस्था केति चेत्, जाग्रदावस्थायां यद् दृष्टं, यत् श्रुतं, तज्जनित-वासनया निद्रा-समये यः प्रपञ्चः प्रतीयते सा स्वप्नावस्था,
सूक्ष्म-शरीराभिमानी आत्मा तैजस इति उच्यते।।

Svapnāvasthā ke'ti cet, jāgradavasthāyaṁ yad dṛṣṭaṁ yat śrutaṁ, tajjanita-vāsanayā nidrā-samaye yaḥ prapañcaḥ pratīyate sā svapnāvasthā,
sūkṣma-śarīrābhimānī ātmā taijasa iti ucyate.

Ke'ti cet if (one asks) what is *svapnāvasthā* the dream state *jāgradavasthāyaṁ* in the waking state *yad dṛṣṭaṁ* that which is seen, *yat śrutaṁ* that which is heard, *tajjanita-vāsanayā* owing to their impressions *nidrā-samaye* during sleep *yaḥ* that which *prapañcaḥ* world *pratīyate* appears *sā svapnāvasthā* that is the dream state; *ātmā* the Self *sūkṣma-śarīrābhimānī* identifying with the subtle body *ucyate* is called *taijasa iti* Taijasa.

What is the dream state?

All that is heard or seen in the waking state become mental impressions. The consequential world that appears during the sleep state is called the dream state.

The Self that identifies itself with the subtle body is called the *Taijasa*.

Svapnāvasthā

As the author of *Tattvabodha* asserts, the experiences of the waking state become the material for dream experiences. This is what Śamkara has written in his commentary to the *Brahma Sūtra* 3.2.6: 'Dreams are a product of the impressions gathered during the waking state, and they are very similar to the waking state. So dreams are *māyā*.'

We have seen how dreams indicate some future happenings. They also behave like *sūcakas*. Thus they have their intrinsic value. Though these are extremely haphazard, they let out the emotions pent up in the sub-conscious. The dream state has been related with the subtle body by the Vedantins. While in the dream state, the soul has nothing to do either with the gross or the causal bodies. When a person dreams, there are rare occasions when he is aware that he is dreaming—dream within dream. Yet dreams have no value of themselves. We cannot build up our lives basing upon some dream of ours.

Recapitulation

The spiritual aspirant, desirous of knowing the Self, is studying the different aspects of his personality. He knows now that he has three bodies, and lives in three states. But he also knows that his ideal is the Fourth state.

Reference:

1. Complete Works, Vol. 2, p. 59

2. see The Encyclopedia Britannica

3. Swami Tapasyananda, *Sri Sarada Devi, the Holy Mother*(Chennai: Ramakrishna Math), p. 215

Chapter 19

THE DEEP SLEEP STATE

Touch the Truth and Return

The three states of the living being are being studied in these sections. The waking state relates to the sense organs and the physical body. The dream state pertains to the mental body. The deep sleep state pertains to the causal body, when the personality has no idea it has a body or mind. It is oblivious of everything. It is 'touching' Brahman then. When the soul returns from deep sleep to waking, it comes from Self or Atman, declares the *Brahma Sūtras* (3.2.8).

The question is, if it goes to the Atman, and touches It, it should become one with the Atman and should not retain an identity. How can the same person go to deep sleep and come back? The scriptures have discussed this aspect. In the *Brahma Sūtras* (3.2.9), this question is asked and answered in this way: 'Since action, memory, and so on are the same before and after sleep. And since the scriptures say so.'

Bṛhadāraṇyaka Upaniṣad (4.3.16) says that the same individual comes back to the waking state. Śaṁkara raises the doubt himself: if a drop of water, thrown into the ocean, can return back. He answers that the analogy is not correct in this case, because it is not a single drop falling into the ocean but something else. The individual is diving into the ignorance-covered Brahman with his karmas and *samskāras*. So he returns the same person after sleep. When one enters the world of samādhi, one comes back enlightened. In deep sleep, it is the ignorant going and coming back.

Holy Mother was asked the same question in a different way. Someone asked her how the enlightened soul can attain Brahman and return back. She gives the example of the swan drinking milk alone from a mixture of milk and water.

The causal body, as we have seen, is nothing but the Truth enveloped by ignorance. The soul that goes to sleep experiences deep sleep almost every day. It is written in the *Chāndogya Upaniṣad* (8.6.3) 'तद्यत्रैतत्सुप्तः समस्तः संप्रसन्नः स्वप्नं न विजानात्यासु तदा नाडीषु सुप्तो भवति तन्न कश्चन पाप्मा स्पृशति तेजसा हि सम्पन्नो भवति; *tadyatraitat suptaḥ samastaḥ saṁprasannaḥ svapnaṁ na vijānātyāsu tadā nāḍīṣu supto bhavati tanna kaścana pāpmā spṛśati tejasā hi sampanno bhavati.* When the soul sleeps in such a way that all the organs are withdrawn, and he becomes completely serene in mind, and does not dream, and remains spread over these nerves.'

Here, nerves are mentioned. These nerves are called *hitā*, and it is said that the mind enters the *hitā* nerve in deep sleep. Where does the soul go to sleep? It is said that through the nerves called *hitā*, the soul enters *purītat*, the heart, and rests there. So in deep sleep the soul is in *purītat* according to the *Bṛhadāraṇyaka Upaniṣad* (2.1.19).

When we experience deep sleep, there is absolutely no awareness of the body or the external world. We are in the dark—literally. Only when we wake up we say we slept well. Scientists say that sleep-walking is a phenomenon happening in the deep sleep state.

अतः सुषुप्त्यवस्था का?

अहम् किमपि न जानामि सुखेन मया निद्राऽनुभूयत
इति सुषुप्त्यवस्था। कारण–शरीराभिमानी आत्मा प्राज्ञ
इति उच्यते ॥

Ataḥ suṣuptyavasthā kā? Ahaṁ kimapi na jānāmi sukhena mayā nidrā'nu-bhūyata iti suṣuptyavasthā. Kāraṇa-śarīrābhimānī ātmā prājña iti ucyate.

Ataḥ now *kā* what is *suṣuptyavasthā* the state of deep sleep? *Ahaṁ* I *na jānāmi* do not know *kimapi* anything; *sukhena* happily *mayā* by me *nidrā'nubhūyata iti* sleep was experienced *suṣuptyavasthā* (to think thus) is called the state of deep sleep. *ātmā* the Self *Kāraṇa-śarīrābhimānī* identifying with the causal body *iti ucyate* is called *prājña* Prājna.

What is the state of deep sleep? 'I do not know anything. I slept happily.' (To think thus) is called the state of deep sleep. The Self, identifying with the causal body, is called Prājna.

We need rest every day. So we go to sleep. First there is dream. Then comes deep sleep. That we pass through these stages is an ancient Indian discovery. Without any instruments our sages discovered everything. What happens in deep sleep? The *jīva* or the ego goes into a shell, as it were. It remains there and returns.

Are swoon and deep sleep the same? Vedanta calls the state of swoon half-sleep. While in deep sleep the soul breathes rhythmically and is in peace, the swoon state is different. It is not waking or deep sleep state. It is not dream state too. So it is a half-sleep state.

Tattvabodha informed us that we have three bodies and three states. The three bodies and their constituents can be classified into five parts using a different method—that of the sheaths. The next chapter discusses this.

Chapter 20

THE FIVE SHEATHS

> The Indivisible Satchidananda—I see It both inside and outside. It has merely assumed this sheath [meaning his body] for a support and exists both inside and outside. I clearly perceive this. .. I see you all as so many sheaths, and the heads are moving.
>
> **—Sri Ramakrishna**[1]

In the previous chapters, where the three bodies were mentioned, the *kośas* or sheaths have also been mentioned. In *Tattvabodha* the discussion on sheaths is begun here.

What is a sheath? It is a covering, a jacket. Just as swords are kept in sheaths, the Atman is enveloped by five sheaths. These five sheaths are divided into three bodies; or the three bodies are 'divided' into five sheaths. These are different ways of looking at the same reality. The idea of the five sheaths is in the Vedas. In the *Taittirīya Upaniṣad* ('Bhrguvalli') these five sheaths are called five 'atmans' or selves. Instead of *kośa,* the term *atman* has been used. The *ānandamaya ātmā* is, however, considered the final attainment. It is perhaps from such Vedic concepts of five sheaths that the *kośa* idea has been developed.

The *Pañcadaśī* (3.1) says that the sheaths are like a cave in which Truth is hidden. It is possible, it says, to know Brahman or Truth, which is hidden in this cave.

The five sheaths are like layers: the outermost is the food sheath, while the innermost is the blissful.

पञ्च कोशाः के?
अन्नमयः प्राणमयः मनोमयो विज्ञानमय आनन्दमयश्च
इति ॥

Pañca kośāḥ ke?
Annamayaḥ prāṇamayaḥ manomayo vijñānamayaḥ ānandamayaśca iti.

Ke What are *pañca kośāḥ* the five sheaths? *Annamayaḥ* The food sheath *prāṇamayaḥ* the life-force or vital sheath *manomayaḥ* the mental sheath *vijñānamayaḥ* the knowledge sheath (and) *ānandamayaśca iti* the blissful sheath.

What are the five sheaths?

The food sheath, the life-force or vital sheath, the mental sheath, the knowledge sheath, and the blissful sheath are the five sheaths.

Sri Ramakrishna explains the five sheaths beautifully:

Chaitanya experienced three states of mind. First, the conscious state, when his mind dwelt on the gross and the subtle. Second, the semi-conscious state, when his mind entered the causal body and was absorbed in the bliss of divine intoxication. Third, the inmost state, when his mind was merged in the Great Cause.

This agrees very well with the five koshas, or 'sheaths', described in the Vedanta. The gross body corresponds to the annamayakosha and the pranamayakosha, the subtle body to the manomayakosha and the vijnanamayakosha, and the causal body to the anandamayakosha. The Mahakarana, the Great Cause, is beyond the five sheaths. When Chaitanya's mind merged in That, he would go into samadhi. This is called the nirvikalpa or jada samadhi.

> While conscious of the outer world, Chaitanya sang the name of God; while in the state of partial consciousness, he danced with the devotees; and while in the inmost state of consciousness, he remained absorbed in samadhi .

Each of these kośas will be taken up in the subsequent chapters.

References

1. Gospel p. 961
2. Gospel, p. 330

Chapter 21

THE FOOD SHEATH

Karmayoga is very hard indeed. In the Kaliyuga it is extremely difficult to perform the rites enjoined in the scriptures. Nowadays man's life is centred on food alone.

—**Sri Ramakrishna**[1]

The Ever-Blissful Saint

They had brought a bullock cart. They had to fill it with sand, to be taken to their master's house. The workers began to dig the sand on the banks of the river. The cart was soon half full. Meanwhile, one of the diggers shouted: 'My spade has struck some animal under the sand. It has come out with fresh blood.' Perhaps some dead fish, they thought. Strange! When the spade was struck again, it brought out a hand, dripping with blood. The worker started to shake with fear and began to howl and cry: 'I have cut a dead body! I have cut a dead body buried here!' But surprisingly enough, the earth in front of them appeared to shake, as if something was shaking of the sand and trying come out.

All the workers stood there, terrified that something ghastly or supernatural was happening. They took courage, dug around and slowly they saw someone come out. It was an alive naked mendicant, hand cut off from the shoulder down, coming out of the sand. They had cut off the hand of a mendicant! The workers had committed the worst blunder a human being could commit. They all fell at the feet of the saint. He was smiling. There was neither pain nor anger in him. He said: 'I don't know when, but I was meditating here and went into samādhi. Sand covered me. You cut off my hand, and the pain made my samādhi break. I am out of the sand now.' Saying this, the saint walked away, even as blood dripped from his shoulder.

This is from the life of Sadāśiva Brahmendra Sarasvatī, the great Advaitin of India.

Sages and Their Struggles

'The rishis of old attained the Knowledge of Brahman. One cannot have this so long as there is the slightest trace of worldliness. How hard the rishis laboured! Early in the morning they would go away from the hermitage, and would spend the whole day in solitude, meditating on Brahman. At night they would return to the hermitage and eat a little fruit or roots. ... But in the Kaliyuga, man, being totally dependent on food for life, cannot altogether shake off the idea that he is the body.'[2]

The greatest hurdle, perhaps, for us in attaining Brahman or Truth is our dear body. We cannot give up identity with the body, as it were. The *Vivekacūḍāmaṇī* (162) says that as long as one does not give up identity with the body, one has no hope of liberation, in spite of his being a great pundit. Therefore the book says (163, 164): 'Never consider the body to be the Atman. If you do, it will be like taking the shadow for the real thing. All troubles are because you confuse the body for the Atman.'

The body is made of food. As doctors declare, our body is in accordance with the food we consume. If our food is good, the body will be healthy. If we eat poor diet, the body will be weak. This far the scientist can go. The spiritual person goes further. He adds that pure food brings a pure body and impure food does otherwise.

We have discussed pure food earlier. The other aspect of pure food is that it is offered to God and partaken as *prasāda* or sacramental food. It is not true that non-vegetarian food is bad, or that it is rejected in the scriptures. Śrī Rāma, Śrī Kṛṣṇa, and almost all avatars were non-vegetatians, and Arjuna too was one such. What Kṛṣṇa meant in the Bhagavad gītā (17.10) was that that food which is defiled should not be offered or eaten.

Eating Pure Food

Sri Ramakrishna says: 'Both the Vedas and the Puranas describe pure food and conduct.'[3] He quotes Guru Nanak and says: 'Nanak once said, "I was about to eat the food of unholy people, when I found it stained with blood."[4]

It is for this reason that our food should be pure. Pure food makes a pure body and pure mind. If the body and mind are pure, one can easily concentrate on God.

What is pure food? The scriptures say that that food which is not defiled by prior eating or impurities like hair, dirt and so on is pure. That food which is cooked by devotees is pure. That food which is earned by noble means is pure. And so on. Food is therefore vital to spiritual aspirants. It is not to appease hunger that we eat but to lead spiritual lives. Moreover, food should be taken in such a way that it is conducive to sadhana. We must eat food like taking medicine—says a saint.

Is the Food Sheath Essential?

The food sheath is impermanent—its span is at the most a hundred years in the case of human beings. Why should it be there at all, if it is impermanent, changing, diseased, and helpless?

We have discussed this issue in the physical body chapter. Our bodies are the gift of our karma, and when the karma is exhausted, we shall be released from them. Secondly, bodies are meant to strive for realization. Thirdly, bodies are meant to work. Fourthly, bodies are meant to know we are all one—all creation is one. Even physically all are one: because it is the five elements which have made all the bodies, and the elements are products of *avidyā*.

अन्नमयः कः?
अन्नरसेनैव भूत्वा अन्नरसेनैव वृद्धिं प्राप्य अन्नरूप–
पृथिव्यां यद् विलीयते तद् अन्नमयः कोशः, स्थूल–
शरीरम् ॥

Annamayaḥ kaḥ? Anna-rasena-eva bhūtvā anna-rasena-eva vṛddhiṁ prāpya annarūpa-pṛthivyāṁ yad vilīyate tad annamayaḥ kośaḥ sthūla-śarīram.

Kaḥ what is *annamayaḥ* the food sheath? *Anna-rasena-eva* by the essence of food *bhūtvā* coming into being *anna-rasena-eva* by the essence of food *vṛddhiṁ prāpya* attaining growth *annarūpa-pṛthivyāṁ* in the earth which is of the nature of food *yad* that which *vilīyate* goes back to *tad* that *sthūla-śarīram* physical body is called *annamayaḥ kośaḥ* the food sheath.

What is the food sheath? That which comes into being owing to the essence of food, that which is sustained by the essence of food, and that which decays or goes back to the earth which also is of the nature of food, is called the food sheath, the physical body.

The Contents of the Food Sheath

The *Vivekacūḍāmaṇī* (87-91) says: 'Skin, flesh, blood, nerves and tendons, fat, marrow, bones and waste—this is what the physical sheath is made up of. What we did in the past has made this body in this manner. We get attached to it, and while we are awake, we get totally involved with the body. 'The constituents of the physical body of the human being too have been studied by ancient Indian medicine experts thoroughly. They had more than 100 types of instruments for surgery, it is said by modern researchers. They could do difficult surgeries with success. They could cure several diseases which were considered complicated even till recently.

All the different beings—their physical bodies—ultimately come from food only. So the body comes into existence, and nourishment makes it grow and develop. When the body dies, it finally becomes food to the earth. So everything pertaining to the body is made of food. Hence it has been called the food sheath.

Why is the Body Important?

This outermost shell or covering envelops the other four coverings, and thereby the Atman. Through sadhana, the outer covering is restrained, the inner coverings too are controlled, and thus the Self becomes revealed. Sri Ramakrishna says: 'After attaining Knowledge some people give up their bodies. After the gold image has been cast in the clay mould, you may either preserve the mould or break it.'[78]

That is the use of the body. We think our bodies are the ultimate things in life. They are not. They are only instruments which help us know the Truth. Once the Truth is known, the outer covering of clay will fall off by itself.

The next section takes up the second sheath.

Further Reading

Complete Works, vol.3, pp.64-69

References:

1. Gospel, p. 143
2. Gospel, p. 103
3. Gospel, p. 564
4. Gospel, p. 162
5. Gospel, p. 164

Chapter 22

THE LIFE-FORCE SHEATH

Who is the Greatest?

Once upon a time, the story goes, there was a secret discussion amongst the several parts of the body like the speech, hearing, mind, sight, and others. Each thought it was great, and that each one was independent. They discussed who was the supreme. *Prāṇa*, the life force or energy, wanted to show them who it really was. So it began to move upwards. The moment *prāṇa* began to move upwards, all the other organs were pulled by it. They helplessly began to follow it. They then realized who was the most powerful one, and addressed *prāṇa* with many supplications: 'O Lord! You are fire, the sun, moon, rains, air, earth, wealth, everything. Just as the axle is vital to a wheel and spokes are dependent on it, we are all dependent on you.' Pleased with their prayers, *prāṇa* returned.[1]

The word *prāṇa* is generally translated as life-breath. But Swamiji says that it is not correct. Even the *Brahma Sūtras* (2.4.9) says:' न वायुक्रिये पृथगुपदेशात्, *na vāyukriye pṛthagupadeśāt*, they are not airs, as they have been discussed separately.' Prāṇa is not merely breath, but it is the energy that is flowing all through the body. It not only runs the body but also runs the cosmos. Such is the power of *prāṇa*. In his *Brahma Sūtras* commentary, Śankara quotes an interesting dialogue from the *Śathapatha Brāhmaṇa* (6.1.1.1). While describing creation, it was said that immediately after creation, the sages were not there. 'Who were the sages (*ṛṣis*)?' asked someone. The reply was that the *prāṇas* were the sages.

'We say, whatever is in this universe has been projected by the vibration of the Prana.... It is the Prana that is moving every part of the body, becoming the different forces. Give up that old idea that God is something that produces the effect and sits on a throne dispensing justice. In working we become exhausted because we use up so much Prana',[2] says Swamiji.

If this energy is controlled and regulated, it can be of immense value to the spiritual aspirant. Any energy runs riot if not controlled. *Prāṇa* too tends to flow downwards if not controlled fully. Therefore one has to control it for the good of one's spiritual progress.

This *prāṇa* along with the organs of action has been termed as the energy sheath. *Tattavabodha* defines the vital sheath:

प्राणमयः कः?

प्राणादि पञ्च वायवः वागादीन्द्रिय–पञ्चकं प्राणमयः ॥

Prānamayah kaḥ?

Prāṇādi pañca vāyavaḥ vāgādi indriya pañcakaṁ prāṇamayaḥ.

Kaḥ what is *prāṇamayaḥ* the life-force sheath? *Prāṇādi* the life-force and the other *pañca vāyavaḥ* five airs, *vāgādi* speech and the other *indriya pañcakaṁ* five sense organs of action (are called) *prāṇamayaḥ* the life-force sheath.

What is the life-force sheath (the vital sheath)? The five airs and the life-force, the organ of speech, and the other sense organs of action are together called the life-force or vital sheath.

Pañca vāyavaḥ

'The Five Airs'. *Prāṇa* is the one energy flowing throughout the body, no doubt. But according to its functions, it has been divided into five aspects or parts. We work, move our limbs, speak, exert, breathe—and all these activities need fuel or energy. This is provided by *prāṇa*. A person may be the most intelligent man, may have countless thoughts; but if he has no energy, he cannot express them. That which keeps the body alive by bringing in oxygen and taking out carbon dioxide and converts food to energy is called *prāṇa*. That which takes out waste from the body is called *apāna*. That which digests the food is called *samāna*. That which spreads the digested food as energy throughout the body, regulates circulation of blood, and regulates the movement of body and senses is called *vyāna*. Finally, that which takes out the soul from the body at the time of death is called *udāna*.

How were the *prāṇas* created? The *Muṇḍaka Upaniṣad* (2.1.8) says: 'सप्त प्राणाः प्रभवन्ति तस्मात् सप्तार्चिषः समिधः सप्त होमाः, *sapta prāṇāḥ prabhavanti tasmāt saptārciṣaḥ samidhaḥ sapta-homāḥ*. From the Creator emerge the seven *prāṇās*.' The *Brahma Sūtras* (2.4.5) raises the question about the number of *prāṇas*. It wants to know how many *prāṇas* are there. In the next aphorism, the clarification comes that there are only five, and seven is figurative. In the *Bṛhadāraṇyaka Upaniṣad* (2.1.20), it is said: 'From the Atman come out all the *prāṇas* just as sparks fly out from the raging fire, or just like the spider brings out its web.'

Swamiji explains the creation of *prāṇas* in this way: 'According to the philosophers of India, the whole universe is composed of two materials, one of which they call Akasha. It is the omnipresent, all-penetrating existence. Everything that has form, everything that is the result of combination, is evolved out of this Akasha.... By what power is this Akasha manufactured into this universe? By the power of Prana. Just as Akasha is the infinite, omnipresent material of this universe, so is this Prana the infinite, omnipresent manifesting power of this universe. At the beginning and at the end of a cycle everything becomes Akasha, and all the forces that are in the universe resolve back into the Prana; in the next cycle, out of this Prana is evolved everything that we call energy, everything that we call force.'[3]

This is the cosmic *prāṇa*. The individual *prāṇas* come from the cosmic *prāṇa*.

We have been told that the five *prāṇas* themselves do not make the sheath; they need something more. That 'something more' are the five organs of action. The vehicle may be ready, but without fuel, it cannot run. The fuel is the *prāṇa*, energy.

Oblations to Vaiśvānara

The five life-forces are not merely energies, they are divinities too, called Vaiśvānara collectively. Vaiśvānara is the universal Self—the collective physical universe plus Brahman. One has to propitiate Vaiśvānara in order to be freed from sins and the dangers of having to be born as insects and birds. Therefore the *Chāndogya Upaniṣad* (5.11) teaches sacrifice to Vaiśvānara. This sacrifice is Agnihotra. The sacrifice is simple. He is to be adored by offering oblations to the five *prāṇas*, that is all. Before beginning to eat, the first few grains are taken and offered to *prāṇa*, saying, 'Oblations to *prāṇa*.' The next oblation is for *apāna*, and sc on. Through this, the aspirant's own eating becomes an offering to the Lord. This purifies the food being taken.

Vāgādi indriya pañcakam

The five senses of action, like speech. These have been discussed before. The five organs of action are the organs of generation and evacuation, the organ of speech, hands, and feet. These, together with the five *prāṇas*, makes up the *prāṇic* sheath or the *prāṇamaya kośa*.

Importance of the *Prāṇamaya Kośa*

In the Chndogya Upaniṣad (5.1.1.), it is said that *prāṇa* is the eldest and the greatest of all: 'यो ह वै ज्येष्ठम् च श्रेष्ठम् च वेद ज्येष्ठश्च ह वै श्रेष्ठश्च भवति, प्राणो वाव ज्येष्ठश्च श्रेष्ठश्च, *yo ha vai jyeṣṭham ca śreṣṭham ca veda jyeṣṭhaḥ ca śreṣṭhaḥ ca bhavati, prāṇo vāva jyeṣṭhaś ca śreṣṭhaśca*. He who knows what is the eldest and the greatest becomes himself eldest and the greatest. The *prāṇa*, verily, is the eldest and the greatest,'

The second sheath is more important than the first one, since it not only accounts for the life of the food sheath but also for its activities. Without the *prāṇa* nothing can function—neither can one perform dharma nor ordinary activities. Further, it is the *prāṇa* that takes the soul out of the body at the time of death. According to the *Brahma Sūtras* (4.2.2-5), the organ of speech merges in the mind at the time of death. The mind merges in the life-force (*prāṇa*). The *prāṇa* then merges in the individual soul. Then the departure from the body takes place. So while the very ordinary souls feel that the body is everything, there are some who understand that beyond the body there is something which is more powerful, and that is *prāṇa*.

This also accounts for the Indian idea that it is neither the blood nor the gene that can bring the bodily characteristics to the newborn child. Scientists believe that the gene contains answers to all their problems. If a person has some disease, he or she has inherited it hereditarily from the parents through the medium of the gene, they say.

Hindu philosophers had long, long ago discarded such ideas because they knew that beyond the body, beyond even the life force called *prāṇa* there is something more which is responsible for all the bodily and environmental effects.

That will be discussed in the next chapter.

References

1. see *Praśna Upaniṣad*, 2.3-6
2. *Complete Works*, Vol. 2, p. 30
3. *Complete Works*, Vol. 1, p. 147

Chapter 23

THE MENTAL SHEATH

It is easy to speak of the body as a sheath, since it is limited and, like a sheath, may contain the Self within. But to speak of the mind as a sheath is difficult. Mind is unlimited. Yet our Vedantic scholars were sure that there was the mental sheath.

This sheath is subtle. Within it are two more sheaths, and then the Atman. This sheath comprises the five organs of knowledge, as will be discussed below.

मनोमयः कोशः कः?

मनश्च ज्ञानेन्द्रिय-पञ्चकं मिलित्वा भवति स मनोमयः कोशः ॥

Manomaya kośaḥ kaḥ?
Manaśca jñānendriya-pañcakaṁ militvā bhavati sa manomayaḥ kośaḥ.

kaḥ what is *manomaya kośaḥ* the mental sheath? *Manaśca* the mind and *jñānendriya-pañcakaṁ* the five organs of knowledge *militvā* together *sa manomayaḥ kośaḥ* is called the mental sheath *bhavati* formed.

What is the mental sheath? The mental sheath is formed of the five organs of knowledge and the mind.

The mind has been defined as *saṁkalpa-vikalpātmakam*—the doubting one. This is the function of the mind. It has to be curious about objects and seek knowledge of them constantly. The mind is impelled by the past tendencies to seek things which were enjoyable in the past again and again. The mind then uses the senses to gain knowledge of the sense objects. For complete knowledge of the thing in itself to be formed, we have to use the other faculties like the intellect and memory.

How is the mind formed? We know that the mind is the subtle body. It is finer in nature. According to the *Chāndogya Upaniṣad* (6.4.1,4), the food we eat is divided into three parts: the grosser part goes out as waste, the gross part becomes muscle and energy in the body, and the subtle part becomes the mind. The mind, says the Upaniṣad, is also made of food.

This is the second sheath of the three in the subtle body.

Chapter 24

THE INTELLECT SHEATH

The intellect sheath is the decisive factor in the personality. It is the intellect, the *buddhi*, that gives us correct knowledge of things. This faculty remains with us till the end. The sharper the intellect, the greater will be the strength of character.

विज्ञानमयः कः?

बुद्धिः ज्ञानेन्द्रिय–पञ्चकं मिलित्वा यो भवति स
विज्ञानमयः कोशः ॥

Vijñāna-mayaḥ kaḥ?
Buddhiḥ jñānendriya-pañcakaṁ militvā yo bhavati sa vijñānamayaḥ kośaḥ.

Kaḥ what is *vijñāna-mayaḥ* the intellect sheath? *Buddhiḥ* when the intellect *militvā* along with *jñānendriya-pañcakaṁ* the five organs of knowledge (come together) *yo bhavati sa* that which is formed *vijñānamayaḥ kośaḥ* is the intellect sheath.

What is the intellect sheath? The intellect, along with the five organs of knowledge, come together, and that which is formed then is the intellect sheath.

There is one point worth noting here. It is said that the intellect sheath is made of the five sense organs like the mental sheath. How can two sheaths share the same parts? There is no difficulty in this because what we call mind or intellect is all the same. When the same inner organ functions as the deciding faculty, we call it intellect. When it wavers, it is the mind. Their locus is the subtle body. Generally, the intellect is said to be situated in the heart region.

The Self is enveloped by the vital breath, mind, and intellect—the *prāṇa, mana* and *vijñāna—maya* sheaths. These three sheaths together form the subtle body—the *sūkṣma śarīra* or *linga śarīra*.

Chapter 25

THE BLISSFUL SHEATH

According to Jainism, in the beginning everything was *suṣama-suṣama,* ever-blissful. Slowly, however, the later stages, like the *suṣama-duṣama,* came into existence. This sheath is called 'blissful' because it is immediately next to the supreme Self—the Atman, which is of the nature of bliss. The sheath is made of ignorance (*māyā*). This sheath, along with the Self, is called the causal body.

आनन्दमयः कः?

एवमेव कारण–शरीर–भूत–अविद्यास्थ–मलिन–सत्त्वं प्रियादि–वृत्तिसहितं सत् आनन्दमयः कोशः ॥

Ānandamayaḥ kaḥ?

Evameva kāraṇa-śarīra-bhūta-avidyāstha-malina-satvam priyādi-vṛtti-sahitam sat ānandamayaḥ kośaḥ.

Kaḥ what is *ānandamayaḥ* the blissful sheath? *Evameva* in this way, *kāraṇa-śarīra-bhūta* that which is in the causal body *avidyāstha-malina-satvam* the impure *Sattva* born of ignorance *priyādi-vṛtti-sahitam sat* having the modifications of dear etc *ānandamayaḥ kośaḥ* is called the blissful sheath.

What is the blissful sheath? That which is in the causal body, which is the impure *sattva* born of ignorance, and has modifications of dear, etc, is called the blissful sheath.

The impure *sattva* quality, which envelops the Self, as it were, has been called the blissful sheath. What is the impurity here? It is the mixture of a little of *rajas* or the limitedness of the *sattva* quality. The causal sheath is *māyā* or *avidyā* enveloping the Self. This ignorance or *avidyā* is made up of *sattva, rajas* and *tamas* according to Vedanta. It is this impure *sattva* quality, which like a sheath has enveloped the Self, that has been termed blissful sheath.

Ignorance is made up of three qualities—*sattva*, *rajas*, and *tamas.* The last two can never come anywhere near the Atman. Only *sattva* quality can come near it. Therefore, *māyā* envelops the Self using her *sattva* quality. In the first stage, Brahman is enveloped, as it were, by *māyā* which is made of pure *sattva*. This is the collective causal state, called Īśvara.

Brahman being enveloped by *māyā* will not be of any 'use'. There should be further developments. So Brahman, as it were, is 'divided' into billions of parts by *māyā*, called the individual Self. This individual Self plus *māyā* is the individual causal body. While pure *sattva* was used to envelop Brahman itself, to divide it and 'create' millions of individual selves, impure *sattva* is used. This individual Self and ignorance together are called the causal body.

Priyādi-vṛtti-sahitam

'Having modifications like dear, etc.' The blissful sheath is so called because it is enveloping the Atman, which is of the nature of Being, Consciousness, and Bliss. Bliss is the nature of Brahman. Bliss is everyone's desire. So any mental modification that arises pertaining to the blissful sheath should be one of love.

Sri Ramakrishna says: 'Man, looking outward, sees the gross; at that time his mind dwells in the *annamayakosha*, the gross body. Next is the subtle body. Functioning through the subtle body, the mind dwells in the *manomayakosha* and the *vijnanamayakosha*. Next is the causal body. Functioning through the causal body the mind enjoys bliss; it dwells in the *anandamayakosha*. This corresponds to the semiconscious state experienced by Chaitanya. Last of all, the mind loses itself in the Great Cause. It disappears. It merges in the Great Cause.'[1]

Recapitulation

1. Life has become meaningless and its sufferings unbearable for some one.

2. He has tried several other methods at overcoming suffering and boredom here, but has failed.

3. He at last comes to know Vedanta, which says that he is failing because he is looking the wrong way for solutions.

4. He is told to venture inward, which is the only way to overcome existential suffering, limitations, bondages, and meaninglessness in life. Meaning cannot be found in the body or the senses he understands.

5. He then becomes an aspirant of Vedanta, by following its principles of (a) knowing what Vedanta contains; (b) performing his daily, occasional and obligatory duties with devotion; (c) avoiding evil deeds and desire-born actions because they once again take him the wrong way; (d) discriminating about what is wrong and what is right; practising dispassion to wrong things, developing the six treasures of fortitude, forbearance, control, etc, and (e) purifying the mind sufficiently to become a *mumukṣu,* the seeker after Truth.

6. Once a person becomes a *mumukṣu,* his next effort will be to know what the Reality is. Is the body real? Is the mind real? Is this cosmos real? What is real? So he approaches a teacher, and serves him with devotion. The teacher tells him that, of the four qualifications needed to know the Truth, he has acquired one, *mumukṣutvam.* The second is to know the subject matter of Vedanta. So the teacher tells him about the gross, subtle, and causal bodies, about

the Self or Atman as being Brahman, and about the five sheaths.

7. The person then realizes that he is not the gross body made of food—the food sheath. He is not the subtle body made also of food but constituted of mental, intellectual, and vital sheaths. And he is also not the causal body made of bliss. He is the Self.

8. Is this Self or Atman the same as the one he held on to all these years, saying 'I am', 'I do', 'I enjoy', 'I suffer' and so on? This will be taken up in the next chapter.

Reference

1. Gospel, p. 604

Chapter 26

'I' NESS AND 'MY'NESS

Introduction

> The feeling of 'Thee and Thine' is the outcome of Knowledge; 'I and mine' comes from ignorance.
>
> —**Sri Ramakrishna** [1]

The author of *Tattvabodha* now begins a new current of thought. He said that there are three bodies and they can be divided into five sheaths. He discussed the five sheaths. The Self has been enveloped by these five sheaths. If the Self could reject these five sheaths one by one it would remain in its own glory, as in Sri Ramakrishna's famous example

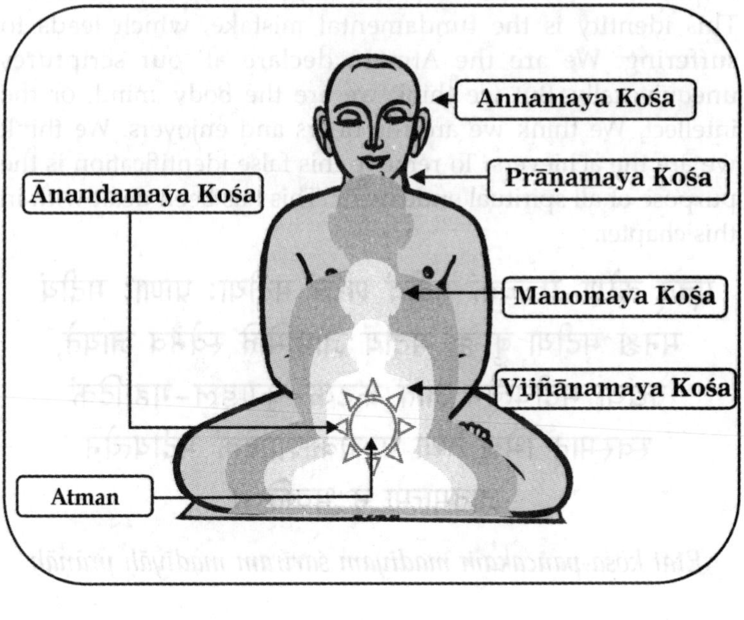

of pealing off the scales of an onion. Unfortunately, however, the problem is with the identification.

Sri Ramakrishna explains this: 'The feeling of "I and mine" has covered the Reality. Because of this we do not see Truth. Attainment of Chaitanya, Divine Consciousness, is not possible without the knowledge of Advaita, Non-duality.'[2]

The five sheaths have no independent existence of themselves. They cannot exist without the Atman. Moreover, the Atman alone is real while these are superimpositions in the absolute sense. This is the fundamental note of the Advaita.

So where lies the problem? It is in false identity. After ignorance envelops the Self, it projects the subtle and gross bodies. The bodies, as we have seen, are products of ignorance. The permutation and combination of the three qualities of ignorance—*sattva, rajas,* and *tamas*—have made the three bodies. So they are inert. The light of the Self falls on the causal and subtle bodies and illumines them. The intellect then begins the confusion. It thinks that it is the Self. The mind thinks it is the Self. And the body thinks it is the Self. This identity is the fundamental mistake, which leads to suffering. We are the Atman, declare all our scriptures unequivocally. But we think we are the body, mind, or the intellect. We think we are the doers and enjoyers. We think we are the achievers. To remove this false identification is the purpose of all spiritual endeavour. This has been dealt with in this chapter.

एतत् कोश–पञ्चकं मदीयं शरीरं मदीयाः प्राणाः मदीयं
मनश्च मदीया बुद्धिः मदीयं ज्ञानमिति स्वेनैव ज्ञायते,
तद्यथा मदीयत्वेन ज्ञातं कटक–कुण्डल–गृहादिकं
स्वस्माद् भिन्नं तथा पञ्चकोशादिकं मदीयत्वेन
ज्ञातमात्मा न भवति ।।

Etat kośa-pañcakaṁ madīyam śarīram madīyāḥ prāṇāḥ

madīyaṁ manaśca madīyā buddhiḥ madīyaṁ jñānamiti svenaiva jñāyate, tadyathā madīyatvena jñātam kaṭaka-kuṇḍala-gṛhādikaṁ svasmād bhinnaṁ tadyathā pañca-kośādikaṁ madīyatvena jñātamātmā na bhavati.

Etat kośa-pañcakaṁ these five sheaths *madīyam śarīram* my body *madīyāḥ prāṇāḥ* my vital breath *madīyaṁ manaśca* my mind *madīyā buddhiḥ* my intellect *madīyaṁ jñānamiti* my knowledge etc; *svenaiva* oneself *tadyathā* just as, (that which is) *jñāyate* known *madīyatvena* as mine *kaṭaka-kuṇḍala-gṛhādikaṁ* the ornaments, the house, etc *svasmād bhinnaṁ* (are) different from me *tadyathā* (and again) just as *pañca-kośādikaṁ* the five sheaths *jñātam* if known as *madīyatvena* mine *na bhavati* do not become. *ātmā* the Self

Even if one has the idea that the house, ornaments, and so on are one's own they do not become the Self. So also if one has the idea like 'this is my body, my vital breath, my mind, my intellect, my knowledge,' and so forth, they do not become the Self.

'Give Up Identification'

Swamiji says: 'Do not identify yourself with anything. Hold your mind free. All this that you see, the pains and the miseries, are but the necessary conditions of this world; poverty and wealth and happiness are but momentary; they do not belong to our real nature at all. Our nature is far beyond misery and happiness, beyond every object of the senses, beyond the imagination; and yet we must go on working all the time. "Misery comes through attachment, not through work."

'As soon as we identify ourselves with the work we do, we feel miserable; but if we do not identify ourselves with it, we do not feel that misery. If a beautiful picture belonging to another is burnt, a man does not generally become miserable; but when his own picture is burnt, how miserable he feels!

Why? Both were beautiful pictures, perhaps copies of the same original; but in one case very much more misery is felt than in the other. It is because in one case he identifies himself with the picture, and not in the other. This "I and mine" causes the whole misery. With the sense of possession comes selfishness, and selfishness brings on misery.

'Every act of selfishness or thought of selfishness makes us attached to something, and immediately we are made slaves. Each wave in the Chitta that says "I and mine" immediately puts a chain round us and makes us slaves; and the more we say "I and mine", the more slavery grows, the more misery increases.'[3]

Sri Ramakrishna says: 'He who has attained this Knowledge of Brahman is a jīvanmukta, liberated while living in the body. He rightly understands that the Atman and the body are two separate things. After realizing God one does not identify the Atman with the body. These two are separate, like the kernel and the shell of the coconut when its milk dries up. The Atman moves, as it were, within the body. When the "milk" of worldly-mindedness has dried up, one gets Self-knowledge. Then one feels that Atman and body are two separate things.'[4]

'What begets egotism? Knowledge or ignorance? It is only the humble man who attains knowledge. In a low place rain-water collects. It runs down from a mound.

'A man achieves neither Knowledge nor liberation as long as he has egotism. He comes back again and again to the world. The calf bellows, "Hamba! Hamba!", that is, "I! I!" That is why it suffers such agony. The butcher slaughters it and the shoe-maker makes shoes from its hide. Besides, its hide is used for the drum, which is beaten mercilessly. Still no end to its misery! At long last a carding machine is made from its entrails. While carding the cotton the machine makes the sound "Tuhu! Tuhu!", that is, "Thou! Thou!" Then the poor calf is released from all suffering. It no longer says, "Hamba!

Hamba!" but repeats, "Tuhu! Tuhu!" The calf says, as it were, "O God, Thou art the Doer and I am nothing. Thou art the Operator and I am the machine. Thou art everything."'[5]

Egotism is born of false identification. We are proud of our physical beauty. But that is so impermanent that a little ailment may destroy it. If physical appearance was everything, all the film personalities of the world would have been the happiest people, and they would have been called 'blissful'. Unfortunately, several film personalities have committed suicide, and they too suffer endlessly. Life is not mere skin-deep philosophy. A little ailment, a small germ, and all the beauty will be gone. Ageing is yet another terror. As we become old, the skin becomes loose, muscles begin to hang, and we look horrible. This is the body. Finally, a single natural calamity and all our life is gone. Our wealth, our property, everything that we boast will go the moment a tornado, typhoon or a cyclone hits. This is all that the physical world has in its store for us.

Then there is the pride of learning. 'I am so-and-so,' 'I am a doctor, an engineer, a PhD,' 'I have so many degrees.' This is yet another false identification. If I think I am big, there will be someone who will be bigger tomorrow. All our so-called learning, intelligence, capacity to achieve things, and so on are there until the body lasts. If something happens to the body somewhere, we are undone. If something happens to the mind, everything is gone. It is said of a great scholar, who was famous for his brilliant memory, that he lost everything in an accident. Alzheimer's is taking its toll heavily all the world over. Such is the glory of memory.

Such is life. Pinning our hopes and life on evanescent things is what is called misery, and we are all doing that.

Holy Mother Sri Sarada Devi says: 'People suffer endless miseries on account of their egoism and at last they say, "Not I, not I; it is Thou, O God! It is Thou!"'[6] This is where religion begins.

A devotee asked Holy Mother once: 'Man cannot do anything by his individual effort. God is doing everything through him.' Holy Mother Sri Sarada Devi replied: 'Yes, that is true. But is one conscious of this always? Blinded by egoism, people think themselves to be independent agents in regard to action. They do not depend on God. He protects one who relies on Him.'[7]

There is another type of egoism. There is a Buddhist story of a rich woman. This rich woman was famous as a pious, calm, loving and gentle person. Her maid servant was poor but saintly. Once this servant decided to test the truth of her mistress' goodness. She came late for work. The mistress scolded her. The next day the same thing happened. On the third day, the rich lady, famous for gentleness beat the maid with a stick. We are pious due to social compulsions.

Swami Vivekananda therefore exhorts everyone to give up false identification. He says: 'What can be a greater giver of peace than renunciation? A little ephemeral worldly good is nothing in comparison with eternal good; no doubt of that. What can bring greater strength than sattva guna (absolute purity of mind)? It is indeed true that all other kinds of knowledge are but non-knowledge in comparison with Self-knowledge. But I ask: How many are there in the world fortunate enough to gain that Sattva Guna? How many in this land of Bharata? How many have that noble heroism which can renounce all, shaking off the idea of "I and mine"? How many are blessed enough to possess that far - sight of wisdom which makes the earthly pleasures appear to be but vanity of vanities? Where is that broadhearted man who is apt to forget even his own body in meditating over the beauty and glory of the Divine?'[8]

In the 16th chapter of the *Bhagavadgītā*, the Lord has discussed this weakness of human beings in detail.

Conclusion

Though we identify ourselves with the five sheaths or the three bodies and remain bound to the world, we cannot be any one of these. While all these undergo birth, death, and so on, the Atman is changeless. The sun can never be confused for a little drop of water on which he shines. So the sages and scriptures warn us repeatedly not to waste our precious lives.

References:

1. *Gospel*, p. 265
2. *Gospel*, p. 308
3. *Complete Works*, Vol. 1, p. 100
4. *Gospel*, p. 719
5. *Gospel*, p. 633
6. *Teachings of Holy Mother*, p. 69
7. *Teachings of Holy Mother*, p. 70
8. *Complete Works*, Vol. 4, p. 404

Chapter 27

THE ATMAN

What Brahman is cannot be described in words. Somebody once said that everything in the world has been made impure, like food that has touched the tongue, and that Brahman alone remains undefiled. The meaning is this: All scriptures and holy books—the Vedas, the Puranas, the Tantras, and so forth—may be said to have been defiled because their contents have been uttered by the tongues of men; but what Brahman is no tongue has yet been able to describe. Therefore Brahman is still undefiled. One cannot describe in words the joy of play and communion with Satchidananda. He alone knows, who has realized it.

—**Sri Ramakrishna**[1]

Adhyāropa or Superimposition

After discussing the different states of being and different bodies, the truth is being told now. What is the truth? Vedantins follow the method of *adhyāropa* and *apavāda* to describe the Truth. Is it possible to pinpoint the Atman? No, say the sages. The Atman is self-revealing. It is not an object to be known. It is the eternal subject. All that the sages do is point out where we are erring—where we have fixed our ego wrongly—and show us the way.

The Vedantins first of all follow the course of superimposition in explaining to us the wrong route we have taken. They say that Brahman is enveloped by *māyā* and thus the three cosmic and individual bodies—causal, subtle, and gross—have appeared. We are identifying ourselves with our gross bodies now, in the waking state. Having shown us the wrong course we have taken, and the wrong place we have reached in our journey, the guidepost, guru, tells us to go back to where we started. This going backwards is *apavāda*. From the gross body, through the subtle and causal, we are told to reach the Truth. The truth is that Atman alone is real, and all else is unreal. This Atman is Brahman.

There is a beautiful mantra in the *Śvetāśvatara Upaniṣad* (6.11):

एको देवः सर्वभूतेषु गूढः सर्वव्यापी सर्वभूतान्तरात्मा ।
कर्माध्यक्षः सर्वभूताधिवासः साक्षी चेता केवलो निर्गुणश्च ॥

Eko devaḥ sarvabhūteṣu gūḍaḥ
sarvavyāpī sarvabhūtāntarātmā |
Karmādhykṣaḥ sarvabhūtādhi-vāsaḥ
sākṣī cetā kevalo nirguṇaśca ||

'There is one God who remains hidden in all beings as the innermost Self. He is all-pervasive and the Ruler of our actions. He is the indweller of all beings, the Witness, the consciousness of all, the One alone, and beyond attributes.'

Such is the Atman. The Upaniṣads declare time and again that it is the One, the Atman, which appears as many. It is the same Self that is in all beings. If I know my Atman, I know everything, because it is the same Self that pervades and has become everything. The *Bṛhadāraṇyaka Upaniṣad* (3.4.1) declares this truth with force: 'यत् साक्षाद् अपरोक्षाद् ब्रह्म य आत्मा सर्वान्तरः, *yat sākṣād aparokṣād brahma ya ātmā sarvāntaraḥ,* That Brahman which is known directly is the same as the Self which is in all beings.'

Tattvabodha begins the discussion on the Atman now.

आत्मा तर्हि कः? सच्चिदानन्द–स्वरूपः ॥

Ātmā tarhi kāḥ? Saccidānanda-svarūpaḥ.

Kāḥ what is *tarhi* then, *ātmā* the Self? *svarūpaḥ* It is of the nature of *saccidānanda* Being-Consciousness-Bliss

What, then, is the Atman?

It is of the nature of Being-Knowledge-Bliss Absolute.

Describing the Atman

The Atman is called Being-Knowledge-Bliss Absolute. This is the best definition or description of the Truth that the sages can give. This is because, the Atman is beyond name and form. The term *sat-cit-ānanda* is not mentioned in any of the major Upaniṣads. The *Tejobindu Upaniṣad* (6.1) mentions this term.

Sometimes the sages or the Vedas have used negative terms to describe the Atman. As for instance, in the *Kena Upaniṣad* (1.2-8) describes the Atman in this way: 'The Atman is the ear of the ear, mind of the mind, speech of the speech, soul of the soul. Neither the eyes nor the speech nor the mind can reach the Self. It is different from all that we know and do not know. Thus we have heard. That which can never be seen, heard, cogitated, and enlivened by the eyes, ears, mind, or *prāṇa* respectively but that which makes these organs function by Its presence is the Atman.'

Swami Vivekananda says: 'The Advaitists, then have no place for the individual soul. They say individual souls are created by Maya. In reality they cannot exist. If there were only one existence throughout, how could it be that I am one, and you are one, and so forth? We are all one, and the cause of evil is the perception of duality. As soon as I begin to feel that I am separate from this universe, then first comes fear, and then comes misery. "Where one hears another, one sees another, that is small. Where one does not see another, where one does not hear another, that is the greatest, that is God. In that greatest is perfect happiness. In small things there is no happiness."'[2]

So the fundamental axiom of Advaita Vedanta is that individuality is false. Not only are the body, mind, intellect,

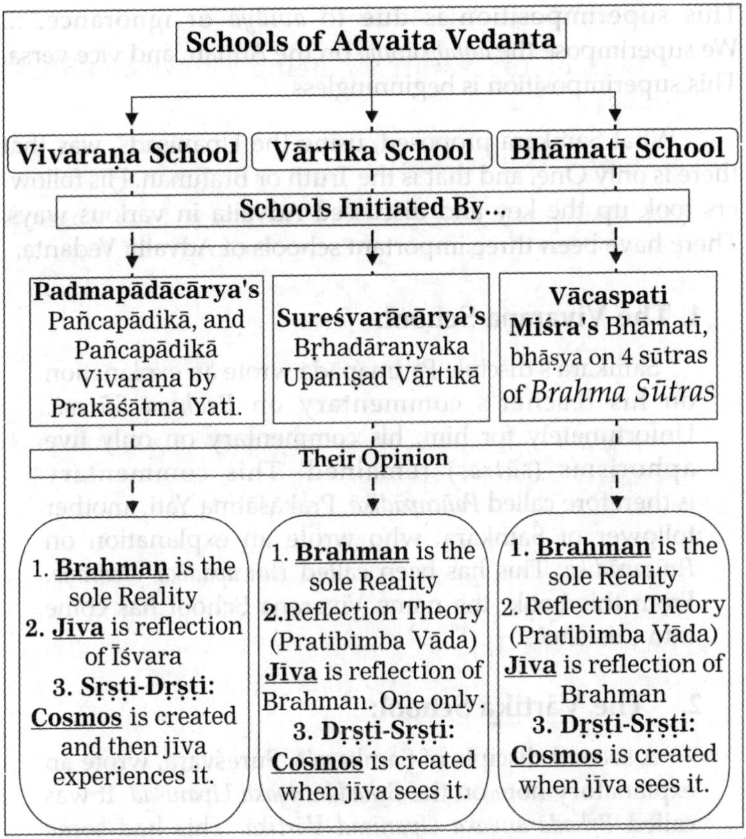

memory, and so on unreal, individual selfhood too is unreal. Thus it is clear that after attainment of the knowledge that we are the Atman, we need not do sadhana further to know that we are Brahman, the Absolute. Knowing the Self is ultimate knowledge.

This is the premise of Saṁkara's famous *adhyāsa bhāṣya,* the introduction to his *Brahma Sūtras* commentary. He says there that the subject and the object, which are respectively called "I" and "you", and are as different as light and darkness, cannot have separate identities, much less, attributes. Thus the superimposition of the subject or its qualities on the object and its qualities—or vice versa—is unthinkable. ...

This superimposition is due to *avidyā* or ignorance. ... We superimpose the *antaḥkaraṇa* on the Atman, and vice versa. This superimposition is beginningless.

What Śaṁkara proposed, using the Upaniṣads, was that there is only One, and that is the Truth or Brahman. His followers took up the key and discussed Advaita in various ways. There have been three important schools of Advaita Vedanta:

1. The Vivaraṇa School:

Śaṁkara's disciple Padmapāda wrote an explanation on his teacher's commentary on *Brahma Sūtras*. Unfortunately for him, his commentary on only five aphorisms (*sūtras*) remained. This commentary is therefore called *Pañcapādikā*. Prakāśātma Yati, another follower of Śaṁkara, who wrote an explanation on *Pañcapādikā*. This has been called *Pañcapādikā Vivaraṇa*. From this book, the name Vivaraṇa School has come into existence.

2. The Vārtikā School:

A second disciple of Śaṁkara's, Sureśvara, wrote an explanatory note on the *Bṛhadāraṇyaka Upaniṣad*. It was called *Bṛhadāraṇyaka Upaniṣad Vārtikā*. This had some novel ideas which made it a school of thought.

3. Bhāmatī School:

The third school of Advaita Vedanta is that of Vācaspati Miśra. Vācaspati Miśra wrote a commentary on the first four aphorisms of the *Brahma Sūtras*. It came to be called *Bhāmatī* after his wife's name. Miśra's wife was so devoted that until her husband completed writing the book, she served him with devotion, though he had altogether forgotten he had a wife. *Bhāmatī* varies from the other two schools in some concepts, and has become a separate school.

These three schools have almost everything in common, but they vary in some points. A few of these are the following:

a. About creation. The Sureśvara School or Vārtikā school holds that creation takes place the moment we see it. When we do not see it, there is no creation. Such is the idea of *dṛṣṭi-sṛṣṭi* theory. The Bhāmatī school says that ignorance of the *jīva* is the cause of creation. The Vivaraṇa School does not accept this and says that the universe is virtually real till one has Brahman knowledge.

b. Jīvahood: The second point is about the nature of the living being. This is what concerns us here. According to Vārtikā and Bhāmatī schools, the individual soul (*jīva*) is the reflection (*pratibimba)* of Brahman. This is called the *pratibimba* theory. This is what is accepted by Śaṁkara also. The other theory is that Īśvara is the *bimba* or source and *jīva* is the *pratibimba.* This is upheld by the Vivaraṇa school. This is not the view held by Śaṁkara.

If the *jīva* is the reflection of Brahman, when the reflection ends there will be Brahman alone.

The Glory of the Atman

Swami Vivekananda says: 'What is this Atman, this soul of man, which is neither the body nor the mind?'[3]

'The difference between man and man, and all things in the whole creation, is not in kind but only in degree. The background, the reality, of everyone is that same Eternal, Ever Blessed, Ever Pure, and Ever Perfect One. It is the Atman, the Soul, in the saint and the sinner, in the happy and the miserable, in the beautiful and the ugly, in men and in animals; it is the same throughout. It is the shining One. The difference is caused by the power of expression. In some It is expressed more, in others less, but this difference of expression has no effect upon the Atman.'[4]

The glory of the Atman has been declared by Swami Vivekananda in these terms: 'What does the Advaitist declare? He says, if there is a God, that God must be both the material and the efficient cause of the universe. Not only is He the creator, but He is also the created. He Himself is this universe. How can that be? God, the pure, the spirit, has become the universe? Yes, apparently so. That which all ignorant people see as the universe does not really exist. What are you and I and all these things we see? Mere self-hypnotism; there is but one Existence, the Infinite, the Ever-blessed One. In that Existence we dream all these various dreams. It is the Atman, beyond all, the Infinite, beyond the known, beyond the knowable; in and through That we see the universe. It is the only Reality. It is this table; It is the audience before me; It is the wall; It is everything, minus the name and form. Take away the form of the table, take away the name; what remains is It. The Vedantist does not call It either He or She—these are fictions, delusions of the human brain—there is no sex in the soul. People who are under illusion, who have become like animals, see a woman or a man; living gods do not see men or women. How can they who are beyond everything have any sex idea? Everyone and everything is the Atman—the Self—the sexless, the pure, the ever - blessed. It is the name, the form, the body, which are material, and they make all this difference.'[5]

How to Know the Self?

The final question is, how can we know the Self? 'How to know the Knower? It cannot be known. How can you see your own Self? You can only reflect yourself. So all this universe is the reflection of that One Eternal Being, the Atman, and as the reflection falls upon good or bad reflectors, so good or bad images are cast up. Thus in the murderer, the reflector is bad and not the Self. In the saint the reflector is pure. The Self — the Atman — is by Its own nature pure.'[6] This is Swamiji's answer.

Since there is only One, the Atman, all our love and hate pertain to the Self alone. In the Upaniṣads [*Bṛhadāraṇyaka Upaniṣad*, 2.4.5] there is the dialogue of Yājñavalkya and Maitreyi, his wife. Yājñavalkya says to her that all our love is Self-based.

Vivekananda says: 'Real existence, real knowledge, and real love are eternally connected with one another, the three in one: where one of them is, the others also must be; they are the three aspects of the One without a second — the Existence-Knowledge-Bliss. When that existence becomes relative, we see it as the world; that knowledge becomes in its turn modified into the knowledge of the things of the world; and that bliss forms the foundation of all true love known to the heart of man.'[7]

The nature of the Self has been mentioned to be *satcidānanda*. Each one of these three terms will be taken up now.

References:

1. *Gospel*, p. 900
2. Complete Works, Vol. 1, p. 364
3. Complete Works, Vol. 2, p. 77
4. Complete Works, Vol. 2, p. 168
5. Complete Works, Vol. 2, pp. 248-9
6. Complete Works, Vol. 2, p. 249
7. Complete Works, Vol.1, p. 58

Chapter 28

BEING (*SAT*)

What is *Sat*?

Swamiji says: 'All the books contained in the Upanishads have one subject, one task before them—to prove the following theme: "Just as by the knowledge of one lump of clay we have the knowledge of all the clay in the universe, so what is that, knowing which we know everything in the universe?"

'The idea of the Advaitists is to generalise the whole universe into one—that something which is really the whole of this universe. And they claim that this whole universe is one, that it is one Being manifesting itself in all these various forms. They admit that what the Sankhya calls nature exists, but say that nature is God. It is this Being, the Sat, which has become converted into all this—the universe, man, soul, and everything that exists. Mind and Mahat are but the manifestations of that one Sat. But then the difficulty arises that this would be pantheism. How came that Sat which is unchangeable, as they admit (for that which is absolute is unchangeable), to be changed into that which is changeable, and perishable? The Advaitists here have a theory which they call Vivarta Vada or apparent manifestation. According to the dualists and the Sankhyas, the whole of this universe is the evolution of primal nature. According to some of the Advaitists and some of the dualists, the whole of this universe is evolved from God. And according to the Advaitists proper, the followers of Shankaracharya, the whole universe is the apparent evolution of God.

'God is the material cause of this universe, but not really, only apparently. The celebrated illustration used is that of the rope and the snake, where the rope appeared to be the snake, but was not really there. The rope did not really change into the snake. Even so this whole universe as it exists is that Being. It is unchanged, and all the changes we see in it are only apparent. These changes are caused by Desha, Kala, and Nimitta (space, time, and causation), or, according to a higher psychological generalisation, by Nama and Rupa (name and form). It is by name and form that one thing is differentiated from another. The name and form alone cause the difference. In reality they are one and the same. Again, it is not, the Vedantists say, that there is something as phenomenon and something as noumenon. The rope is changed into the snake apparently only; and when the delusion ceases, the snake vanishes.

'When one is in ignorance, he sees the phenomenon and does not see God. When he sees God, this universe vanishes entirely for him. Ignorance or Maya, as it is called, is the cause of all this phenomenon—the Absolute, the Unchangeable, being taken as this manifested universe. This Maya is not absolute zero, nor non-existence. It is defined as neither existence nor non-existence. It is not existence, because that can be said only of the Absolute, the Unchangeable, and in this sense, Maya is non-existence.'[1]

सत् किम्?

कालत्रयेऽपि तिष्ठतीति सत् ॥

Sat kim?
Kālatraye'pi tiṣṭhtīti sat.

kim what is *Sat* Being? *Kālatraye'pi* in all the three times (past, present and future) *tiṣṭhtīti* It remains (and therefore it is) *sat* Being.

What is Being? Reality remains in all the three times—past, present, and future—and so it is called *Sat*.

Kālatraya

'The Three Times'. The three times are the past, present and future. The present is the standard for judging the other two. For us, the future is dark. But for the gods, the three times are one. They move in all these three with equal ease. So the concept of the three times is relative. It is in the minds of the living beings only. What about the Self then? It is beyond the idea of time. The Self was not born; it shall not die. So it is always there.

The word *sat* means being; it was also translated a few years ago as existence. *Sat* is a statement of fact. 'To be' means 'is'. This is the most essential fact of something—that it is. The Atman can never be the opposite. The *Bhagavadgītā* (17.26) gives these meanings to *sat:* 'The word indicates being, is used regarding someone being good, and for indicating auspiciousness.' In the general sense, the word *sat* is used to indicate goodness: *sadguṇa* means good quality. So it has been called *sat*, being. Sri Ramakrishna goes further and says: 'The Vedas speak of Satchidananda Brahman. Brahman is neither one nor two; It is between one and two. It cannot be described either as existence or as non-existence; It is between existence and non-existence.'[2]

References

1. Complete Works, Vol. 1, pp. 362-3
2. Gospel, p. 659

Chapter 29

CONSCIOUSNESS (*CIT*)

[Brahman] has no attributes but is Existence, Knowledge, and Bliss—Absolute. Existence, we have seen, is the very ultimate generalisation which the human mind can come to. Knowledge does not mean the knowledge we have, but the essence of that, that which is expressing itself in the course of evolution in human beings or in other animals as knowledge. The essence of that knowledge is meant, the ultimate fact beyond, if I may be allowed to say so, even consciousness. That is what is meant by knowledge and what we see in the universe as the essential unity of things.

—Swami Vivekananda[1]

The word consciousness is being used recently. Earlier, *cit* was translated as knowledge. The first qualification of that which is beyond mind and thought was 'being'. Its second attribute is 'consciousness'. That is, it is the opposite of inertia. Whatever awareness, knowledge, lack of ignorance, and so on we notice are because of this consciousness. 'According to Vedanta, the three fundamental factors of consciousness are, I exist, I know, and I am blessed. The idea that I have no want, that I am restful, peaceful, that nothing can disturb me, which comes from time to time, is the central fact of our being, the basic principle of our life; and when it becomes limited, and becomes a compound, it manifests itself as existence phenomenal, knowledge phenomenal, and love. Every man exists, and every man must know, and every man is mad for love. He cannot help loving. Through all existence, from the lowest to the highest, all must love. The I, the internal thing-in-itself, which, combining with mind, manufactures existence, knowledge, and love, is called by the Vedantists, Existence absolute, Knowledge absolute, Bliss absolute.'[2]

चित् किम्?

आनन्द–स्वरूपः ॥

Cit kim?
Ānanda-svarūpaḥ.

kim what is *cit* consciousness ? *Ānanda-svarūpaḥ* It is Bliss itself.

What is consciousness? It is (of the nature of) Bliss itself.

Swami Vivekananda asked his disciple if he knew that Vedanta gave the terms *sat*, *cit* and *ānanda* for Brahman. The disciple said yes. Then Swami Vivekananda explained the terms to him: 'The phrase Sat-chit-ananda means—sat, i.e. existence, Chit, i.e. consciousness or knowledge, and Ananda, i.e. bliss which is the same as love. There is no controversy between the Bhakta and the Jnani regarding the Sat aspect of Brahman. Only, the Jnanis lay greater stress on His aspect of Chit or knowledge, while the Bhaktas keep the aspect of Ananda or love more in view. But no sooner is the essence of Chit realised than the essence of Ananda is also realised. Because what is Chit is verily the same as Ananda.'[3]

How can one realize such a consciousness? Sri Ramakrishna says: 'Through the awakening of the inner consciousness one realizes the All-pervading Consciousness.'[4]

What is *ānanda*? This will be discussed in the next part.

References

1. Complete Works, Vol. 1, pp. 372-3
2. Complete Works, Vol. 2, pp. 458-9
3. Complete Works, Vol.7, p. 385
4. *Gospel*, p. 734

Chapter 30

BLISS (*ĀNANDA*)

'I am Full of Bliss'

Once upon a time Brahmā had a desire to come down to earth and lead the life of living beings, his own creation. He chose, not the body of a human being, but that of the pig. To be a swine is not all that bad. But the moment Brahmā became the pig, he became engrossed with the pig life. He married a good-looking sow and raised a wonderful family. He grunted and hunted food for the family day and night. He was thrilled whenever he moved about in ditchwater. The sweet fragrance of the ditchwater, the germs and worms that flowed in it, everything appealed to the Brahmā-pig. He was full of bliss.

The gods above were concerned. They had waited long for their leader, Brahmā, to return home, but he was busy on the earth. Deciding to call him back, the gods came down, stood near the ditch where the pig family's residence was, and called upon Brahmā to return home. 'No, I shall not,' replied Brahmā firmly. 'I am full of bliss here, and I have a beautiful family with a obedient wife and well-educated children. The way my eldest son swims in ditchwater is exciting. I shall not come back.' The gods were puzzled and worried too. How to bring back the chief of their clan to senses? At last they hit upon a plan. One of the gods tore apart the pig body, and the moment the body was gone, out came Brahmā, laughing at his own foolishness of attachment to ditchwater-bliss.

Bliss is Everywhere

There is an aphorism in *Brahma Sūtras* (3.3.11), which says that bliss should be understood as all-pervasive, for the simple reason that Brahman is all-pervasive. Everything is bliss. Everywhere there is bliss. 'मधुवाता ऋतायते मधुक्षरन्ति सिन्धवः …*madhu-vātā ṛtāyate madhu-kṣaranti sindhavaḥ*…, the air spreads sweetness, the waters exude sweetness, everything is sweetness,' says the Ṛg Veda.

We have to know first of all the correct meaning of bliss. We get this from the authority of Sri Ramakrishna himself: 'Let me tell you something. There are three kinds of ānanda, joy: the joy of worldly enjoyment, the joy of worship, and the Joy of Brahman. The joy of worldly enjoyment is the joy of "woman and gold", which people always enjoy. The joy of worship one enjoys while chanting the name and glories of God. And the Joy of Brahman is the joy of God-vision. After experiencing the joy of God-vision the rishis of olden times went beyond all rules and conventions.'[1]

Swamiji adds further: 'The freedom which the saint seeks is very different from that which the robber seeks; the freedom loved by the saint leads him to the enjoyment of infinite, unspeakable bliss, while that on which the robber has set his heart only forges other bonds for his soul.'[2]

What we call bliss in the ordinary sense of the word, therefore, is another form of pain alone. There is no persistent bliss in this world. If we think there is momentary bliss, it will be followed by misery. Yet why do we seek bliss here?

This is because our nature is bliss. Our essential nature is one of bliss since we are Being-Consciousness-Bliss Absolute Itself. In deep sleep, when we are aware of nothing else but the causal body, we enjoy a faint taste of that bliss. The taste lingers. So we search for bliss always. Swamiji explains this: 'We do not believe that there will come a time when there will be all happiness and no unhappiness.

Now and then we know a moment of supreme bliss, when we ask nothing, give nothing, know nothing but bliss. Then it passes, and we again see the panorama of the universe moving before us....'[3]

Swamiji once spoke regarding why we should seek that immortal bliss: 'Having once realised that Supreme Bliss, one is no more overwhelmed by pleasure and pain of this world. Men being fettered by base lust-and-wealth cannot enjoy that Bliss of Brahman.' There was a disciple who was listening to these words of Swami Vivekananda. He asked him: 'If it is so, and if we are really of the essence of the Supreme Brahman, then why do we not exert ourselves to gain that Bliss? Why do we again and again run into the jaws of death, being decoyed by this worthless snare of lust-and-wealth?'

Swamiji repied to him: 'You speak as if man does not desire to have that Bliss! Ponder over it, and you will see that whatever anyone is doing, he is doing in the hope of gaining that Supreme Bliss. Only, not everyone is conscious of it and so cannot understand it. That Supreme Bliss fully exists in all, from Brahma down to the blade of grass. You are also that undivided Brahman. This very moment you can realise if you think yourself truly and absolutely to be so. It is all mere want of direct perception.

'That you have taken service and work so hard for the sake of your wife also shows that the aim is ultimately to attain to that Supreme Bliss of Brahman. Being again and again entangled in the intricate maze of delusion and hard hit by sorrows and afflictions, the eye will turn of itself to one's own real nature, the Inner Self. It is owing to the presence of this desire for bliss in the heart, that man, getting hard shocks one after another, turns his eye inwards—to his own Self. A time is sure to come to everyone, without exception, when he will do so—to one it may be in this life, to another, after thousands of incarnations.'[4]

It is clear, therefore, that we are all seeking supreme bliss that is within us. Most of us are unaware of it and looking the wrong way. To be conscious and seek that source of everlasting bliss is our goal. Hence the Vedanta, a perfectly scientific system, comes forward to awaken us.

आनन्दः कः?

सुख–स्वरूपः ।

Ānandaḥ kaḥ?
Sukha-svarūpaḥ.

Kaḥ what is *ānandaḥ* Bliss? *Sukha-svarūpaḥ* It is happiness itself.

What is Bliss?

It is of the nature of absolute happiness.

A senior monk of the Ramakrishna Order remarked once that while the Vedas declared that everything is *ānanda,* bliss, the Buddha remarked that everything is *duḥkha,* sorrow. This is the basic difference between the two paths.

The *Pañcadaśī* says (11.13): 'All beings are born of bliss and live by it, pass on to It and are finally re-absorbed in it. There is therefore no doubt that Brahman is bliss.'

In the phenomenal state, when we have the body, mind, and Self, we think this universe, specially this world, is full of misery. But when the Self is attained, when the mirage is discovered, there is only bliss.

Swami Vivekananda declares: 'We are "Existence, Knowledge, Bliss" (Sachchidananda). Existence is the last generalisation in the universe; so we exist, we know it; and bliss is the natural result of existence without alloy. Now and then we know a moment of supreme bliss, when we ask nothing, give nothing, and know nothing but bliss. Then it passes and we again see the panorama of the universe going on before us and we know it is but a "mosaic work set upon God, who is the background of all things".

'When we return to earth and see the Absolute as relative, we see Sachchidananda as Trinity—father, Son, Holy Ghost. Sat = the creating principle; Chit = the guiding principle; Ananda = the realising principle, which joins us again to the One.'[5]

One day, Dr Mahendralal Sarkar had come to visit Sri Ramakrishna. 'Suddenly Sri Ramakrishna went into a spiritual mood and said to Dr Sarkar: "Mahindra Babu, what is this madness of yours about money? Why such attachment to wife? Why such longing for name and fame? Give up all these, now, and direct your mind to God with whole-souled devotion. Enjoy the Bliss of God."'[6] Engaging oneself in doing good to others, forgetting the ideal, was not the way Sri Ramakrishna taught. He spoke of the greatest philanthropist of his times, Ishvara Chandra Vidyasagar: 'One needs sadhana. Mere study of the scriptures will not do. I noticed that though Vidyasagar had no doubt read a great deal, he had not realized what was inside him; he was satisfied with helping boys get their education, but had not tasted the Bliss of God. What will mere study accomplish?'[7] Therefore, *Tattvabodha* declares now that the Self has to be known.

References

1. Gospel, p. 478
2. Complete Works, Vol.1, p. 109
3. Complete Works, Vol., 5, p. 284
4. Complete Works, Vol. 5, p. 393
5. Complete Works, Vol. 8, p. 11
6. Gospel, p. 915
7. Gospel, p. 779

Chapter 31

KNOW THYSELF

Dialogue in Heaven

There was a beautiful story in one of the books we read recently. It is about an interview in heaven. It seems a person went to heaven and knocked at the gates.

The gatekeeper asked him: 'Who are you?'

The person answered: 'I am Mr So-and –so.'

Gatekeeper: 'I did not want your name on earth. Who are you?'

Person: 'You want to know my occupation? I was a businessman before I died.'

Gatekeeper: 'I did not want to know what you were doing. Who are you?'

Person: 'Oh, I am Mrs So-and-so's husband.'

Gatekeeper: 'I don't want whose husband you were. Who are you?'

The dialogue continued for a long time. At last, the gatekeeper said: 'So you do not know who you are? Then go back and know who you are.'

Why Should we Know Ourselves?

'Both happiness and misery are chains, the one golden, the other iron; but both are equally strong to bind us and hold us back from realising our true nature. The Atman knows neither happiness nor misery. These are mere "states", and states must ever change. The nature of the soul is bliss and peace unchanging. We have not to get it; we have it;

let us wash away the dross from our eyes and see it. We must stand ever on the Self and look with perfect calmness upon all the panorama of the world. It is but baby's play and ought never to disturb us,' says Swami Vivekananda.[1]

Long ago, the Delhpic Oracles have declared: 'Know Thyself.' This was taken up by Socrates and other Greek philosophers as the standard of a meaningful life. Mysticism begins when the Truth within is revealed to us—in whichever language, that of the devotee's, as the vision of God, or of the jñāni, as the realization of Truth. Swami Brahmanandaji remarked that spiritual life begins with samādhi.

The Self is clouded by ignorance. Our efforts are not to *know* but to remove the clouds. Then knowledge stands self-revealed. If knowledge had a beginning, it would have an end, and once again we would have been deluded. So knowledge is always there. We are ignorant of it, that is all.

Taitvabodha now asks us to strive to know the Truth.

एवम् सच्चिदानन्दस्वरूपं आत्मानं विजानीयात् ॥

Evam saccidānanda-svarūpaṁ ātmānaṁ vijānīyāt.

Evam Of such a nature *saccidānanda-svarūpaṁ* that which is Being-Consciousness-Bliss *ātmānaṁ* the Self *vijānīyāt* should be known.

The Self, which is of such a nature of Being-Consciousness-Bliss, should be known.

Since time immemorial, we have been thinking that we are the body and are taking repeated births. There has been no end to our coming and going. We have been enduring endless suffering—thinking that this is called life. However, there has been one thing: hope, that someday, sometime, we may be happy. This vain hope has been leading us nowhere. Rather, it has been taking us round and round.

Sri Ramakrishna explains this very well: 'But the souls that are entangled, involved in worldliness, never come to their senses. They lie in the net but are not even conscious that they are entangled. If you speak of God before them, they at once leave the place. They say: "Why God now? We shall think of Him in the hour of death." But when they lie on their deathbeds, they say to their wives or children: "Why have you put so many wicks in the lamp? Use only one wick. Otherwise too much oil will be burnt." While dying they think of their wives and children, and weep, "Alas! What will happen to them after my death?"

'The entangled souls repeat those very actions that make them suffer so much. They are like the camel, which eats thorny bushes till the blood streams from its mouth, but still will not give them up. Such a man may have lost his son and be stricken with grief, but still he will have children year after year. He may ruin himself by his daughter's marriage, but still he will go on having daughters every year. And he says: "What can I do? It's just my luck!" When he goes to a holy place he doesn't have any time to think of God. He almost kills himself carrying bundles for his wife. Entering the temple, he is very eager to give his child the holy water to drink or make him roll on the floor; but he has no time for his own devotions. These bound creatures slave for their masters to earn food for themselves and their families; and they earn money by lying, cheating, flattery. They laugh at those who think of God and meditate on Him, and call them lunatics.

"So you see how many different kinds of men there are. You said that all men were equal. But how many varieties of men there are! Some have more power and some less.'[2]

In order to become powerful and strong, we should seek God. Strength of character, strength of purity, strength of aspiration, and finally, the strength of God—will all be ours if we seek the Truth, promise the saints.

Recapitulation

1. The seeker of Truth has been told that he is not the physical, mental, or the causal body. He is something different from all these.

2. He has been told that he is the supreme Self, the Atman, which is beyond sorrow, pain, misery, dualities, and bondage. He has also been told that Atman alone exists, and every other thing is a mere superimposition.

3. What is the nature of that Atman? It is of the nature of Being-Consciousness-Bliss—the three fundamental qualities, which say everything about Reality.

4. That alone is Being, that alone is Consciousness, and that alone is Bliss. So the seeker has to give up all that is false and seek that alone.

In the forthcoming chapters, *Tattvabodha* begins a new theme: it is about the cosmos.

Suggested Reading

1. Swami Brahmananda, *The Eternal Companion*
2. *Jnana Yoga* lectures by Swami Vivekananda
3. *For Seekers of God*, Swami Shivananda

References

1. Complete Works, Vol. 8, p. 28
2. Gospel, pp. 630-1

Chapter 32

TWENTYFOUR COSMIC PRINCIPLES

According to the philosophers of India, the whole universe is composed of two materials, one of which they call Akasha. It is the omnipresent, all-penetrating existence. Everything that has form, everything that is the result of combination, is evolved out of this Akasha. It is the Akasha that becomes the air, that becomes the liquids, that becomes the solids; it is the Akasha that becomes the sun, the earth, the moon, the stars, the comets; it is the Akasha that becomes the human body, the animal body, the plants, every form that we see, everything that can be sensed, everything that exists. It cannot be perceived; it is so subtle that it is beyond all ordinary perception; it can only be seen when it has become gross, has taken form. At the beginning of creation there is only this Akasha. At the end of the cycle the solids, the liquids, and the gases all melt into the Akasha again, and the next creation similarly proceeds out of this Akasha.

—Swami Vivekananda[1]

Cosmic Creation

Tattvabodha has a definite plan. It initially discussed the creation of the living individual, and now it takes up the cosmic creation.

We have seen that the creation of the individual soul follows the procedure of causal through the subtle to the gross. The same process is followed in the creation of the cosmic form also. In the following pages, the discussion on Advaitic concept of creation (*vyāvahārika*) has been mentioned.

Before going to that, a schematic representation of the Sāmkhyan concept is given below.

Tattvabodha introduces the topic of creation now.

अथ चतुर्विंशति-तत्त्वोत्पत्ति-प्रकारं वक्ष्यामः ॥

Atha catur-viṁśati tattvotpatti-prakāraṁ vakṣyāmaḥ

Atha now *catur-viṁśati* the twentyfour *tattvotpatti* principles, their birth; *prakāraṁ* method *vakṣyāmaḥ* we shall discuss.

Now we shall discuss the method of the birth of the twentyfour cosmic principles.

Caturvimśati

'Twenty-four'. The idea that there are 24 cosmic principles was a gift of the Sānkhyans to Vedanta. Sānkhya is the oldest philosophy in India, according to tradition. Of the six systems of Indian philosophy, Sānkhya and Yoga are a group, Nyāya and Vaiśeṣika are a group, and Pūrva and Uttara Mīmāmsā are a group.

Sānkhya was the discovery of Kapila—the great sage of the ancient times. His philosophy is that there are two eternal principles. One is the Self, called Puruṣa, and the other is not-Self, called Prakṛti. Puruṣas are countless, while Prakṛti is one. Each one of our Self or Soul is a Puruṣa. Kapila believed in God too, but later Sānkhyans have perhaps sidelined Īśvara.

Keeping the Puruṣa aside, Sānkhyans count 24 cosmic principles. These are shown in the diagram next page. This is the scheme of the Sānkhyan cosmology. From Prakṛti downwards, we have the cosmic intelligence called *mahat.* This *mahat* is a collective form of individual intelligence also. Then comes cosmic and individual *ahamkāra* or ego. From ego rises the five 'they alone' or *tanmātras*—the fundamental five elements. From them comes the cosmic and individual mind. The *tanmātras* give rise to the 10 sense organs—five sensory and five motor. This completes the creation process.

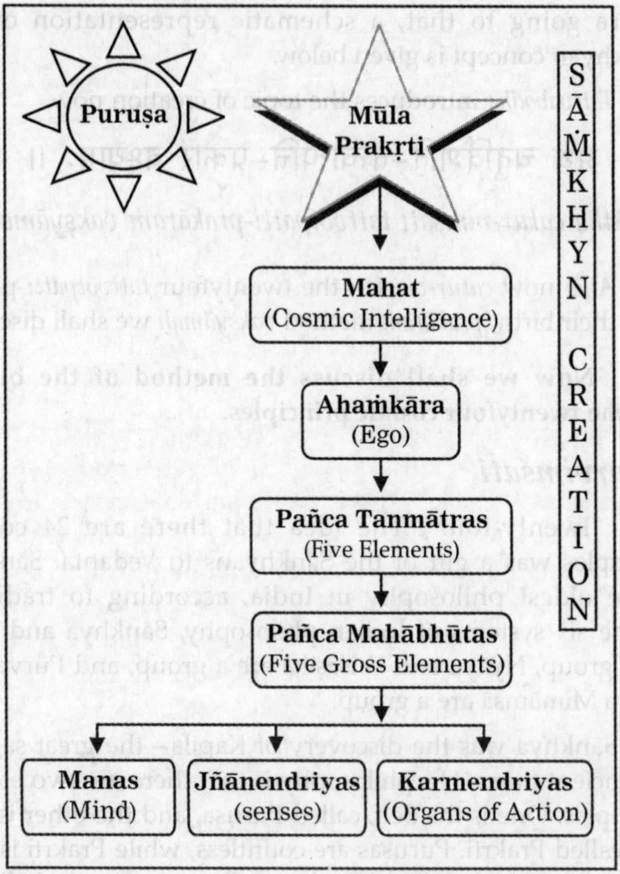

This scheme was by and large acceptable for the Vedantins. With some changes, they have adapted it for the *vyāvahārika* or practical purposes. However, the Vedantin is careful to note that unlike in Sānkhya, there is no dualism of Puruṣa and Prakṛti in Advaita Vedanta.

This scheme of creation or projection is the Sāmkhyan scheme. The Advaitin says that the desire to be many that is in Īśvara is the seed of creation: 'बहु स्याम् प्रजायेयेति, *bahusyām prajāyeyeti*, May I become many.' This desire is called *sisṛkṣā* or the desire to create. In the Vedas it has been declared that God assumes countless forms using his *māyā*: 'इन्द्रो मायाभिः पुरुरूप ईयते, *indro māyābhiḥ pururūpa īyate*.'

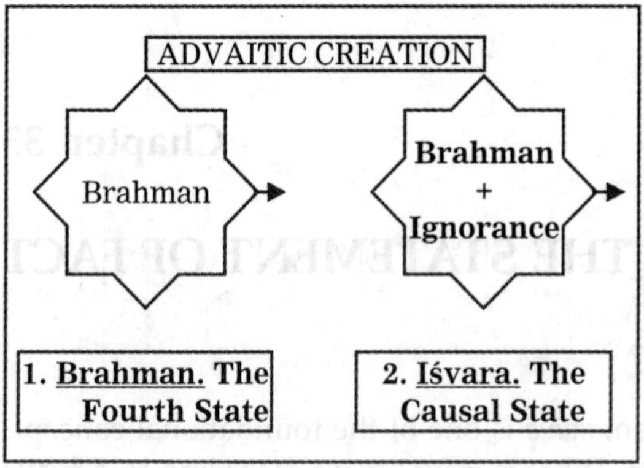

Desire is the seed, and hence it is called ignorance or *māyā.* This seed will be hidden in Īśvara at the time of dissolution, and during creation, Īśvara, endowed with the power of *māyā,* projects the universe. From causal to gross, the projection needs a material and some intelligence. Both are God Himself. So Brahman is the efficient and material cause of the universe. If God was not the material of the universe, how could we know Him by knowing anything in this universe? If a lump of clay is known all clay is known—says the Upaniṣads, while giving the example of creation. So Brahman or God creates everything and pervades everything. And hence He is everything. Owing to ignorance we do not see Him but see the name and form alone.

References:

1. Complete Works, Vol.1, p. 147

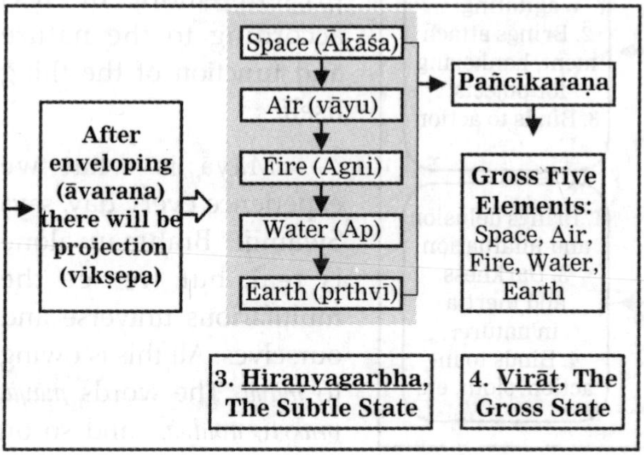

Chapter 33

MĀYĀ OR THE STATEMENT OF FACT

What is *māyā*?

After Brahman, *māyā* is one of the foundational concepts of Advaita Vedanta. What is *māyā*? *Māyā* according to Advaita Vedanta is that power which veils the Truth and makes It appear as many. *Māyā* consists of three qualities, *sattva, rajas* and *tamas*. Since *māyā* is made of three qualities, all of its projection (or creation)—from Space down to the blade of grass—is made of the three qualities too. In every atom of the universe, gross or subtle, the three qualities are present—more or less according to the nature and function of the thing itself.

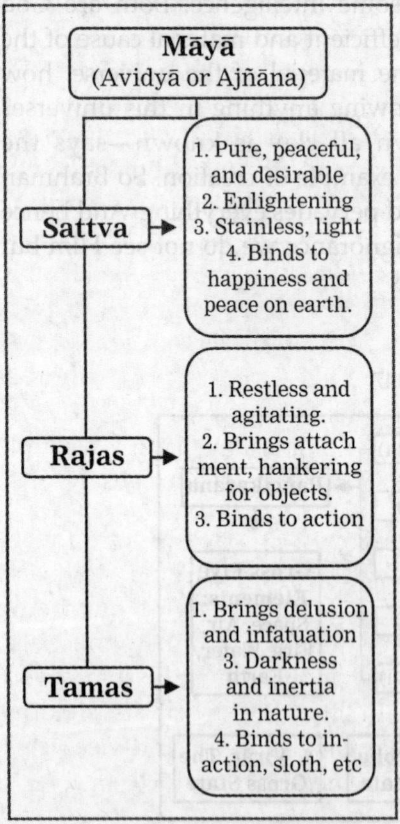
Māyā
(Avidyā or Ajñāna)
Sattva
1. Pure, peaceful, and desirable
2. Enlightening
3. Stainless, light
4. Binds to happiness and peace on earth.
Rajas
1. Restless and agitating.
2. Brings attach ment, hankering for objects.
3. Binds to action
Tamas
1. Brings delusion and infatuation
3. Darkness and inertia in nature.
4. Binds to in-action, sloth, etc

Māyā is what we experience every day, says Swamiji. Brahman alone is real, but we see the multifarious universe and ourselves. All this is owing to *māyā*. The words *māyā, prakṛti, avidyā,* and so on are synonyms. The *prakṛti* of Sānkhyans is a real entity, but that of Advaita is relatively real.

Māyā is explained in a beautiful verse of *Pañcadaśī* (6.130): 'Māyā is looked upon in three different ways: (a) from the viewpoint of self-knowledge, it is negligible (*tucca*); (b) from the viewpoint of reasoning, it is indefinable (*anirvacanīyā*); and (c) from the viewpoint of ordinary people, it is real (*vāstva*).'

That is, it is real for the people of the world; indefinable for the scholars because they are midway between Self-knowledge and ignorance; and worthless for the person of Self-knowledge.

Swami Vivekananda defines *māyā* in a unique way: 'Almost all of you have heard of the word Maya. Generally it is used, though incorrectly, to denote illusion, or delusion, or some such thing. But the theory of Maya forms one of the pillars upon which the Vedanta rests; it is, therefore, necessary that it should be properly understood. I ask a little patience of you, for there is a great danger of its being misunderstood.... When the Hindu says the world is Maya, at once people get the idea that the world is an illusion. This interpretation has some basis, as coming through the Buddhistic philosophers, because there was one section of philosophers who did not believe in the external world at all. But the Maya of the Vedanta, in its last developed form, is neither Idealism nor Realism, nor is it a theory. It is a simple statement of facts—what we are and what we see around us.'[1]

Swami Vivekananda continues: '...Maya is not a theory for the explanation of the world; it is simply a statement of facts as they exist, that the very basis of our being is contradiction, that wherever there is good, there must also be evil, and wherever there is evil, there must be some good, wherever there is life, death must follow as its shadow, and everyone who smiles will have to weep, and vice versa. Nor can this state of things be remedied.'[2]

Brahman and Śakti are One

We must note here in passing that according to Sri Ramakrishna *māyā* is the Divine Mother, who creates, preserves and destroys the universe. When She is doing all these she is the Divine Mother or Śakti. When She is static, She is Brahman. So Brahman and Śakti are one, he says. Thus the negative connotation for *avidyā* or *māyā* in Advaita has been transmuted to positive something by Sri Ramakrishna. However, according to some scholars, Śaṅkara also considers *māyā* to be divine (*daivī*) and says that She creates etc. This he does in his *Bhagavadgitā* commentary, (see introduction).

Tattvabodha now takes up the question of *māyā*.

ब्रह्माश्रया सत्त्वरजस्तमोगुणात्मिका माया अस्ति,
ततः आकाशः सम्भूतः,
आकाशाद् वायुः वायोः तेजः, तेजस आपः,
अद्भ्यः पृथिवी ॥

Brahmāśrayā sattva-rajas-tamoguṇātmikā māyā asti, tataḥ ākāśaḥ sambhūtaḥ, ākāśād vāyuḥ vāyoḥ tejaḥ tejasa āpaḥ, adbhyaḥ pṛthivī.

Brahmāśrayā That which has Brahman as the Support; *sattva-rajas-tamoguṇātmikā* of the nature of equipoise, activity and lethargy; *māyā* Māyā *asti* is there. *Tataḥ* from her *ākāśaḥ* Space *sambhūtaḥ* is born. *ākāśād* from space *vāyuḥ* air *vāyoḥ* from air *tejaḥ* fire *tejasa* from fire *āpaḥ* the waters, *adbhyaḥ* from the waters *pṛthivī* the earth.

There is (something) that has Brahman as the support, called ignorance. Its three qualities are equilibrium (*sattva*), activity (*rajas*) and inertia (*tamas*). From her springs space; from space comes air; from air comes fire; from fire comes waters; from the waters come the earth.

Brahmāśrayā

'Supported by Brahman.' What is the locus of *māyā* or ignorance? This is a question that bothers the Advaitin a lot. There is only One Reality, and that is Brahman, they have declared. Yet they have to give some position

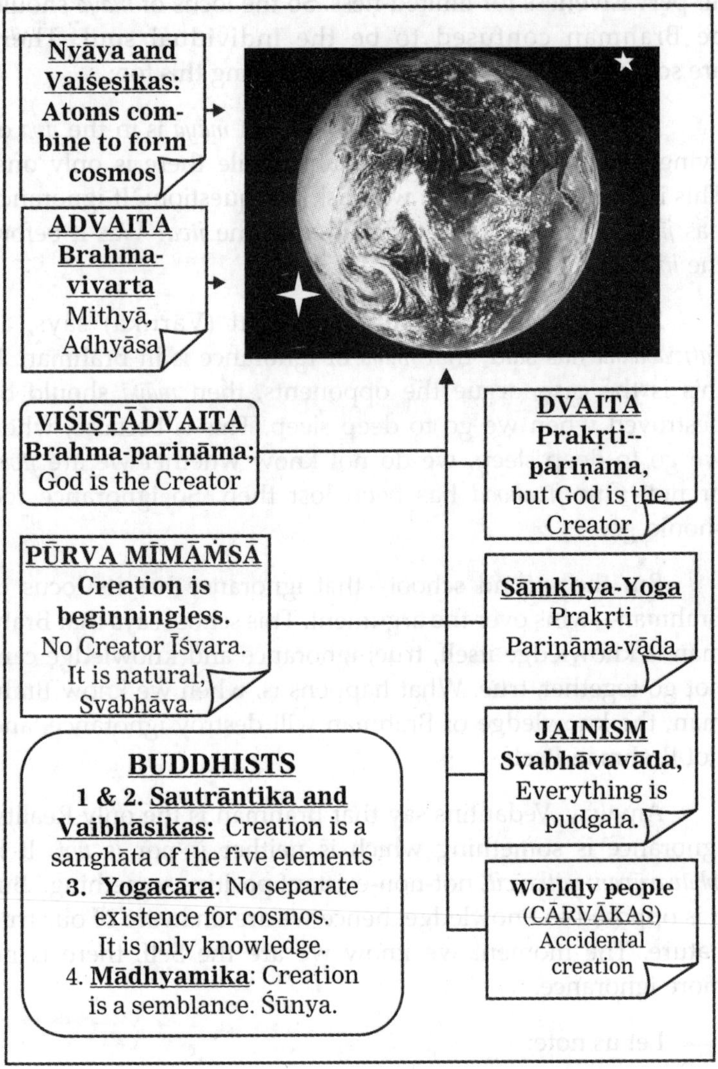
Nyāya and Vaiśeṣikas:
Atoms combine to form cosmos
ADVAITA
Brahma-vivarta
Mithyā, Adhyāsa
VIŚIṢṬĀDVAITA
Brahma-pariṇāma;
God is the Creator
PŪRVA MĪMĀṀSĀ
Creation is beginningless.
No Creator Īśvara.
It is natural, Svabhāva.
BUDDHISTS
1 & 2. Sautrāntika and Vaibhāsikas: Creation is a sanghāta of the five elements
3. Yogācāra: No separate existence for cosmos. It is only knowledge.
4. Mādhyamika: Creation is a semblance. Śūnya.
DVAITA
Prakṛti--pariṇāma,
but God is the Creator
Sāṁkhya-Yoga
Prakṛti Pariṇāma-vāda
JAINISM
Svabhāvavāda,
Everything is pudgala.
Worldly people
(CĀRVĀKAS)
Accidental creation

to *māyā,* which is experienced in our day-to-day lives. How to explain it? There are different opinions about the locus of *māyā.* The general conscensus is that when Brahman is confused to be an individual soul, *jīva,* the trouble has begun. Whether the individual sees the universe or Brahman is secondary. The primary problem is to confuse all-pervasiveness for limited-ness. So the locus of *māyā* should be Brahman confused to be the individual soul. There are schools of thought in Advaita regarding this too:

1. One school (Vivaraṇa) holds that *māyā* is in the *jīva* or living being, so the *jīva* sees many while there is only one. This is rejected by others, who ask this question: 'If ignorance has *jīva* as its locus, when did it enter the *jīva*? Was it before the *jīva* was created, or after?'

2. The second school of thought (Vārtikā) says, as *Tattvabodha* has said, that *māyā* or ignorance is in Brahman. If this is the case, argue the opponents, then *māyā* should be destroyed when we go to deep sleep. This is because, when we go to deep sleep, we do not know whether we are *jīva*s or not. Our *jīvahood* has been lost then. So ignorance too should go.

But the second school—that ignorance has its locus in Brahman—wins over the argument. This school says that Brahman is knowledge itself, true; ignorance and knowledge cannot go together, true. What happens is, when we know Brahman, the knowledge of Brahman will destroy ignorance, and not Brahman Itself.

Anyway, Vedantins say that Brahman is the only Reality. Ignorance is something which is neither *is* nor *is not*. It is *'bhāvarūpam yatkiñcit*, not-non-existant positive something.' But it is opposed to knowledge, hence we are unaware of our true nature. The moment we know we are the Self, there is no more ignorance.

Let us note:

1. Śaṁkara never denied the universe in the ordinary or practical sense (*vyavahāra*).

2. Śaṁkara denied absolute existence for the universe. 'Brahman is real, the universe is unreal' is an experience in the highest state.

3. The universe, which we experience in the three states of existence, is real for the three states, and has been created by *māyā*. That highest state, where the universe is negated, is called absolute (*paramārtha*). In the practical state (*vyavahāra*), the universe is real.

4. *Māyā* is something positive, to be sublated in knowledge.

5. So long as dualistic ideas are cherished, there is *māyā*.

One or Many

Is ignorance one or many? This is another puzzle for the Advaitins. Some say there is only one, but others say there are many. But Śaṁkara says this *māyā* is something inexplicable, impossible to comprehend. It is one. The moment we wish to know her, she is gone.

Are *jīvas* or living beings one or many? This is yet another puzzle. The Vedantins are divided in this aspect: The dṛṣṭi-sṛṣṭi school, which says that creation takes place when one sees it, say there is only one soul, and with its liberation, every problem under the sun is solved. The other school, sṛṣṭi-dṛṣṭi school, says that there are many souls and they are created, and they should strive for liberation. In liberation, there is only One. Generally, Advaitins say that *jīva* for the enlightened is only one, for that enlightened soul never sees duality. For the ignorant, *jīvas* are countless.

Process of Cosmic Creation

The fundamental point to be noted is that *māyā* or ignorance has two qualities: it covers and projects. If it had just covered the Truth, perhaps the problems would have been less. But it projects too. What does *māyā* project? It projects the universe. The material cause of the universe, of course, is Brahman itself. But *māyā* projects it.

Brahman + *māyā* = Īśvara. After this, the first product of Īśvara is space (*ākāśa*) or Sound (*śabda tanmātra*) for the quality of space is sound. From space comes air (*vāyu*) or Touch (*sparśa tanmātra*). From air comes fire (*agni*) or form (*rūpa tanmātra*). From fire comes water (*āp*) or Taste (*rasa tanmātra*). From water comes earth (*pṛthvī*) or Smell (*gandha tanmātra*).

In the *Brahma Sūtras*, there is an interesting discussion about whether or not space was created. Can one create space? Everything else can be created in space, but can space itself be created? Hence the opponents of this theory say: 'न वियदश्रुते:, *na viyadaśruteḥ*, Space is not created, since this is not heard of at all.' To this, the Vedantin replies: 'अस्ति तु, *asti tu*, But such a mention is there!' Where is it mentioned? In the Upaniṣads [*Taittirīya Upaniṣad*, 2.1.2] it is said that 'आत्मन आकाश: सम्भूत:, *ātmana ākāśaḥ sambhūtaḥ*, space was born from the Atman.' Further, all the things created or superimposed should come from Brahman, for the Vedas say that when Brahman is known, all else is known. So Brahman is the source of space. From space come the other four fundamental elements.

These five elements, however, are the fundamental elements. They are not seen or experienced. They are in *their* causal state.

These fundamental elements go to form the individual (*vyaṣṭi*) subtle bodies, as we have seen before. From

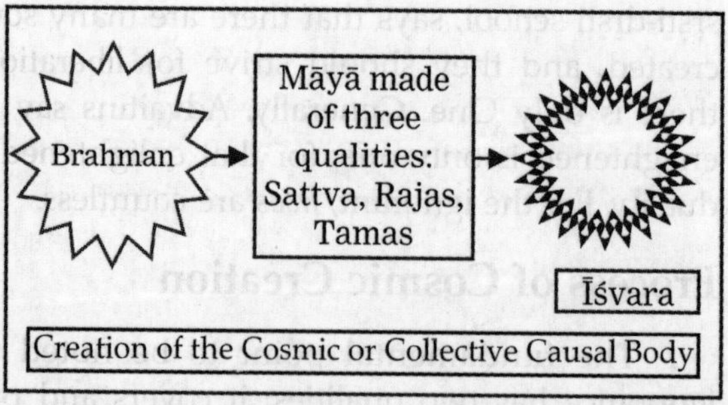

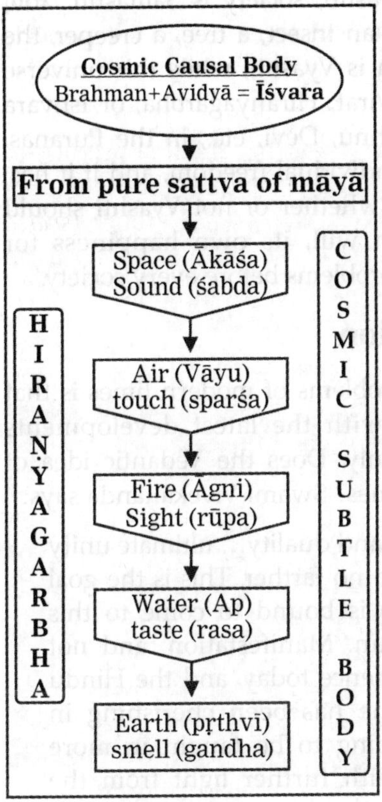

the five subtle elements we have the 19 constituents of the individual subtle body. These 19 are: intellect, mind, memory, ego, five sense organs, five organs of action, and five life-forces. The collective form (*samaṣṭi*) of all the individual subtle bodies put together is called the cosmic subtle body or *Hiranyagarbha*. We should be careful to note here that the individual is only a miniscule part of the cosmic whole. Since *Hiraṇyagarbha* is the collection of subtle bodies, and has collective intelligence, He is called cosmic Intelligence or cosmic *mahat*. So *Hiraṇyagarbha* is the subtle cosmic universe and the source of the gross physical universe.

Swami Vivekananda says: 'The body is the form, and the mind or the Antahkarana is the name, and sound-symbols are universally associated with Nama (name) in all beings having the power of speech. In the individual man the thought-waves rising in the limited Mahat or Chitta (mind-stuff), must manifest themselves, first as words, and then as the more concrete forms. In the universe, Brahma or Hiranyagarbha or the cosmic Mahat first manifested himself as name, and then as form, i.e., as this universe.'[3]

Swami Vivekananda further makes the 'collective' idea clear here: 'The aggregate of many individuals is called Samashti (the whole), and each individual is called Vyashti (a part). You and I—each is Vyashti, society is Samashti. You, I, an animal, a bird, a worm, an insect, a tree, a creeper, the earth, a planet, a star — each is Vyashti, while this universe is Samashti, which is called Virat, Hiranyagarbha, or Ishvara in Vedanta, and Brahma, Vishnu, Devi, etc., in the Puranas. Whether or not Vyashti has individual freedom, and if it has, what should be its measure, whether or not Vyashti should completely sacrifice its own will, its own happiness for Samashti—are the perennial problems before every society.'

Manifestation or Creation

One of the important problems of modern times is that if philosophy does not go with the latest developments of science, it is mythology only. Does the Vedantic idea of cosmology stand the test of times? Swami Vivekananda says:

> … through multiplicity and duality… ultimate unity is reached. Religion can go no farther. This is the goal of all science. All science is bound to come to this conclusion in the long run. Manifestation, and not creation, is the word of science today, and the Hindu is only glad that what he has been cherishing in his bosom for ages is going to be taught in more forcible language, and with further light from the latest conclusions of science.[4]

From what latest developments in astrophysics say, the idea of the so-called big bang that happened 10,000,000,000 years ago is the best-possible theory. The steady-state theory and others have been questioned by the expansion of the universe. Yet science has to go a long way—from observation to experimentation and further still.

References:

1. Complete Works, Vol. 2, p. 89.
2. Complete Works, Vol. 2, p. 97
3. Complete Works, Vol. 3, p. 57
4. Complete Works, Vol. 1, p. 15

Chapter 34

CREATION OF INDIVIDUAL SUBTLE BODY

Introduction

We have already discussed the creation of the individual subtle body in the previous chapter, as well as earlier. The author of *Tattvabodha* takes up this aspect here.

एतेषां पञ्च–तत्त्वानां मध्ये
आकाशस्य सात्त्विकांशात् श्रोत्रेन्द्रियं सम्भूतम् ।
वायोः सात्त्विकांशाद् त्वगिन्द्रियं सम्भूतम् ।
अग्नेः सात्त्विकांशाद् चक्षुरिन्द्रियं सम्भूतम्।
जलस्य सात्त्विकांशाद् रसनेन्द्रियं सम्भूतम् ।
पृथिव्याः सात्त्विकांशात् घ्राणेन्द्रियं सम्भूतम् ।

Eteṣām pañca-tattvānāṁ madhye ākāśasya sāttvikāṁśāt śrotrendiryam saṁbhūtam. Vāyoḥ sāttvikāṁśād tvagindriyaṁ saṁbhūtam. Agneḥ sāttvikāṁśād cakṣurindriyaṁ saṁbhūtam. Jalasya sāttvikāṁśād rasanendriyaṁ saṁbhūtam. Pṛthivyāḥ sāttvikāṁśād ghrāṇendriyaṁ saṁbhūtam.

Eteśām of these *pañca-tattvānāṁ* five elements *madhye* in *sāttvikāṁśāt ākāśasya* of space being made of equipoise or sattva quality *śrotrendiryam* the sense of hearing is *saṁbhūtam* born. *sāttvikāṁśād vāyoḥ* of the equilibrium quality of air *tvagindriyaṁ* the sense of touch is *saṁbhūtam* born. *Agneḥ sāttvikāmśād* of the equipoise of fire *cakṣurindriyaṁ* the sense of sight *saṁbhūtam* are born. *sāttvikāmśād jalasya* of the sattva quality of water *rasanendriyaṁ* the sense of taste *saṁbhūtam* is born. *sāttvikāmśād pṛthivyāḥ* of the sattva quality of earth *ghrāṇendriyaṁ* the sense of smell is *saṁbhūtam* born.

Of these five elements, the sattva of space gives birth to the sense of hearing. The sense of touch is born of the sattva quality of air. The sense of sight is born of the sattva of fire. From the sattva of water the sense of taste is born. And from the sattva of earth the sense of smell is born.

एतेषां पञ्चतत्त्वानां समष्टि–सात्विकांशात् मनो–
बुद्ध्यहंकार–चित्त–अन्तःकरणानि सम्भूतानि ॥

Eteṣām pañca-tattvānāṁ samaṣṭi-sāttvikāṁśād mano-buddhyaham-kāra-citta-antaḥkaraṇāni saṁbhūtāni.

Eteṣām pañca-tattvānāṁ of these five elements *samaṣṭi-sāttvikāṁśād* combined sattva quality *mano-buddhyaham-kāra-citta-antaḥkaraṇāni saṁbhūtāni* the mind, intellect, ego, memory, and inner organs are born.

With the combined sattva quality of all these elements the mind, intellect, ego, memory, and inner organs are born.

The formation of the 17 cosmic elements is being described here. There are three basic divisions in this projection. The five sense organs belong to one group, the five organs of action belong to the second, and the intellect and mind belong to the third.

The five fundamental elements are projected by *māyā*. We know that *māyā* consists of *sattva, rajas,* and *tamas*. So its products too will naturally have these three qualities. Of the three, the sense organs—sight, taste, touch, smell, and sound—

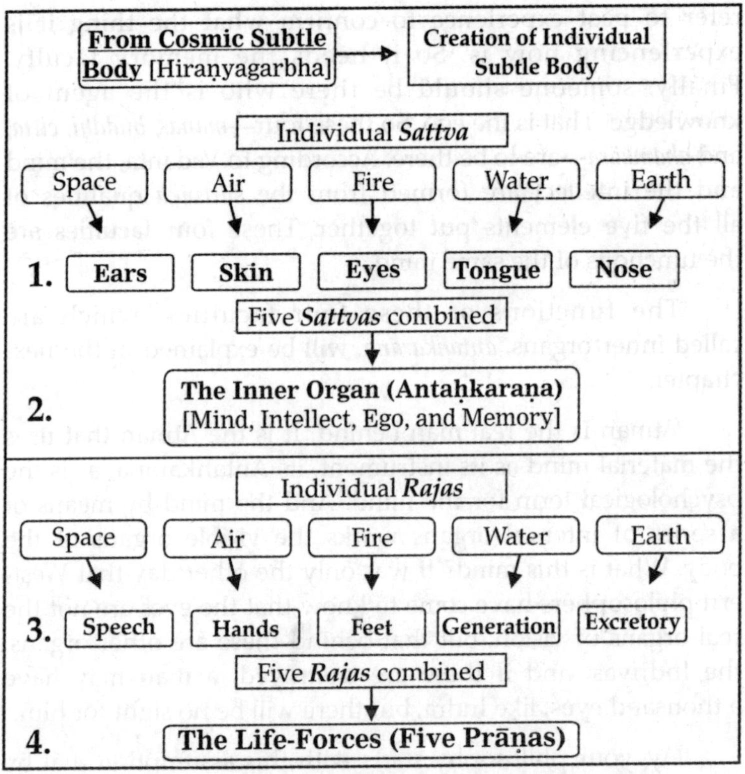

are created by the *sāttvika* portion of the five basic elements, each one contributing to its respective sense. Space is related to sound, so from space comes the sense of hearing. Water is related to taste. So the sense of taste has come from it. The sense of touch has come from air. The sense of smell has come from earth. Finally, the sense of form has come from fire.

Thus we have the cosmic elements and the five sense organs. The sense organs, we remember, are in the subtle body and not in the gross body. The gross sense organs are just apertures. The sense organs bring information about the outer world constantly. Something has to receive the message. Who is to do that?

Here comes the function of the mind. The mind passes on the message to the intellect. The intellect, in its turn, has to refer to past experience to confirm what the thing it is experiencing now is. So it needs the memory faculty. Finally, someone should be there who is the agent of knowledge. That is the ego. So these four—*manas, buddhi, citta,* and *ahamkāra*—are to be there. According to Vedanta, the mind and the intellect are formed from the *sāttvika* qualities of all the five elements put together. These four faculties are the functions of the same mind.

The functions of these four faculties, which are called inner organs, *antahkaraṇa*, will be explained in the next chapter.

'Atman is the real man behind. It is the Atman that uses the material mind as its instrument, its Antahkarana, as is the psychological term for the mind. And the mind by means of a series of internal organs works the visible organs of the body. What is this mind? It was only the other day that Western philosophers have come to know that the eyes are not the real organs of vision, but that behind these are other organs, the Indriyas, and if these are destroyed, a man may have a thousand eyes, like Indra, but there will be no sight for him.

'Ay, your philosophy starts with this assumption that by vision is not meant the external vision. The real vision belongs to the internal organs, the brain-centres inside. You may call them what you like, but it is not that the Indriyas are the eyes, or the nose, or the ears. And the sum total of all these Indriyas plus the Manas, Buddhi, Chitta, Ahamkara, etc., is what is called the mind, and if the modern physiologist comes to tell you that the brain is what is called the mind, and that the brain is formed of so many organs, you need not be afraid at all; tell him that your philosophers knew it always; it is one of the very first principles of your religion,' says Swami Vivekananda.[1]

References:

1. Complete Works, Vol. 3, pp. 401-2

Chapter 35

THE MIND, INTELLECT, ETC

The Function of the Mind

We begin with Swami Vivekananda's words:

The organs (Indriyas), together with the mind (Manas), the determinative faculty (Buddhi), and egoism (Ahamkara), form the group called the Antahkarana (the internal instrument). They are but various processes in the mindstuff, called Chitta. The waves of thought in the Chitta are called Vrittis (literally "whirlpool").

What is thought? Thought is a force, as is gravitation or repulsion. From the infinite storehouse of force in nature, the instrument called Chitta takes hold of some, absorbs it and sends it out as thought. Force is supplied to us through food, and out of that food the body obtains the power of motion etc. Others, the finer forces, it throws out in what we call thought. So we see that the mind is not intelligent; yet it appears to be intelligent. Why? Because the intelligent soul is behind it.

You are the only sentient being; mind is only the instrument through which you catch the external world.

The unknowable furnishes the suggestion that gives a blow to the mind, and the mind gives out the reaction in the form of a book, in the same manner as when a stone is thrown into the water, the water is thrown against it in the form of waves. The real universe is the occasion of the reaction of the mind.[1]

Tattvabodha defines the *antaḥkaraṇa* or the inner organ now:

संकल्प–विकाल्पात्मकं मनः,

निश्चयात्मिका बुद्धिः, अहंकर्ता अहंकारः,

चिन्तनकर्तृ चित्तम्,

मनसो देवता चन्द्रमाः,

बुद्धेः ब्रह्मा, अहंकारस्य रुद्रः, चित्तस्य वासुदेवः ॥

Saṁkalpa-vikalpātmakaṁ manaḥ, niścayātmikā buddhiḥ, ahaṁkartā ahaṁkāraḥ, cintanakartā cittam, manaso devatā candramāḥ, buddheḥ brahmā, ahaṁkārasya rudraḥ cittasya vāsudevaḥ.

Manaḥ the mind is *saṁkalpa-vikalpātmakam* that which wavers, *buddhiḥ* the intellect is *niścayātmikā* decisive, *ahaṁkāraḥ* the ego *ahaṁkartā* is the creator of the sense of I, *cittam* the memory *cintanakartā* is that which makes us cogitate, *manaso* of the mind *devatā* the deity is *candramāḥ* the moon, *buddheḥ* of the intellect (it is) *brahmā* Brahmā, *ahaṁkārasya* of the ego *rudraḥ* Rudra; *cittasya* of the memory *vāsudevaḥ* Vāsudeva.

The mind is that which wavers, the intellect is the decisive faculty; the ego is the creator of the sense of "I", the memory is that which makes us cogitate. The deity of the mind is the moon; that of the intellect is Brahmā; that of the ego is Rudra; and that of the memory is Vāsudeva.

Swami Vivekananda himself is the best teacher in this regard. He has mentioned the functions of these four faculties in this manner: 'Well then, we have to understand now what is meant by this Manas, Buddhi, Chitta, Ahamkara, etc. First of all, let us take Chitta. It is the mindstuff—a part of the Mahat—it is the generic name for the mind itself, including all its various states.

'Suppose on a summer evening, there is a lake, smooth and calm, without a ripple on its surface. And suppose some one throws a stone into this lake. What happens? First there is the action, the blow given to the water; next the water rises and sends a reaction towards the stone, and that reaction takes the form of a wave. First the water vibrates a little, and immediately sends back a reaction in the form of a wave. The Chitta let us compare to this lake, and the external objects are like the stones thrown into it. As soon as it comes in contact with any external object by means of these Indriyas—the Indriyas must be there to carry these external objects inside—there is a vibration, what is called Manas, indecisive.

'Next there is a reaction, the determinative faculty, Buddhi, and along with this Buddhi flashes the idea of Aham and the external object. Suppose there is a mosquito sitting upon my hand. This sensation is carried to my Chitta and it vibrates a little; this is the psychological Manas. Then there is a reaction, and immediately comes the idea that I have a mosquito on my hand and that I shall have to drive it off. Thus these stones are thrown into the lake, but in the case of the lake every blow that comes to it is from the external world, while in the case of the lake of the mind, the blows may either come from the external world or the internal world. This whole series is what is called the Antahkarana.'[2]

The Deities

While discussing the sense organs, we have discussed the gods presiding over each sense organ. *Tattvabodha* says here that each of the four faculties of the mind has a deity presiding over it. Since the times of the Vedas, the concept of the deities has been there. The Vedic sages adored and prayed to hundreds of gods and goddesses. However, they knew fully well that these gods and goddesses were representations of that one Supreme. In the *Bṛhadāraṇyaka Upaniṣad* (3.9) a sage by name Vidagdha Śākalya asks Yājñavalkya as to how many gods are there. Yājñavalkya answers that there are 3,333 gods.

Again and again the same question is repeated, and Yājñavalkya goes on reducing the count. At last it comes to One only. Then Vidagdha Śākalya asks him to explain his reduction of the number of the gods. Yājñavalkya replies satisfactorily.

'What are these gods? They mean certain states, certain offices. For instance, Indra the king of gods, means a certain office; some soul which was very high has gone to fill that post in this cycle, and after this cycle he will be born again as man and come down to this earth, and the man who is very good in this cycle will go and fill that post in the next cycle. So with all these gods; they are certain offices which have been filled alternately by millions and millions of souls, who, after filling those offices, came down and become men.'[3]

The Vedantic scholars have perhaps taken the idea of the gods from the Vedas. According to Advaita Vedantins, the eye is ruled by Candra, the moon, the intellect is ruled by Brahmā; the ruler of ego is Rudra; and that of the memory is Vāsudeva.

We are dependent. This is one of the important lessons from this. Though we think we can use our minds as we wish, it is not possible to do so because there is a cosmic connection.

References:

1. Complete Works, Vol.1, p. 201
2. Complete Works, Vol. 3, p. 403
3. Complete Works, Vol. 2, p. 243

Chapter 36

THE ORGANS OF ACTION

Creation from Space, etc

After discussing the sense organs and the *antahkaraṇa*, *Tattvabodha* now considers the functional aspect of the individual. The senses may bring knowledge, all right. The mind may decipher them. The ego may identify itself with them. Yet nothing can happen until the organs of action, specially the hands, feet, and speech act.

The organs of action are considered now. These organs are also situated in the subtle body. Yet they are called the *bahiḥkaraṇas* or external instruments. They have their outlets in the body. *Tattvabodha* discusses their creation now.

एतेषां पञ्चतत्त्वानां मध्ये आकाशस्य राजसांशात्
वागिन्द्रियं सम्भूतम् । वायोः राजसांशात् पाणीन्द्रियं
सम्भूतम् । वह्नेः राजसांशात् पादेन्द्रियं सम्भूतम् ।
जलस्य राजसांशात् उपस्थेन्द्रियं सम्भूतम्। पृथिव्याः
राजसांशात् गुदेन्द्रियं सम्भूतम् ।

Eteṣām pañca-tattvānāṁ madhye ākāśasya rājasāmśāt vāgendiryam sambhūtam. Vāyoḥ rājasāmśāt pāṇīndriyaṁ sambhūtam. Vahneḥ rājasāmśāt pādendriyaṁ sambhūtam. Jalasya rājasāmśāt upasthendriyaṁ sambhūtam. Pṛthivyāḥ rājasāmśāt gudendriyaṁ sambhūtam

Eteśām of these *pañca* five *tattvānāṁ* elements *madhye rājasāmśāt* from the *rajas* (or dymanic) quality *ākāśasya* of the space *vāgendiryam* the organ of speech *sambhūtam* is born. *Rājasāmśāt vāyoḥ* of the dynamic quality of air *pāṇīndriyaṁ sambhūtam* the organ of holding (hand) is born. *rājasāmśāt* of the dynamic quality of *vahneḥ* fire *pādendriyaṁ* the organ of movement (legs) *sambhūtam* is born. *rājasāmśāt jalasya* of the rajas quality of water *upasthendriyaṁ* the organ of enjoyment is *sambhūtam* born. *rājasāmśāt pṛthivyāḥ* of the rajas quality of earth *gudendriyaṁ* the organ of evacuation *sambhūtam* is born.

From these five basic elements, of the *rajas* of space the organ of speech is born. From the dynamic quality (*rajas*) of air the organ of clasping (hand) is born. From the dymanic quality of fire the organ of movement is born. Of the dynamic quality of water the organ of enjoyment is born. Of the dynamic quality of earth the organ of evacuation is born.

The quality of *rajas* is dynamism. While *sattva* is equilibrium, *rajas* is dynamism. The third, *tamas*, is inertia. All the three are essential in order to balance the organism or creation. If there was no *sattva*, none could control the actions of the individual or the cosmos because everything would have been chaotic. If there was no *tamas* or inertia, there would be chaos again. And if there was no *rajas*, there would be only static equilibrium.

The organs of action, as their name signifies, are action prone. Hence *rajas* of the five *tanmātras* have been used to make them.

The author of *Tattvabodha* follows the traditional account to say that the organs of evacuation and generation, respectively, are created by the *rajas* portions of the earth and water. The hands are formed by the *rajas* of air. The legs are formed by the *rajas* of fire. Finally, speech is formed by the *rajas* of space. Such a creation takes place because each organ of action has one predominant quality—and thus an element—in it.

Recapitulation

The Product	The Creator
Īśvara	Brahman + Avidyā
Cosmic Creation	
The Five Subtle Elements (Tanmātras)—Sound, Touch, Form, Taste, Smell	Projection of Consciousness enveloped by Avidyā
The Five Gross Elements (Mahābhūtas)—Space, Air, Fire, Water, Earth	The Permutation and Combination (Pañcīkaraṇa) of Tanmātras
Individual Creation	
The Five Senses (Ear, Skin, Eye, Tongue, Smell)	From the individual sattva of the five tanmātras respectively
The Antaḥkaraṇa (Manas, Buddhi, Aham, Citta)	From the collective sattva of the tanmātras
The Five prāṇas (prāṇa, apāna, udāna, samāna, vyāna)	From the individual rajas of the tanmātras
The Five Organs of Action (vāk, pāṇi, pāda, pāyū, upastha)	From the collective rajas of the tanmātras
The Gross Cosmos is	pṛthvī
The Gross Individual is	created from food

Chapter 37

THE LIFE FORCES (*PRĀṆAS*)

Prāṇa and the Gods

Once upon a time there was a fight between the gods and the demons. The fight was a long and fierce one. The gods, unable to overcome the demons quickly, thought of a way to vanquish them. They held on to their great treasure, the blessed Omkāra, or Praṇava, which is the greatest representation of Brahman, the Sound Brahman, the Path to Immortality, and the source of Bliss. This Omkāra is also called Udgītha in the Vedas. The gods thought that by contemplating on Omkāra they could destroy the demons. So they began contemplating on Omkāra as the source of strength— *Prāṇa. Prāṇa* is the life-force, so they thought they could become powerful. *Prāṇa* comes and goes out of the nose. While the gods thought they were meditating thus, the demons injected evil into the nose. The gods changed the locus and meditated on the *prāṇa* in the eye. That too the demons pierced with evil. Twice did the gods fail.

Then the gods went to the secret chamber of the heart, and meditated on *prāṇa* in the mind. Even that the demons pierced with evil. That is, the nose, eye, and mind see evil and good owing to this piercing. Since these three became impure because of evil, the gods meditated on *prāṇa* as the presiding deity. That is, when they resorted to *prāṇa* itself for power instead of depending on other senses, the demons failed. When the demons came to pierce the *prāṇa* they were pulverized.

This is an allegorical story from the *Chāndogya Upaniṣad*

(1.2). This is a meditation. The idea is, life-force or *prāṇa* is pure. It is not tainted like the senses or the mind.

Prāṇa: Its Importance

In his eagerness to give a thrust to Advaita, Śrī Śaṁkara considers everything as ultimately leading to Brahman alone. For instance, he does not appear to give the importance that is due for *prāṇa*. Just as Brahman pervades everything at the Spirit level, at the subtle level everything is pervaded by *Prāṇa*. Advaita equates it with Brahman. But Swami Vivekananda gives it the vital place it demands in his *Raja Yoga* lectures.

Swami Vivekananda says: 'There is nothing occult in the air that we take in with our breath and assimilate to purify the blood; the action is merely a motion. This motion can be reduced to the unit movement we call Prana; and everywhere, all movements are the various manifestations of this Prana. This Prana is electricity, it is magnetism; it is thrown out by the brain as thought. Everything is Prana; it is moving the sun, the moon, and the stars.'[1]

How is the Prāṇa produced initially? *Tattvabodha* says:

एतेषां समष्टिराजसांशात् पञ्च-प्राणाः सम्भूताः ॥

eteṣāṁ samaṣṭi-rājasāṁśāt pañca-prāṇāḥ sambhūtāḥ.

Samaṣṭi-rājasāṁśāt combined dynamic quality *eteṣāṁ* of these *pañca-prāṇāḥ sambhūtāḥ* are born.

Of the dynamic quality of all these together, the five life-breaths are born.

Swami Vivekananda gives us the importance of Prāṇa:

'This body is made of particles which we call matter, and it is dull and insentient. So is what the Vedantists call the fine body. The fine body, according to them, is a material but transparent body, made of very fine particles, so fine that no microscope can see them. What is the use of that? ... The fine body is also material, only very fine matter; and just as this gross body is the instrument that works the gross forces, so the fine body is the instrument that works the fine forces.

'From where do all these forces come? According to Vedanta philosophy, there are two things in nature, one of which they call Akasha, which is the substance, infinitely fine, and the other they call Prana, which is the force. ... Akasha is like the water, and everything else in the universe is like blocks of ice, made out of that water, and floating in the water, and Prana is the power that changes this Akasha into all these various forms. The gross body is the instrument made out of Akasha, for the manifestation of Prana in gross forms, as muscular motion, or walking, sitting, talking, and so forth. That fine body is also made of Akasha, a very fine form of Akasha, for the manifestation of the same Prana in the finer form of thought. ... God is eternal. Nature is also eternal, but changefully eternal. The material of nature — prana and Akasha — is eternal, but it is changing into different forms eternally.'[2]

Suggested Reading

Swami Vivekananda's Raja Yoga Lectures

References:

1. Complete Works, Vol. 2, p. 30
2. Complete Works, Vol. 1, p. 396

Chapter 38

PAÑCĪKARAṆA

Introductory

We have discussed the Advaitic concept of creation. Brahman alone is real, and everything is a superimposition—this is the Advaitic concept of the cosmos. The same Reality is seen by two individuals in two diametrically opposite ways. The realized soul sees it as nothing but Brahman, the one Reality. The ignorant see it as the cosmos.

Since we cannot understand the Reality and think that this universe is real and solid, the Vedantins have conceived a method of explaining creation to us. The Vedantins say that there is only one Supreme State — Brahman. But, for the ignorant, there are the other three states as well. In all, there can only be four states or *avasthas*. These are the three states of experience and one Absolute State. The chart on p.253 will help recapitulate the Advaitic concept of creation.

The Story of Creation

What is told here is all a repetition now. Yet for comprehension, repetition is good, they say.

The story of creation is directly related to *pañcīkaraṇa*. From the *jñāni's* viewpoint—the *pāramārthika* or spiritual viewpoint—there is neither creation nor destruction; It is all one single Whole. From the ignorant one's point of view—the *vyavahārika* viewpoint—creation is there and so is destruction. In order to know what *pañcīkaraṇa* is, we should remember the two viewpoints, which lead us to the four states and the process of creation. First there is Brahman or Reality alone and nothing else. This is the absolute viewpoint. *Māyā* envelops Brahman and creates the confusion. Not only does she envelop Brahman but also projects the universe. Hence *māyā* is said to have two powers: enveloping (*āvaraṇa*) and projecting (*vikṣepa*).

What does *māyā* project? It projects the three states, which we mentioned above. The state when *māyā* envelops Brahman, as it were, has been called the causal or *suṣupti* state. Consciousness enveloped by ignorance is called Īśvara. The projecting power of ignorance then continues its play, and thus there is projected the subtle state. In this state, Brahman as covered by ignorance has been called Hiraṇyagarbha. From the subtle state, there is further projection into the gross state. Brahman enveloped by ignorance in the gross state is called Virāṭ.

Māyā has three qualities: *sattva* or equilibrium, *rajas* or intense activity, and *tamas* or inertia. Using these three qualities, *māyā* projects the universe from Īśvara down to Virāṭ. The purely *sattva* quality is what envelops Brahman. Then begins the work of *tamas*. This *tamas* is used for further creation.

The projection of *māyā* begins with its creating *ākāśa* or space, then *vāyu* or air, then *tejas* or energy, then *ap* or waters, then *pṛthvī* or matter. These are the five fundamental units of creation. They have both the subtle as well as the gross aspects. The first projection of *māyā*, which envelops Brahman, are the five subtle elements, called *pañca tanmātra* ('The Supreme Five Alone'). From space (*ākāśa*) forwards, the five fundamental elements become grosser. Yet they are not perceptible. These five fundamental elements interact to form the gross elements called (*mahābhūtas*). This interaction has been called *pañcīkaraṇa*.

एतेषां पञ्चतत्त्वानां तामसांशात पञ्चीकृत–पञ्चतत्त्वानि भवन्ति ।

Eteṣāṁ pañca-tattvānāṁ tāmasāṁśāt pañcikṛta pañca-tattvāni bhavanti.

Tāmasāṁśāt of the inertia portion *eteṣāṁ pañca-tattvānāṁ* of the five elements *pañcīkṛta* the fivefold-multiplied *pañca-tattvāni bhavanti* five elements come into being.

From the inertia (*tamas*) portion of the five elements the fivefold multiplied (*pañcīkṛta*) five elements come into being.

पञ्चीकरणं कथमिति चेत्, एतेषां पञ्च महाभूतानां
तामसांश-स्वरूपं एकैकं भूतम् द्विधा विभज्य
एकमेकमर्धं पृथक् तूष्णीं व्यवस्थाप्य अपरमर्धं चतुर्धा
विभज्य स्वार्धं अन्येषु अर्धेषु स्वभाग-चतुष्टय-
संयोजनं कार्यम्, तदा पञ्चीकरणम् भवति। एतेभ्यः
पञ्चीकृत-महाभूतेभ्यः स्थूल-शरीरं भवति, एवम्
पिण्ड-ब्रह्माण्डयोः ऐक्यं सम्भूतम् ॥

Pañcīkaraṇam kathamiti cet, eteṣāṁ pañca mahābhūtānāṁ
tāmasāṁśa-svarūpam ekaikaṁ bhūtaṁ dvidhā vibhajya
ekamekamardhaṁ pṛthak tūṣṇīm vyavasthāpya
aparamardhaṁ caturdhā vibhajya svārdhaṁ anyeṣu ardheṣu
svabhāga-catuṣṭaya-saṁyojanaṁ kāryam, tadā
pañcīkaraṇaṁ bhavati. Etebhyaḥ pañcīkṛta-mahābhūtebhyaḥ
sthūla-śarīraṁ bhavati, evaṁ piṇḍa-brahmāṇḍayoḥ aikyaṁ
sambhūtam.

kathamiti cet If it is asked how does *pañcīkaraṇam* pañcīkaraṇa takes place, *eteṣāṁ pañca mahābhūtānāṁ* of these five gross elements *tāmasāṁśa-svarūpam ekaikaṁ bhūtaṁ* each one of the inertia portion *dvidhā vibhajya* is divided into two; *ekamekamardhaṁ* and each half is *pṛthak tūṣṇīm vyavasthāpya* kept aside as it is *aparamardhaṁ caturdhā vibhajya* and the other half is divided further into four parts; *svārdhaṁ anyeṣu ardheṣu* its other half with the halves each of others *svabhāga-catuṣṭaya-saṁyojanaṁ kāryam* and its one-half with the half of others to be mixed, *tadā pañcīkaraṇaṁ bhavati* then it becomes *pañcīkaraṇa. Etebhyaḥ pañcīkṛta-mahābhūtebhyaḥ* of these fivefold multiplied gross physical elements *sthūla-śarīraṁ bhavati* the physical body comes into being, *evaṁ piṇḍa-brahmāṇḍayoḥ aikyaṁ sambhūtam* and in this way the union of the microcosmic and the macrocosmic.

If it is asked how *pañcīkaraṇa* takes place, (it is said:) Each of the inertia portion of the five gross elements is divided into two halves. One half is kept aside. The other half is further divided into four parts. Each one of the four parts is put into the half of the other four elements. In this way, these fivefold multiplied gross physical elements give birth to the physical body and thus the union of the microcosmic and macrocosmic bodies takes place.

The process of *pañcīkaraṇa* is mathematical. There are five fundamental subtle elements—earth, fire, water, air, and space. Divide the five into half each. Keep one half of each separately. Taking the other halves of the five elements, divide them further into four parts. So there is one big half, and four small parts of each element. Now, bring one small piece each of four elements and put them along with the fifth big piece. Thus there will be one big piece and four small pieces of different elements. They combine and form the five gross elements—space, air, water, fire and earth. These five elements are what we see, experience, and *are*. So the becoming of the gross from subtle involves *pañcīkaraṇa*. These gross elements have been called the five *mahābhūtas* or great elements. The following picture will depict the method of *pañcīkaraṇa*.

Is this method of explaining creation Vedic? Oh yes! This is based on the Vedic *trivṛt-karaṇa* or 'the combination of the three'.

'एकैकं त्रिवृतं त्रिवृतं करवाणि, *ekaikaṁ trivṛtaṁ trivṛtaṁ karavāṇi,* they should be divided and added thrice three times,' says the *Chāndogya Upaniṣad* (6.3.2). Based on this Vedic dictum,

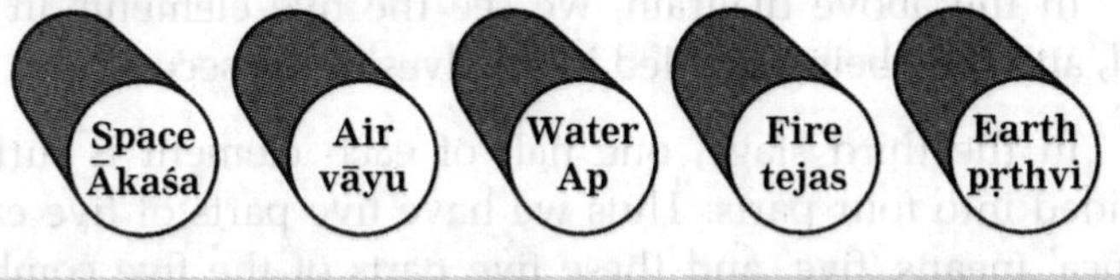

Stage I: **The Five Fundamental Elements in their subtle form**

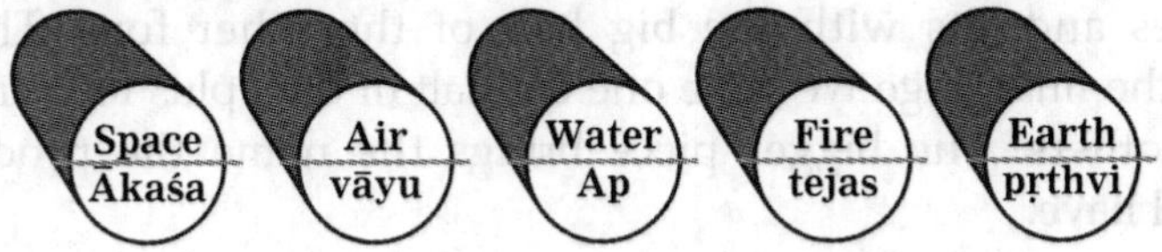

Stage II: **The First Division into Half**

the system of *pañcīkaraṇa* has been developed by Vedanta. While only three—*tejas* (fire), *ap* (water) and *anna* (food)—were considered in the Vedas (and hence three), the five tanmātras, the fundamental elements of creation, are considered here. Tanmātras, as we have seen earlier, are not precisely space, air, and others, but their faculties like sound (*śabda*), touch (*sparśa*), form (*rūpa*), taste (*rasa*), and smell (*gandha*).

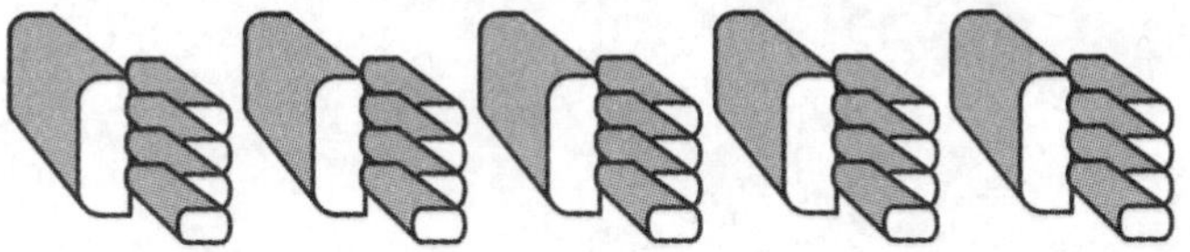

Stage III: **The Second Half Divides into Four parts**

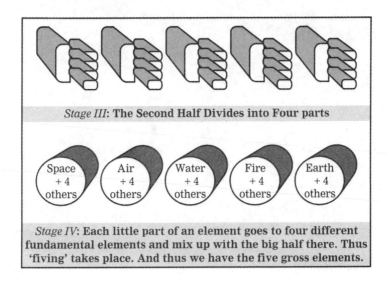

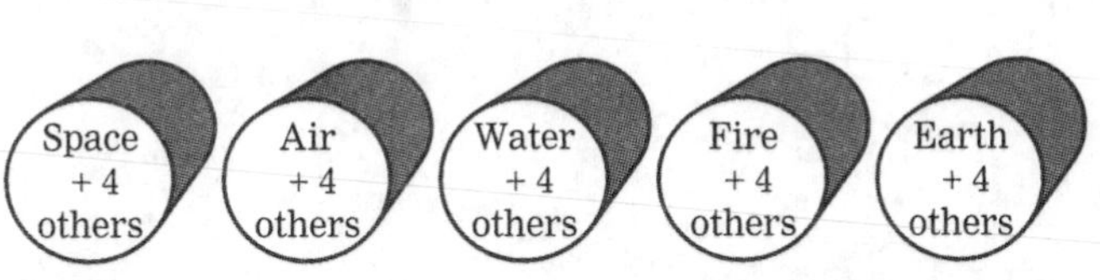

Stage IV: **Each little part of an element goes to four different fundamental elements and mix up with the big half there. Thus 'fiving' takes place. And thus we have the five gross elements.**

In the above diagram, we see the five elements in the first, and they being divided into halves in the second.

In the third stage, one half of each element is further divided into four parts. Thus we have five parts of five each. 'Pañca' means 'five' and these five parts of the five combine with one another in this way: Each little part of an element goes and sits with the big half of the other four. Thus, in the final stage we have one big half of one, plus four small of others. The bigger piece brings the name the product will have.

This is the method in which the cosmic subtle becomes the cosmic gross. Thus we have the cosmos. Considering the big bang theory and the others as latest discoveries, we might say that the idea of the gross returning to the subtle, and the subtle becoming the gross, was known to the Hindus long, long ago.

Chapter 39

THE *JĪVA*

'Who are you?'

The day dawned. Birds began singing sweetly. The little girl, who would be eager to listen to the singing, was in a different mood today. That blessed day had arrived at last, for which she had been waiting so long. The Buddha, on his way to Lumbini, was in the village that morning, and would be delivering a sermon soon. She would be seeing the Buddha today! How happy she was!

She finished all her household work quickly. But her father, a weaver, told her: 'My child, after your work is over, come to the workplace. I am not well. You will have to run the loom today.' A little girl, but all the work for her. Yet there was no remorse or sadness. She did everything at home cheerfully. Now she ran. Her father's shop was at the other end of the village. So she would stop, listen to the Buddha, and run to her father.

There, under the tree sat the Lord. Calmness incarnate. Smiling and speaking to the assembled few. The girl stood like a statue, looking at the Lord. The sermon stopped abruptly. The Buddha was talking to her now. What a surprise! What a joy! 'Who are you, my child?' All eyes turned towards her now. 'Oh, the weaver's daughter. No mother. Good girl. Works the whole day....,' someone was giving her biodata. But the Buddha did not want that. 'Who are you, my child?' The girl nodded in the negative: 'I don't know.' The assembly was aghast. She does not know who she is! Arrogant girl. The Buddha smiled. 'Where did you come from?' The girl nodded in the negative. She did not know. The Buddha asked her: 'Where are you going?' Again negative reply. No answer, just a nod that she did not know.

The Buddha stood up, came to her, and blessed her. She fell at the Lord's feet, and wept bitter tears. 'Ah! Cries for mother,' said the villagers. But she was happy. She ran now.

Her father was dozing on the loom, but it was running. In her joy, she rushed in, and cried to her father: 'Father, I saw Him!' Before she knew what she did, she had slipped and fallen on the loom. The axle had pierced her heart. And she was gone.

After the light is uncovered, whether or not the clay covering remains is of little consequence.

The Individual Soul

After the first question as to who made all these stars and planets and trees and rivers, i.e, who is God, the next question that bothered ancient people was, 'Who am I?' Were they what they appeared to be? They saw their dear one lying in front of them. Everything was there as it was before, but just because that lying person did not breathe, they called the person 'dead'. What went out? Who went out? Who is the real person then? What was in all the time? The ancient people of India were quick enough to discover that the body is not the real person. It is only an instrument made of clay, they realized. How madly we ignorant people hold on to this clay thing and play with it! How much we strive to please it! All our valuable lives are spent in pleasing this dirty little body! Yet we die. The greatest surprise in the world, said the eldest Pāṇḍava, Dharmarāja, was that even though we see people dying every day, we think we are to live eternally here. This is the wonder of wonders.

If body is not the real person, who is it? This eternal puzzle of the individual being has been answered by different schools in different ways. Every school of thought has this concept. Yet each school differs from the other in its idea of the *jīva.* Swami Vivekananda gives a synoptic view of all the views in his lecture titled 'Steps of Hindu Philosophic Thought', and we shall quote at length from him:

What the Dualists Say

'So far we see that man is a being, who has first a gross body which dissolves very quickly, then a fine body which remains through aeons, and then a Jiva. This Jiva, according to the Vedanta philosophy, is eternal, just as God is eternal. … The gross body is a compound of Akasha and Prana and, therefore, will be decomposed. The fine body will also be decomposed, after a long time, but the Jiva is simple, and will never be destroyed. … The whole of nature comprising millions and millions of souls is under the will of God. God is all-prevading, omniscient, formless, and He is working through nature day and night. The whole of it is under His control. He is the eternal Ruler. So say the dualists.

Then the question comes: If God is the ruler of this universe, why did He create such a wicked universe, why must we suffer so much? They say, it is not God's fault. It is our fault that we suffer. Whatever we sow we reap. … The Jiva has been existing for all time, was never created. It has been doing all sorts of things all the time. Whatever we do reacts upon us. … So the Jiva goes on enjoying and suffering, and doing all sorts of things.

Death and Rebirth For Dualists

'What comes after death? All these Vedanta philosophers admit that this Jiva is by its own nature pure. But ignorance covers its real nature, they say. As by evil deeds it has covered itself with ignorance, so by good deeds it becomes conscious of its own nature again. Just as it is eternal, so its nature is pure. The nature of every being is pure.

When through good deeds all its sins and misdeeds have been washed away, then the Jiva becomes pure again, and when it becomes pure, it goes to what is called Devayana. Its organ of speech enters the mind. You cannot think without words. Wherever there is thought, there must be words. As words enter the mind, so the mind is resolved into the Prana, and the Prana into the Jiva. Then the Jiva gets quickly out of the body, and goes to the solar regions.

Various Spheres of the Universe

'This universe has sphere after sphere. This earth is the world sphere, in which are moons, suns, and stars. Beyond that there is the solar sphere, and beyond that another which they call the lunar sphere. Beyond that there is the sphere which they call the sphere of lightning, the electric sphere, and when the Jiva goes there, there comes another Jiva, already perfect, to receive it, and takes it to another world, the highest heaven, called the Brahmaloka, where the Jiva lives eternally, no more to be born or to die. It enjoys through eternity, and gets all sorts of powers, except the power of creation. There is only one ruler of the universe, and that is God. No one can become God; the dualists maintain that if you say you are God, it is a blasphemy. All powers except the creative come to the Jiva, and if it likes to have bodies, and work in different parts of the world, it can do so. If it orders all the gods to come before it, if it wants its forefathers to come, they all appear at its command. Such are its powers that it never feels any more pain, and if it wants, it can live in the Brahmaloka through all eternity. This is the highest man, who has attained the love of God, who has become perfectly unselfish, perfectly purified, who has given up all desires, and who does not want to do anything except worship and love God.

'There are others that are not so high, who do good works, but want some reward. They say they will give so much to the poor, but want to go to heaven in return. When they die, what becomes of them? The speech enters the mind, the mind enters the Prana, the Prana enters the Jiva, and the Jiva gets out, and goes to the lunar sphere, where it has a very good time for a long period. There it enjoys happiness, so long as the effect of its good deeds endures. When the same is exhausted, it descends, and once again enters life on earth according to its desires. In the lunar sphere the Jiva becomes what we call a god, or what the Christians or Mohammedans call an angel. These gods are the names of certain positions; for instance, Indra, the king of the gods, is the name of a position; thousands of men get to that position.

So the Jivas go to heaven, and have a very good time, except now and then when the demons give them a chase. In our mythology it is said there are demons, who sometimes trouble the gods. In all mythologies, you read how these demons and the gods fought, and the demons sometimes conquered the gods, although many times, it seems, the demons did not do so many wicked things as the gods. In all mythologies, for instance, you find the Devas fond of women. So after their reward is finished, they fall down again, come through the clouds, through the rains, and thus get into some grain or plant and find their way into the human body, when the grain or plant is eaten by men.

In the Deva form they make no Karma at all; only man makes Karma. Karma means work which will produce effect. When a man dies and becomes a Deva, he has only a period of pleasure, and during that time, makes no fresh Karma; it is simply a reward for his past good Karma. When the good Karma is worked out, then the remaining Karma begins to take effect, and he comes down to earth. He becomes man again, and if he does very good works, and purifies himself, he goes to Brahmaloka and comes back no more.

The animal is a state of sojourn for the Jiva evolving from lower forms. In course of time the animal becomes man. It is a significant fact that as the human population is increasing, the animal population is decreasing. The animal souls are all becoming men.

What the Qualified Non-Dualists Say

Next comes the higher Vedantic philosophy which says, that this cannot be. God is both the material and the efficient cause of this universe. If you say there is a God who is an infinite Being, and a soul which is also infinite, and a nature which is also infinite, you can go on multiplying infinites without limit which is simply absurd; you smash all logic. So God is both the material and the efficient cause of the universe; He projects this universe out of Himself. [How can he create degenerate things?] Our answer is: just as I am a soul and have a body, and in a sense, this body is not different from me, yet I, the real I, in fact, am not the body. For instance, I say, I am a child, a young man, or an old man, but my soul has not changed. It remains the same soul. Similarly, the whole universe, comprising all nature and an infinite number of souls, is, as it were, the infinite body of God. He is interpenetrating the whole of it. He alone is unchangeable, but nature changes, and soul changes. He is unaffected by changes in nature and soul. In what way does nature change? In its forms; it takes fresh forms. But the soul cannot change that way. The soul contracts and expands in knowledge. …

This is the second theory. The first is called dualism. … This represents a higher stage of religious development and goes by the name of qualified monism. In dualism, the universe is conceived as a large machine set going by God, while in qualified monism, it is conceived as an organism, interpenetrated by the Divine Self.

What the Non-Dualists Say

The last are the non-dualists. They raise the question also, that God must be both the material and the efficient cause of this universe. The material cause is the cause become effect; the effect is nothing but the cause in another form. Wherever you see an effect, it is the cause reproduced. If the universe is the effect, and God the cause, it must be the reproduction of God. If you say that the universe is the body of God, and that the body becomes contracted and fine and becomes the cause, and out of that the universe is evolved, the non-dualists say that it is God Himself who has become this universe.

'Now comes a very fine question. If this God has become this universe, you and all these things are God. Certainly. This book is God, everything is God. My body is God, and my mind is God, and my soul is God. Then why are there so many Jivas? Has God become divided into millions of Jivas? Does that one God turn into millions of Jivas? Then how did it become so? How can that infinite power and substance, the one Being of the universe, become divided? It is impossible to divide infinity. How can that pure Being become this universe? If He has become the universe, He is changeful, and if He is changeful, He is part of nature, and whatever is nature and changeful is born and dies. If our God is changeful, He must die some day. Take note of that. Again, how much of God has become this universe? If you say X (the unknown algebraical quantity), then God is God minus X now, and, therefore, not the same God as before this creation, because so much has become this universe.

'So the non-dualists say, "This universe does not exist at all; it is all illusion. The whole of this universe, these Devas, gods, angels, and all the other beings born and dying, all this infinite number of souls coming up and going down, are all dreams." There is no Jiva at all. How can there be many? It is the one Infinity. As the one sun, reflected on various pieces of water, appears to be many, and millions of globules of water reflect so many millions of suns, and in each globule will be a perfect image of the sun, yet there is only one sun, so are all these Jivas but reflections in different minds. These different minds are like so many different globules, reflecting this one Being. God is being reflected in all these different Jivas. But a dream cannot be without a reality, and that reality is that one Infinite Existence. You, as body, mind, or soul, are a dream, but what you really are, is Existence, Knowledge,

Bliss. You are the God of this universe. You are creating the whole universe and drawing it in. Thus says the Advaitist.'[1]

From this very long quotation from Swami Vivekananda, we get a clear picture of the basic concepts of the *jīva* in the world. The last theory that Swami Vivekananda mentions is the Advaita theory of *pratibimba* or reflection. This is what is discussed here by *Tattvabodha.*

स्थूल–शरीराभिमानी जीव–नामकं ब्रह्म–प्रतिबिम्बं
भवति; स एव जीवः प्रकृत्या स्वस्मादीश्वरं भिन्नत्वेन
जानाति, अविद्योपाधिः सन आत्मा जीव उच्यते ।

Sthūla-śarīrābhimānī jīva-nāmakaṁ brahma-pratibimbaṁ bhavati; sa eva jīvaḥ prakṛtyā svasmādīśvaraṁ bhinnatvena jānāti, avidyopādhiḥ san ātmā jīva ucyate.

Sthūla-śarīrābhimānī that which identifies with the gross physical body *jīva-nāmakaṁ* and is called jiva *brahma-pratibimbaṁ bhavati* becomes the image of Brahman; *sa eva jīvaḥ* that jiva itself *jānāti* knows that *svasmādīśvaraṁ* from itself Īśvara is *prakṛtyā* by nature *bhinnatvena* different, *avidyopādhiḥ san ātmā jīva ucyate* the Self with the conditioning of ignorance is called jīva.

That which identifies with the gross physical body and is called the *jīva* is the image of Brahman. That *jīva* itself thinks that Īśvara is by nature different from it. The Self with the conditioning of ignorance is called the *jīva.*

Schools of Advaita on the *Jīva*

There are three schools of Advaita Vedanta. We have discussed them in an earlier chapter. We have seen that two schools—Bhāmatī and the Vārtikā—say that the *jīva* is the image (*pratibimba*) of Brahman. The third school, Vivaraṇa, says that *jīva* is the image of Īśvara and not Brahman. This is called *ābhāsa-vāda* or the theory of falsity.

What does this mean? In the first school, it will suffice if I know that I am the reflection of Brahman and when ignorance goes, I am Brahman Itself. According to the Vivaraṇa School, both the image and the original have to be transcended to know Brahman—the *jīva* should know it is an image of Īśvara, reject Īśvara also, and then reach Brahman. So *Tattvabodha* considers the *pratibimba* theory alone.

Locus of the *Jīva*

Where is the *jīva* located? It is not the physical body, but it identifies itself with the physical body and says, "I am strong", "I am tall", "I am handsome", and so on. So it is not the physical body.

Is it the mind? It cannot be the mind because mind falls under the category of the subtle body, and we have seen that mind, which is indecisive, cannot be the reflection of Brahman. The intellect too cannot be the *jīva,* because that too is subtle body alone. The subtle body is created by using the five fundamental elements and they will come to an end one day. The reflection of Brahman is not created and shall never end. So it should be different.

The causal body is the *jīva*. Ignorance has enveloped the soul, which is the reflection of Brahman. When the body dies, the *jīva* travels from this body to another, carrying with it the subtle body also.

Our aim is to know that this *jīva-hood* is nothing but a mere reflection. What we are proudly holding on to and struggling all our millions of lives is but a shadow!

This knowledge is enough to take us to supreme knowledge, the Truth, says Vedanta.

Recapitulation

A seeker of Truth, purified by several spiritual practices, possessing the six treasures needed for a *mumukṣu*, goes to an illumined teacher.

The teacher teaches him by the method of superimposition (*adhyāropa*), and de-superimposition (*apavāda*). Thus the disciple learns how his body, mind, and the causal self have been created. He also learns how the cosmos has come into being, and that while the visible cosmos is gross, it has a subtle and a causal counterpart too.

The seeker then learns that he should strive to know the Truth. The Truth is hidden by untruth or falsity, called *avidyā*. This ignorance has enveloped the Self and so the idea of 'individuality' has come. In order to give up this false 'individuality' and attain the true individuality, which is Brahman, the aspirant is to know what Truth is.

Is this truth God? The next chapter will discuss this.

Reference:

1. Complete Works, Vol. 1, pp. 396-402

Chapter 40

ĪŚVARA

Swamiji on Īśvara

'Who is Ishvara? *Janmadyasya yatah* —"From whom is the birth, continuation, and dissolution of the universe,"—he is Ishvara—"the Eternal, the Pure, the Ever-free, the Almighty, the All-knowing, the All-merciful, the Teacher of all teachers"; and above all, *Sa Ishvarah anirvachaniya-premasvarupah* —"He the Lord is, of His own nature, inexpressible Love." These certainly are the definitions of a Personal God. Are there then two Gods — the "Not this, not this," the Sat-chitananda, the Existence-knowledge-bliss of the philosopher, and this God of Love of the Bhakta? No, it is the same Sat-chit-ananda who is also the God of Love, the impersonal and personal in one. It has always to be understood that the Personal God worshipped by the Bhakta is not separate or different from the Brahman. All is Brahman, the One without a second; only the Brahman, as unity or absolute, is too much of an abstraction to be loved and worshipped; so the Bhakta chooses the relative aspect of Brahman, that is, Ishvara, the supreme Ruler.'

—Swami Vivekananda[1]

Tattvabodha now discusses Īśvara, the supreme God of all religions of the world. Hinduism, Christianity, Islam, Sikhism, Zoroastrianism, and other religions revere this God—the Creator, [Preserver, and Destroyer] of the cosmos. It is this God who has created human beings in his own divine image. Buddhists reject this God. It is this God that incarnates on the earth again and again. It is this God who sports in the world for the good of the devotee. It is this God who destroys evil and restores good.

Sri Ramakrishna's Concept of God

We read in the *Life of Swami Vivekananda:* 'A couple of days before the Master's [Sri Ramakrishna's] passing away, when Narendra and a few others were standing by his bed at night, a curious thought flashed across Naren's mind: "The Master has said many a time that he is an Incarnation of God. If he now says in the midst of the throes of death, in this terrible moment of human anguish and physical pain, 'I am God Incarnate', then I will believe." No sooner had Naren thought this than the Master turned towards him and, summoning all his energy, said, "O my Naren, are you not yet convinced? He who was Rama, He who was Krishna, He Himself is now Ramakrishna in this body: not in your Vedantic sense [according to which each soul is potentially divine], but actually so."'[2]

The universality of Sri Ramakrishna is evident in his concept of God. He never limited God, saying 'this much alone'. There is an interesting conversation in the *Gospel* between Sri Ramakrishna and Kedar:[3]

Kedar: "It is said in the *Bhagavata* that Vyasa asked God's forgiveness for his three transgressions. He said: 'O Lord, Thou art formless, but I have thought of Thee in my meditation as endowed with form; Thou art beyond speech, but I have sung Thee hymns; Thou art the All-pervading Spirit, but I have made pilgrimages to sacred places. Be gracious, O Lord, and forgive these three transgressions of mine.'"

Sri Ramakrishna: "Yes, God has form and He is formless too. Further, He is beyond both form and formlessness. No one can limit Him."

To some devotee who was conversing with him, Sri Ramakrishna gave the ideal in this manner:

'Well, what suits your taste—God with form or the formless Reality? But to tell you the truth, He who is formless is also endowed with form. To His bhaktas He reveals Himself as having a form. It is like a great ocean, an infinite expanse of water, without any trace of shore. Here and there some of the water has been frozen. Intense cold has turned it into ice. Just so, under the cooling influence, so to speak, of the bhakta's love, the Infinite appears to take a form. Again, the ice melts when the sun rises; it becomes water as before. Just so, one who follows the path of knowledge—the path of discrimination—does not see the form of God any more. To him everything is formless. The ice melts into formless water with the rise of the Sun of Knowledge. But mark this: form and formlessness belong to one and the same Reality.'[4]

Such is the grand conception of God that Sri Ramakrishna gives to the world. If a person worships stones and images, that is good. If someone worships the formless, that too is good. There is a wrong idea that Hindus worship millions of gods and goddesses. Hindus worship one God in millions of forms and names. God can have countless names and forms. Why do Hindus worship the image? To this question, Swamiji has replied wonderfully. He says that if one can worship the photographs of one's elders—parents and others—though they may not be in the photographs, why should the Hindu not worship God? The principle is the same.

Further, Hinduism is perhaps the only religion which says that even the Vedas are lower, so far as the illumined soul is concerned. The Hindu scriptures repeatedly assert that the worship of God in the image is the lowest form of worship, and to see Him in all beings is the highest.

Tattvabodha now gives the definition of 'God'.

मायोपाधिः सन् ईश्वर इत्युच्यते। एवम् उपाधि-भेदात्
जीव-ईश्वर-भेद-दृष्टिः यावत् पर्यन्तं तिष्ठति, तावत्

पर्यन्तम् जन्म–मरणादि रूप संसारो न निवर्तते,
तस्मात् कारणात् न जीवेश्वरयोः भेदबुद्धिः कार्या ॥

Māyopādhiḥ san īśvara ityucyate. Evam upādhi-bhedāt jīva-īśvara-bheda-dṛṣṭiḥ yāvat paryantaṁ tiṣṭhati, tāvat paryantam janma-maraṇādi rūpa samsāro na nivartate, tasmāt kāraṇāt na jīveśvaryoḥ bhedabuddhiḥ kāryā.

Māyopādhiḥ san īśvara ityucyate having the false attribute of māyā it is called Īśvara. *Evam upādhi-bhedāti* in this way, due to the difference in qualities *yāvat paryantaṁ* as long as *jīva-īśvara-bheda-dṛṣṭiḥ* the knowledge of the difference of jīva and Īśvara *tiṣṭhati* remains, *tāvat paryantam* till then *janma-maraṇādi rūpa samsāro na nivartate* worldliness of the form of birth and death will not go, *tasmāt kāraṇāt* therefore *na jīveśvaryoḥ bhedabuddhiḥ kāryā* one should never differentiate between jīva and Īśvara.

In this manner, that which has the false attribute of *māyā* is called Īśvara. Owing to the difference in qualities (sattva etc), so long as the knowledge of the difference between the jiva and Īśvara remains, worldliness in the form of birth and death will not go. Therefore one should never differentiate between *jīva* and Īśvara.

Swami Vivekananda was asked by some admirers in Europe about the exact position of Īśvara in Vedanta. He replied: 'Ishvara is the sum total of individuals, yet He is an Individual, as the human body is a unit, of which each cell is an individual. Samashti or collected equals God; Vyashti or analysed equals the Jiva. The existence of Ishvara, therefore, depends on that of Jiva, as the body on the cell, and vice versa. Thus, Jiva and Ishvara are coexistent beings; when one exists, the other must. Also, because, except on our earth, in all the higher spheres, the amount of good being vastly in excess of the amount of evil, the sum total (Ishvara) may be said to be all-good. Omnipotence and omniscience are obvious qualities and need no argument to prove from the very fact of totality. Brahman is beyond both these and is not a conditioned state; it is the only Unit not composed of many units, the principle which runs through all from a cell to God, without which nothing can exist; and whatever is real is that principle, or Brahman. When I think I am Brahman, I alone exist; so with others. Therefore, each one is the whole of that principle.'[5]

Brahman as the only Reality is the contribution of Advaita Vedanta. All other schools consider Brahman to be Īśvara alone. Even Rāmānuja considers Brahman to be one whose *pariṇāma* or transformation is this universe and jiva. So Brahman undergoes transformation. He is Īśvara there also. Yet Advaita qualifies Īśvara as *sarveśvara* (the supreme Lord), *sarvajña* (all-knowing), *sarvaśakta* (all-powerful) and *sarva-niyantā* (Controller).

There is an Upaniṣad devoted to Īśvara, and that is the *Īśa Upaniṣad.* Its very first mantra says that all this is pervaded by Īśvara.

Īśvara and Brahman are non-different, says Swami Vivekananda, in the sense that everything is that one ultimate Reality alone. Yet, he says that one has to transcend the stage of personal God to reach the Absolute. That was what Sri Ramakrishna did when he was practising Advaita Sadhana. He was unable to transcend the personal God. His teacher, Totapuri, told him to take a firm step and cut the image of the personal God with the sword of knowledge. Ramakrishna did that, and he attained *nirvikalpa samādhi.* After the highest experience, Sri Ramakrishna accepted both Eternal as well as the Sportive non-Eternal, Formless as well as Form, Brahman as well as Śakti.

Swamiji says that we should transcend the personal God: 'Vedanta is necessary because neither reasoning nor books can show us God. He is only to be realised by superconscious perception, and Vedanta teaches how to attain that. You must get beyond personal God (Ishvara) and reach the Absolute Brahman. God is the perception of every being: He is all there is to be perceived. … Brahmavidya is the highest knowledge, knowing the Brahman; lower knowledge is science.'[6]

Advaita places Iśvara at a lower state than Brahman because Iśvara is *ajñānopahita-caitanya,* Consciousness enveloped by ignorance. Iśvara according to Advaita is the sumtotal of all the individual causal bodies.

We shall conclude by quoting the greatest authority in such subjects, Swamiji, again: 'Ramanuja divides the universe into Chit, Achit, and Ishvara—man, nature, and God; conscious, subconscious, and superconscious. Shankara, on the contrary, says that Chit, the soul, is the same as God. God is truth, is knowledge, is infinity; these are not qualities. Any thought of God is a qualification, and all that can be said of Him is "Om tat sat".

'Shankara further asks, can you see existence separate from everything else? Where is the differentiation between two objects? Not in sense-perception, else all would be one in it. We have to perceive in sequence. In getting knowledge of what a thing is, we get also something which it is not. The differentiae are in the memory and are got by comparison with what is stored there. Difference is not in the nature of a thing, it is in the brain. Homogeneous one is outside, differentiae are inside (in the mind); so the idea of "many" is the creation of the mind. …

'We are but the reflections of that Atman; and Atman and Brahman are one.

'When you talk and think of the Absolute, you have to do it in the relative; so all these logical arguments apply. In Yoga, perception and realisation are one. Vishishtadvaita, of which Ramanuja is the exponent, is seeing partial unity and is a step toward Advaita. Vishishta means differentiation. Prakriti is the nature of the world, and change comes upon it. Changeful thoughts expressed in changeful words can never prove the Absolute. You reach only something that is minus certain qualities, not Brahman Itself; only a verbal unification, the highest abstraction, but not the non-existence of the relative.'[7]

'Ishvara is to be known from the Vedanta; all Vedas point to Him (who is the Cause; the Creator, Preserver and Destroyer). Ishvara is the unification of the Trinity, known as Brahma, Vishnu, and Shiva, which stand at the head of the Hindu Pantheon,' says Swami Vivekananda.[8]

References:

1. Complete Works, Vol. 3, p. 37
2. *Life of Swami Vivekananda,* Vol.1, p. 183
3. Gospel, p. 192
4. Gospel, p. 370
5. Complete Works, Vol. 5, pp. 269-70
6 Complete Works, Vol. 7, pp. 41-2.
7 Complete Works, Vol. 7, pp. 54-55.
8. Complete Works, Vol. 7, p. 46

Chapter 41

'YOU ARE THAT'

The Vedanta claims that there has not been one religious inspiration, one manifestation of the divine man, however great, but it has been the expression of that infinite oneness in human nature; and all that we call ethics and morality and doing good to others is also but the manifestation of this oneness. There are moments when every man feels that he is one with the universe, and he rushes forth to express it, whether he knows it or not. This expression of oneness is what we call love and sympathy, and it is the basis of all our ethics and morality. This is summed up in the Vedanta philosophy by the celebrated aphorism, Tat Tvam Asi, "Thou art That". ...I am the Infinite, only I am not conscious of it now; but I am struggling to get this consciousness of the Infinite, and perfection will be reached when full consciousness of this Infinite comes.

—Swami Vivekananda[1]

Introductory

After this long discussion on the various aspects of Vedanta, *Tattvabodha* has made it clear to us that we are not the body, not the mind, not the intellect, not the *prāṇas,* and not the causal body also. We are something beyond. The goal of life is to know that. There is a beautiful statement regarding this in the *Gospel of Sri Ramakrishna:* 'Therefore I say again that work is only the first step. It can never be the goal of life. Devote yourself to spiritual practice and go forward. Through practice you will advance more and more in the path of God. At last you will come to know that God alone is real and all else is illusory, and that the goal of life is the attainment of God.'[2]

Sri Ramakrishna also says: 'The jīva is nothing but the embodiment of Satchidānanda. But since māyā, or ego, has created various upadhis, he has forgotten his real Self. ...One can get rid of the ego after the attainment of Knowledge. On attaining Knowledge one goes into samādhi, and the ego disappears.'[3]

Steps to the Attainment

Scriptures are meant to guide us, ignorant persons. They know our problems and difficulties and compassionately take us step by step along the path.

Tattvabodha began with what Vedanta is, and took us through various concepts of creation and finally told us we *jīvas* are reflections of Brahman: that we have no independent entity. We are nothing but Brahman itself—that infinite Being-Consciousness-Bliss absolute—and not limited, suffering, weak, timid creatures.

How to know that? That is the next step. Fundamentally, we are *not* going to know that we are Brahman; we are only removing obstacles to that knowledge we already possess. These obstacles are the products of ignorance.

Advaita is a special tradition in this regard. It says to us: 'Come prepared and ready to the guru. He says a few things, and you are liberated.' The preparation is everything. To become a *mumukṣu* is everything. The rest is left to the teacher. Hence the teacher is revered immensely in Advaita.

An aspirant begins his journey along the spiritual path by striving to purify his mind, controlling his senses and mind, thinking constantly of his Self, and approaching the teacher. The teacher will teach him the *mahāvākya* or sadhana which will guide him to Truth. The main quest is to know who we really are. It is this *mahāvākya* that illumines us.

Are we God Himself?

We are in our quest to know the Truth. We are aware that we are not the body or mind. We are told we are the Supreme. What is that Supreme? The one greatest power left is God. Are we God? God, according to Advaita, is Īśvara. Are we Īśvara?

Vedanta clarifies to us that the first step is to know that we are not equal to Īśvara or God. Why? This chapter gives the reason:

ननु साहंकारस्य किञ्चित् ज्ञस्य जीवस्य,
निरहंकारस्य सर्वज्ञस्य ईश्वरस्य
तत्त्वमसीति महावाक्यात्
कथमभेद-बुद्धिः स्यादुभयोः विरुद्ध-धर्माक्रान्तत्वात् ॥
इति चेत् न ॥

Nanu sāhaṁkārasya kimcit jñasya jīvasya nirahaṁkārasya sarvajñasya iśvarasya tattvamasīti mahāvākyāt kathamabheda-buddhiḥ syādubhayoḥ viruddha-dharmākrāntatvāt. Iti cet na.

Nanu sāhaṁkārasya now, with ego *kimcit* a little *jñasya* knowing *jivasya* living being *nirahaṁkārasya* (and) egoless *sarvajñasya* all-knowing *iśvarasya* God *mahāvākyāt* like the great sentence *tattvamasīti* 'You are That' *kathamabheda-buddhiḥ syād* how could there be non-difference *ubhayoḥ viruddha dharmākrāntatvāt* because both are of opposing natures. *Iti cet na,* if it is said so, no.

Now how can there be non-difference—as the great statement 'You are That' says—between the living being with ego and limited knowledge, and the all-knowing God without ego, since both are opposite in nature? If it is said so, no.

Sāhaṁkārasya-nirahaṁkārasya; Kimcit-jñasya Sarvajñasya:

'With Ego'-'Without Ego'; 'With limited knowledge'-'Omniscient' . The limited beings, ourselves, are embodiments of ego. We have thus limited ourselves to small circles. We are very proud of ourselves and our little achievements. We build up our own little worlds and our egos. Our edifice is false and so is our base.

The Unlimited, Īśvara, is egoless. God is a circle whose centre is everywhere, as Swamiji remarks. This is the fundamental difference between *Īśvara* and *jīva*. The second fundamental difference between us is, we are of limited intellect and knowledge, while Īśvara is all-knowing. Īśvara is the sumtotal of all souls and more. He is the creator, preserver, and destroyer of the universe and much more. The *jīva* is a limited being with no such powers.

How can the two be one? How can the lamp and the Sun be one?

So the comparison between Īśvara and ourselves, and calling ourselves Īśvara, would be nothing but impudence. Yet the Upaniṣads declare that we are That. The guru teaches that we are That. What is the meaning of 'That'? This will be discussed in the next chapter. But before going to that, we shall discuss the statement which calls us 'That'.

Sentences

When two or more meaningful words are placed in a meaningful order, a meaningful sentence is created. As they say, a sentence should at least have a subject and a predicate. Sentences should convey some complete meaning. There are sentences and sentences. 'Go there,' is as much a sentence as 'Pray to God.' But one has a very ordinary connotation while the other has a deep significance. An ordinary speaker may go on talking for hours—beating around the bush—but may not be able to convey what he wants to say at all. Another speaker may say a few words and fill the listeners' hearts with joy and minds with understanding. A great author uses a few sentences to convey his ideas clearly, whereas, an ordinary writer may write a huge book to convey nothing.

Take this sentence for example: 'Jack and Jill went up the hill.' There was a hill and two children climbed up that hill. That is all the meaning it conveys. This is a meaningful sentence, called *samsrṣṭārtha vākya* in Sanskrit. There are three different 'things' here: Jack, Jill, and the hill. But there is a connection between the word 'hill' and the children, and their going up.

Take this sentence: 'Dense white fumes.' Here the sentence, though somewhat meaningful, goes to say something about fumes alone. Such sentences are called *akhaṇḍārtha vākyas*.

According to philosophers, any sentence should have three qualities for it to convey correct, comprehensible, and complete meaning. These are the following:

A. *Yogyatā*—meaningful connection between the words in a sentence ('John horse cricket' are merely three words but have no interconnectedness).

B. *Āsakti*—timely pronouncement of words, i.e., syntactical expression with proper timing (to say 'I' today, and 'shall' tomorrow and 'eat' ten days later will not do);

C. *Ākāñkṣā*—the meaningful expression of words ('While carrying the bucket' is all right as a sentence, but the question, what next, remains).

So the words in a sentence should be arranged syntactically well, pronounced at the right moments, and must not give room for ambiguity. The mutual relationship between words and phrases should be strong for a sentence to be complete.

Vākyas and *Mahāvākyas*

Ordinary sentences, called *vākyas,* convey ordinary meanings. But there are some rare sentences that can convey a huge philosophy in just a few words. These are called great sentences (*mahāvākyas*). The difference between a *vākya* and a *mahāvākya* is that while the ordinary sentence conveys a direct or an implied meaning only, a great sentence can liberate an individual.

The Vedas are divided into four groups—Ṛg Veda, Yajur Veda, Sāma Veda, and Atharva Veda. Each Veda has several Upaniṣads as its end portion or culmination. There are more than 108 Upaniṣads, of which four contribute a great sentence each. ***Tat Tvam Asi*** is from *Chāndogya Upaniṣad* (6.9.4). ***Ahaṁ Brahmāsmi*** is from *Bṛhadāraṇyaka Upaniṣad* (1.4.10). ***Ayam Ātmā Brahma*** is from *Māṇḍūkya Upaniṣad* (2). And ***Prajñānaṁ Brahma*** is from *Aitareya Upaniṣad* (5.3). These sentences are generally taught to monks and nuns by their monastic teachers. This is because, Advaita was predominantly a monastic tradition though, of late, all study and try to practise it.

The guru teaches this sentence to the disciple. The disciple may, if he is a fit aspirant, become illumined the moment he hears it. How? According to Advaitins, the moment the sentence is heard, its meaning flashes in the competent aspirant, and a mental modification arises in the mind, which is called the *akhaṇḍākāra-ākārita vṛtti* 'the modification of the shape of the Immutable.' This *vṛtti* (a) destroys ignorance enveloping the Self or Atman; (b) destroys the products of ignorance like the mind; and (c) itself gets destroyed. If the aspirant is not ready, he may meditate on its meaning and be liberated in time.

Of all the four great sentences, *tat tvam asi* is famous. It was told by his teacher to Śvetaketu, a mere child, and the child became illumined. It means 'You are That'. Swami Vivekananda was also fond of it, it appears. For he says:

'But this is my attempt, my mission in life, to show that the Vedantic schools are not contradictory, that they all necessitate each other, all fulfil each other, and one, as it were, is the stepping-stone to the other, until the goal, the Advaita, the Tat Tvam Asi, is reached.'[4] The author of *Tattvabodha* has used that great sentence here.

By listening to this statement from the spiritual teacher, the general aspirant is confused initially. Who is he, really? Is he Īśvara? Īśvara and jīva cannot be one and the same because there are differences in knowledge and egos. As human beings, a professor and an idiot may be the same; but we cannot equate them in everything. We cannot, for instance, ask the idiot to give classes.

Īśvara and jīva are the same because their essence is the same. They are two because of the enveloping ignorance. Hence their difference. They are essentially Brahman.

This will be dealt with in the next section.

We shall end this section by quoting from Swami Vivekananda:

> There is only One Being, One Existence, the ever-blessed, the omnipresent, the omniscient, the birthless, the deathless. ... Wherever there are two, there is fear, there is danger, there is conflict, there is strife. When it is all One, who is there to hate, who is there to struggle with? When it is all He, with whom can you fight? This explains the true nature of life; this explains the true nature of being. This is perfection, and this is God. As long as you see the many, you are under delusion. "In this world of many he who sees the One, in this ever-changing world he who sees Him who never changes, as the Soul of his own soul, as his own Self, he is free, he is blessed, he has reached the goal." Therefore know that thou art He; thou art the God of this universe, "Tat Tvam Asi" (That thou art).'[5]

References

1. Complete Works, Vo1. 1, p. 389-90
2. Gospel, p. 453
3. Gospel, p. 169
4. Complete Works, Vol. 3, p. 324
5. Complete Works, Vol. 2, p. 236

Chapter 42

THE MEANING OF 'YOU'

Reading the Real Meaning

What is the meaning of 'Thou art That' or, in modern language, 'You are That'? By 'That', Īśvara is not meant—this was clear in the previous section. What 'That' really means will be discussed in the next section. In this section the word *tvam* or 'You' is being dealt with.

There are two ways of looking at things: the direct and the indirect. A sentence can convey a direct meaning or an implied meaning. 'Hari, go home,' is a direct sentence which has no implied meaning. The meaning is clear. Such a direct-meaning sentence is called *vācyārtha vākya*. There are some sentences which have implied meanings. As for instance: 'John is a lion.' The boy John cannot be a lion. But the implied meaning is important here: John is as brave as the lion. This sentence is called *lakṣyārtha vākya*. A third group of sentences is the *vyañgyārtha vākya,* which means ironical statements.

In the sentence 'You are That', we should use the second method—*lakṣyārtha* or implied meaning—to get the correct meaning of the sentence. This will be discussed in the present section.

स्थूल-सूक्ष्म-शरीराभिमानी त्वम्-पद-वाच्यार्थं;
उपाधि-विनिर्मुक्तम् समाधि-दशासम्पन्नम् शुद्धम्
चैतन्यं त्वम्पद-लक्ष्यार्थः ॥

sthūla-sūkṣma-śarīrābhimānī tvam-pada vācyārtham

upādhi-vinirmuktam samādhi-daśāsampannaṁ śuddham caitanyaṁ tvaṁ pada lakṣyārthaḥ.

sthūla-sūkṣma-śarīrābhimānī that which identifies with the gross and subtle bodies, *tvam-pada vācyārthaṁ* is called 'you'; (but) *tvaṁ pada lakṣyārthaḥ* (that which) is indicated by the word 'you' is *śuddham caitanyaṁ* pure consciousness *upādhi-vinirmuktam* freed from all attributes *samādhi-daśāsampannaṁ* and attained in the state of samādhi.

That which identifies itself with the gross and subtle bodies is called 'you' in the direct sense; but that which is really implied by the word 'you' (are not these) but the pure consciousness, freed from all attributes and attained in the state of samādhi.

The Direct Meaning

In the sentence 'You are That', the direct meaning of the word 'you' will naturally be the person standing before the teacher. The teacher tells his disciple: 'You are That.' By 'you' the ordinary disciple naturally understands that the teacher means him. By 'him', again, the body-mind complex is understood.

If the disciple of Vedanta, who has purified himself by practising intense sadhana and has come to the teacher after great struggle, takes only the direct meaning of the word and thinks that by 'you' his body-mind complex is meant, he is wrong. The teacher is a knower of Brahman. He looks through the apparent personality into the true Self. By 'you', therefore, the implied meaning is the 'Atman', the Self.

The Implied Meaning

The implied meaning (*lakṣyārtha*) of the word 'you' is the Atman. The body-mind complex is not meant here. 'You, i.e., the Atman, are That—*Tvam asi Tat.*' Swami Vivekananda says: 'The Vedas cannot show you Brahman, you are That already;

they can only help to take away the veil that hides the truth from our eyes. The first veil to vanish is ignorance; and when that is gone, sin goes; next desire ceases, selfishness ends, and all misery disappears. This cessation of ignorance can only come when I know that God and I are one; in other words, identify yourself with Atman, not with human limitations.'[1]

Implied meanings can be of three forms:

1. *Jahat-lakṣaṇa*: Here the direct meaning of the sentence is to be given up and its indirect meaning is to be accepted. 'He flew to London' does not mean that human beings can fly. The direct meaning should be discarded here.

2. *Ajahat-laksaṇa:* This is the opposite of the first. Here, the direct meaning is to be accepted. But if the direct meaning is unclear, indirect meaning too is considered. 'India wins the match.' Here India as a nation cannot play, but a few chosen citizens play and win. Yet, the direct meaning is not altogether silly as in the first case.

3. *Jahat-ajahat-laksaṇa*: This is also called *bhāga-lakṣaṇa.* This is the correct way of reading sentences as 'You are That'. We have to give up one part of the direct meaning, and consider one part of the indirect meaning. That is, we must discard unnecessary details and consider only the gist or the root of the thing. 'He is that Devadatta.' Which Devadatta? Of some place, seen at some point of time, about whom the discussion is on. When he arrives, we remark that this is that Devadatta whom we are discussing. Here, the essence is Devadatta. So the other details are discarded. That Devadatta and this Devadatta might have been separated by time and place. But they are one essentially.

Thus, in the sentence 'You are That,' other details of 'you', like body and mind, are discarded.

Having understood that the implied meaning of 'you' is the Atman, the disciple should know the real meaning of 'That'.

Reference:

5. Complete Works, Vol. 7, p. 46

Chapter 43

THE MEANING OF 'THAT'

The Meaning of 'That'

Having known that the individual is nothing but the Atman, the next step is to know what 'That' is. It has been decided that 'That' is not Īśvara. The implied meaning (*lakṣyārtha*) should be searched for here also.

This section clarifies the true meaning of 'That or *tat*'.

एवम् सर्वज्ञत्वादि-विशिष्ट ईश्वरः तत्पद-वाच्यार्थः।
उपाधिशून्यं शुद्ध-चैतन्यं तत्पद-लक्ष्यार्थः । एवञ्च
जीवेश्वरयोः चैतन्यरूपेणाऽभेदे बाधकाभावः ॥

Evaṁ sarvajñatvādi-viśiṣṭa īśvaraḥ tatpada-vācyārthaḥ.
Upādhi-śūnyaṁ śuddha-caitanyaṁ tatpada-lakṣyārthaḥ.
Evamca jīveśvarayoḥ caitanya-rūpeṇābhede bādhakābhāvaḥ.

Evaṁ in this manner *sarvajñatvādi-viśiṣṭa* He who is qualified by the powers of all-knowingness, *īśvaraḥ* the Lord *tatpada-vācyārthaḥ* is called 'That'. *tatpada-lakṣyārthaḥ* but that which is indicated by 'That' is *śuddha-caitanyaṁ* pure consciousness *upādhi-śūnyaṁ* which is freed from all attributes. *Evamca jīveśvarayoḥ* in this manner is living beings and God *bādhakābhāvaḥ* are non-different *caitanya-rūpeṇābhede* (since) there is non-difference in consciousness.

In this manner, He who is qualified by the powers of all-knowingness, the Lord, is understood by 'That' in its direct meaning. But that which is truly implied by 'That' is the pure Consciousness, which is freed from all attributes.

In this way, God and living beings are non-different, since there is non-difference in Consciousness.

When the disciple listens to the *mahāvākya* from his teacher, he understands that by *tvam* his true Self, the Atman, is meant. He rejects the meaning of Īśvara from *tat* or 'That'. So what remains is Brahman. It cannot be anything lower.

Thus he understands that Brahman is Atman. The same reality is there in him and in the cosmos. the division, the bifurcation, the duality are all myth. When the disciple understands that he is infinite, he merges into samādhi. This is the culmination of his sadhana.

Words and Their Power

Can a mere statement of the Vedas do so much? Of course! Words carry power. Ordinary words have ordinary power, but some words are so powerful that they can destroy our illusion and ignorance. They should, however, be uttered by powerful souls. In the *Upadeśa Sāhasrī* (18.172), it is said: 'Just as the sentence "You are the tenth person" produces such knowledge, the sentence "You are That" produces instant effect.'

A remarkable incident in the annals of spiritual history is reported of Swami Vivekananda, which we quote from his life:

> Speaking of this one day to Sharatchandra [his disciple], Swamiji suddenly exclaimed: 'Keeping before you the national ideal of renunciation which comes of devotion to the Lord, you have to work fearlessly with the strength of a lion, heedless of the fruits of action and without caring for criticism. Let Mahavira be your ideal. See how, with unbounded faith in the name of Rama, he—the prince of the self-controlled ones, wise and sagacious—crossed the ocean in one bound,defying death! You have to mould your lives after that high ideal, thinking yourselves the servants of the Lord."

> ... Speaking in this strain the Swami came downstairs and sat on the canvas cot under the mango tree in the courtyard, facing west, as he often did. His eyes were luminous; his whole frame seemed alive with some strange spiritual consciousness. Pointing to the Sannyasis and Brahmacharis about him, he exclaimed: 'And where will you go to seek Brahman? He is immanent in all beings. Here, here is the visible Brahman! Shame on those who, disregarding the visible Brahman, set their minds on other things! Here is the Brahman before you as tangible as a fruit in your hand! Can't you see! Here — here — here is the Brahman!' He spoke these words in such an inspiring way that over all present there came the peace and insight of deep meditation. They stood like marble statues, so motionless and hushed in silence had they become! Swami Premananda, after his bath in the Ganga, was on his way to the shrine for worship. Hearing the words of his brother-monk he fell into a state of absorption and became motionless. After a quarter of an hour the Swami said to him, 'Now go for worship.' Then only did Premananda regain normal consciousness.
>
> That scene was unforgettable. Everyone in the monastery was struck with amazement at the power of the beloved Leader who, with a word, could raise the minds of all present to the heights of Supreme Insight.

The Vedas have the inherent power because they are words of realized masters. And the Veda is Brahman Itself. Ordinary words and mantras are different in this sense. The mantras have inherent potencies, which act upon the soul from within and destroy the ignorance. Swami Vivekananda says: 'There are certain sacred words called Mantras, which have power, when repeated under proper conditions, to produce these extraordinary powers. We are living in the midst of such a mass of miracles, day and night, that we do not think anything of them. There is no limit to man's power, the power of words and the power of mind.'[2]

'What are these Mantras? The whole of this universe has, according to Indian philosophy, both name and form (Nama-Rupa) as its conditions of manifestation. In the human microcosm, there cannot be a single wave in the mindstuff (Chittavritti) unconditioned by name and form. If it be true that nature is built throughout on the same plan, this kind of conditioning by name and form must also be the plan of the building of the whole of the cosmos. "As one lump of clay being known, all things of clay are known", so the knowledge of the microcosm must lead to the knowledge of the macrocosm.'[3] This is the power of Vedanta.

Recapitulation

1. The aspirant, ready for spiritual instruction, arrives at the doors of the teacher. The teacher tells him about the Truth and the superimposition.

2. The disciple learns that, his own body and mind included, everything is fleeting, and Brahman alone is the Reality. The guru then gives him the *mahāvākya*. The fit aspirant merges into samādhi instantly.

Suggested Reading

1. *Self-Knowledge,* based on Śaṅkara's *Atmabodha.*

2. *Upadeśa Sāhasrī,* chapter on 'Tat Tvam Asi'

References:

1. *The Life of Swami Vivekananda,* Vol. 2, pp. 630-1

2. Complete Works, Vol. 1, p. 290

3. Complete Works, Vol. 3, pp. 56-7

Chapter 44

THE LIBERATED-IN-LIFE

Jīvanmukti

'Jīvanmukti' is 'liberation in life'. There is an apparent contradiction in terms here. Life means bondage, *mukti* means liberation. How can contradictions co-exist? How can there be bondage and liberation at the same time?

The concept of *jīvanmukti* is not a creation of Advaitins. It was there in the Vedas. There are many mantras in the Upaniṣads which speak of liberation in life. *Chāndogya* (7.25.2) says: '*ātmaratiḥ, ātmakrīḍaḥ,* He delights in his own Self, sports in his own Self.' The *Katha* (2.1.15) says: 'Just as pure water poured into pure water becomes non-different, so does the Self of the person of knowledge.' 'अविभागेन दृष्टत्वात्, *avibhāgena dṛṣṭatvāt*, the liberated soul is inseparable from Brahman,' says *Brahma Sūtras* (4.4.4). Further, *Brahma Sūtras* (4.4.9) says that the liberated soul is free from all injunctions. He has no one to rule over him: 'अतएव चानन्याधिपतिः *ata eva caananyādhipatiḥ*.'

The *Brahma Sūtras* (3.4.50) declares that a *jīvanmukta* lives like a child: 'अनाविष्कुर्वन्नन्वयात्, *anāviṣkurvan-anvayāt*, without pomp, the enlightened should live like a child.' In the *Bṛhadāraṇyaka Upaniṣad* (3.5.1) it is said that 'Persons of knowledge, after enlightenment, live in the world without attachment for anything, having overcome all sorrow and suffering, and take to mendicancy. The knowers of Brahman live like children.'

The oft-quoted mantra is *tasya tāvadeva ciram*.... Advaitins developed this idea, but they too are divided in this. While some say *jīvanmukti* is possible, others say that it is not.

Śrī Śaṁkara writes in several places that *jīvanmukti* is possible. In his commentary to a *Bhagavad Gītā* verse (2.51), he writes that while living in the body, the person of knowledge will attain liberation. Of the other schools of thought, like the Nyāya, Sānkhya, and others, accept liberation in life. Among the chief opponents of *jīvanmukti,* Rāmānuja is one. How can somebody still living in the body be called liberated, he asks.

The concept of *jīvanmukti* is true and real because Sri Ramakrishna, Holy Mother, and Swami Vivekananda accept them. Sri Ramakrishna says several times: 'If by the grace of God a man but once realizes that he is not the doer, then he at once becomes a Jīvanmukta. Though living in the body, he is liberated. He has nothing else to fear.'[1] Sri Ramakrishna gives a beautiful example of the *jīvanmukta*: 'Suppose an office clerk has been sent to jail. He undoubtedly leads a prisoner's life there. But when he is released from jail, does he cut capers in the street? Not at all. He gets a job as a clerk again and goes on working as before. Even after attaining Knowledge through the guru's grace, one can very well live in the world as a Jīvanmukta.'[2]

The Method of Attaining Knowledge

Elsewhere, we have mentioned that all knowledge, whether external or internal, is had in the form of mental modifications, called *vṛtti*. Every knowledge comes in the form of a *vṛtti*. Even Brahman knowledge comes in the form of *vṛtti* according to Vedanta. Such a *vṛtti* or mental modification has been called *brahmākārā-vṛtti*. This is the ultimate *vṛtti* that rises in the mind, before the mind merges into samādhi.

Can one attain Brahman knowledge? No, one cannot. If knowledge of the Atman or Brahman is attained by effort or other means, it will go. That which comes, goes. That which is born will die. So Brahman knowledge should also come to an end some day. But once a person becomes enlightened, there is no more ignorance for him. He is forever enlightened. So Brahman knowledge is neither born, nor acquired.

It is always there. According to Vedanta we have only forgotten this knowledge. It has been enveloped by ignorance.

Brahmākārā-vṛtti destroys ignorance and leaves. Knowledge shines of itself.

The Process of Awakening

The guru tests the disciple's intensity of devotion to Truth initially. As Sri Ramakrishna says, the seeker should pant for liberation. Then alone can teachings bear fruit. The disciple succeeds in all tests. The teacher then tells his disciple about *adhyāropa* or superimposition. He tells the disciple how *māyā* has superimposed herself on Brahman, as it were, and so the Truth has come to him (in the disciple's form), lamenting that It is ignorant. The teacher next discusses *apavāda* or de-superimposition. Yes, Brahman has been enveloped by *avidyā* or ignorance. How to overcome it?

There are methods. One is meditation on the Reality, assuming It to be like a fish in the vast ocean, or a bird in the sky. Such meditations are suggested because while a devotee can concentrate on beautiful forms of God, the seeker of knowledge has no such symbols of Truth. These, then, are his symbols.

Apart from meditation, the disciple is told to enquire into the Truth. This is called *vicāra*. 'Who am I?' is the standard question for the Advaitin.

The other method is giving the great *upadeśa* or advice—giving the *mahāvākya*. Of the four great sentences, the teacher may give any one to the disciple. The disciple could either be enlightened instantly, or later.

The moment the disciple listens to the guru, there awakens in his heart the idea that he is not the limited, sorrowing, and suffering body or mind. He is the eternal, pure, ever-free, Self or Brahman itself. This is not mere conviction. It is a positive *vṛtti* that awakens in the mind. This is not indirect knowledge—like the ones we have from books.

Books tell us we are Brahman. We read them time and again. Yet nothing happens. But in the case of such a *vṛtti*, there is the awakening of direct knowledge or perception (*aparokṣa*).

This *vṛtti* will make Brahman as its subject. It destroys the ignorance that envelops It. Thus there is the flash of knowledge. This is the explanation of the Vedanta. The Vedantins give this example: when the threads in a piece of a cloth are burnt, the cloth too is burnt. So also, when ignorance is destroyed, all the effects of ignorance—mind, intellect, etc—also are destroyed automatically. The *vṛtti* too is destroyed! What remains, remains.

This is the culmination of Vedanta.

Swami Vivekananda summarizes all this beautifully in his talks with a disciple of his: 'The direction of the mind which always runs after the senses has to be turned within. The mind has to be killed. The body is but gross—it dies and dissolves into the five elements. But the bundle of mental impressions, which is the mind, does not die soon. It remains for some time in seed-form and then sprouts and grows in the form of a tree—it takes on another physical body and goes the round of birth and death, until Self-knowledge arises. Therefore I say, by meditation and concentration and by the power of philosophical discrimination plunge this mind in the Ocean of Existence-knowledge-bliss Absolute. When the mind dies, all limiting adjuncts vanish and you are established in Brahman.'[3]

What happens next? This is being explained in this section:

एवं च वेदान्त–वाक्यैः सद्गुरु–उपदेशेन सर्वेष्वपि भूतेषु
येषां ब्रह्म–बुद्धिरुत्पन्ना, ते जीवन्मुक्ता इत्यर्थः ॥

Evam ca vedānta-vākyaiḥ sadguru-upadeśena sarveṣvapi bhūteṣu yeṣāṁ brahma-buddhirutpannā, te jīvanmuktā ityarthaḥ.

Evam ca so also *sadguru-upadeśena* by the teachings of a great teacher *vedānta-vākyaiḥ* through the texts of Vedanta *yeṣāṁ* for those *brahma-buddhirutpannā* who have the understanding of Brahman *sarveṣvapi bhūteṣu* in all the living beings *te jīvanmuktā ityarthaḥ* are called liberated in life.

So also due to the teachings of a supreme teacher, those who have, with the help of the texts of Vedanta, developed the understanding of Brahman in all the living beings, are called 'liberated in life'.

Sadguru-upadeśa

Of the greatest gifts of God, three have been considered supreme—human birth, desire for liberation, and the company of an illumined soul. He or she who has all these is indeed blessed. The gift of a *sadguru* is very difficult to be had. There are teachers and teachers, but to obtain a teacher who is a knower of the Vedas (*śrotriya*), sinless (*avṛjina*), without desires (*akāma-hata*), and a knower of Brahman (*brahmajña*) is near to impossible. But if the disciple is ready, somehow the guru also comes at the right time.

The teachings of such a teacher are called his *upadeśa*. As we saw before, the teacher teaches only out of extreme compassion—he has no other motive because for him who is a knower of Truth, this world is equal to a mud-puddle. He wants nothing. Yet the disciple, out of reverence, serves him. The teacher tells him about the Truth. This will work in the mind of the disciple and destroy his ignorance. His limitedness will go.

Swami Vivekananda was the greatest of such teachers. And how fortunate should be the soul who became his disciple! One such disciple asked Swami Vivekananda what should be the process of meditation in the path of knowledge. The conversation is reported as it is:

> Disciple: Yes, sir, but meditation must base itself on some object?

Swamiji: You yourself will be the object of your meditation. Think and meditate that you are the omnipresent Atman. "I am neither the body, nor the mind, nor the Buddhi (determinative faculty), neither the gross nor the subtle body"— by this process of elimination, immerse your mind in the transcendent knowledge which is your real nature. Kill the mind by thus plunging it repeatedly in this. Then only you will realise the Essence of Intelligence, or be established in your real nature. Knower and known, meditator and the object meditated upon will then become one, and the cessation of all phenomenal superimpositions will follow. This is styled in the Shastras as the transcendence of the triad or relative knowledge (Triputibheda). There is no relative or conditioned knowledge in this state. When the Atman is the only knower, by what means can you possibly know It? The Atman is Knowledge, the Atman is Intelligence, the Atman is Sachchidananda. It is through the inscrutable power of Maya, which cannot be indicated as either existent or non-existent, that the relative consciousness has come upon the Jiva who is none other than Brahman. This is generally known as the conscious state. And the state in which this duality of relative existence becomes one in the pure Brahman is called in the scriptures the superconscious state and described in such words as, it is like an ocean perfectly at rest and without a name".

'...Viewed from the transcendent standpoint, everything appears to be unreal — religious creeds, and works, I and thou, and the universe — everything is unreal! Then only it is perceived: "I am the only reality; I am the all-pervading Atman, and I am the proof of my own existence." ... I have seen that state, realised it. You also see and realise it and preach this truth of Brahman to all. Then only will you attain to peace.

'While speaking these words, Swamiji's face wore a serious expression and he was lost in thought. After some time he continued: "Realise in your own life this knowledge of Brahman which comprehends all theories and is the rationale of all truths, and preach it to the world. This will conduce to your own good and the good of others as well. I have told you today the essence of all truths; there is nothing higher than this."'[4]

Seeing Brahman in All

In one of his glorious letters, Swami Vivekananda writes: 'When there comes affliction in the heart, when the storm of sorrow blows all around, and it seems light will be seen no more, when hope and courage are almost gone, it is then, in the midst of this great spiritual tempest, that the light of Brahman within gleams. Brought up in the lap of luxury, lying on a bed of roses and never shedding a tear, who has ever become great, who has ever unfolded the Brahman within? Why do you fear to weep? Weep! Weeping clears the eyes and brings about intuition. Then the vision of diversity—man, animal, tree—slowly melting away, makes room for the infinite realisation of Brahman everywhere and in every thing. Then—

समं पश्यन् हि सर्वत्र समवस्थितमीश्वरम् ।
न हिनस्त्यात्मनात्मानं ततो याति परां गतिम् ॥

"Verily, seeing the same God equally existent everywhere, he does not injure the Self by the self, and so goes to the Supreme Goal."'[5]

We generally speak of seeing God in everything and everyone. As if it was all so easy. Unless we have seen God within, which is Brahman itself, how can we see it without? Yet for those who know the ideas and ideals of Ramakrishna-Vivekananda, faith in their teachings can bring the faith too that all beings are manifestations of God. So the true aspirant will strive to overcome ignorance first, and then sees light everywhere.

The *Jīvanmukta*

Swami Vivekananda says:

One day I was very thirsty and I wanted to have a drink at one of these lakes; but when I approached that lake it vanished. Immediately with a blow came into my brain that idea that this was a mirage about which I read all my life; and then I remembered and smiled at my folly, that for the last month all the beautiful landscapes and lakes I had been seeing were this mirage, but I could not distinguish them then.

The next morning I again began my march; there was the lake and the landscape, but with it immediately came the idea, "This is a mirage." Once known it has lost its power of illusion. So this illusion of the universe will break one day. The whole of this will vanish, melt away. This is realisation.

Philosophy is no joke or talk. It has to be realised; this body will vanish, this earth and everything will vanish, this idea that I am the body or mind will for some time vanish, or if the Karma is ended it will disappear, never to come back; but if one part of the Karma remains, then as a potter's wheel, after the potter has finished the pot, will sometimes go on from the past momentum, so this body, when the delusion has vanished altogether, will go on for some time. Again this world will come, men and women and animals will come, just as the mirage came the next day, but not with the same force; along with it will come the idea that I know its nature now, and it will cause no bondage, no more pain, nor grief, nor misery. Whenever anything miserable will come, the mind will be able to say, "I know you as hallucination."

When a man has reached that state, he is called Jīvanmukta, "living-free", free even while living. The aim and end in this life for the Jnana-yogi is to become this Jīvanmukta, "living-free."

He is Jīvanmukta who can live in this world without being attached. He is like the lotus leaves in water, which are never wetted by the water. He is the highest of human beings, nay, the highest of all beings, for he has realised his identity with the Absolute, he has realised that he is one with God. So long as you think you have the least difference from God, fear will seize you, but when you have known that you are He, that there is no difference, entirely no difference, that you are He, all of Him, and the whole of Him, all fear ceases. "There, who sees whom? Who worships whom? Who talks to whom? Who hears whom? Where one sees another, where one talks to another, where one hears another, that is little. Where none sees none, where none speaks to none, that is the highest, that is the great, that is the Brahman." Being That, you are always That. What will become of the world then? What good shall we do to the world? Such questions do not arise. "What becomes of my gingerbread if I become old?" says the baby! "What becomes of my marbles if I grow? So I will not grow," says the boy! "What will become of my dolls if I grow old?" says the little child! It is the same question in connection with this world; it has no existence in the past, present, or future.

If we have known the Atman as It is, if we have known that there is nothing else but this Atman, that everything else is but a dream, with no existence in reality, then this world with its poverties, its miseries, its wickedness, and its goodness will cease to disturb us. If they do not exist, for whom and for what shall we take trouble? This is what the Jnana-Yogis teach. Therefore, dare to be free, dare to go as far as your thought leads, and dare to carry that out in your life.'[6]

In the beginning of this chapter we have discussed the positive and negative views about *jīvanmukti.* We have mentioned there that Sri Ramakrishna and Swami Vivekananda accept *jīvanmukti*. They had firsthand experience of things.

Sri Ramakrishna defines the state of *jīvanmukti*: 'He who has attained this Knowledge of Brahman is a jīvanmukta, liberated while living in the body. He rightly understands that the Atman and the body are two separate things. After realizing God one does not identify the Atman with the body.'[7]

Further Reading

1. *Vivekacūḍāmaṇī*, the portion on *jīvanmukti.*

2. Selections from *Jīvanmukti-Viveka.*

3. *Muktikopaniṣad,* 2nd chapter

References:

1. Gospel, p. 169
2. Gospel, p. 233
3. Complete Works, Vol. 7, p. 195
4. Complete Works, Vol. 7, pp. 196-7
5. *Bhagavad Gītā* 13.28
6. Complete Works, Vol. 3, p. 10-11
7. Gospel, p. 719

Chapter 45

WHO IS A *JĪVANMUKTA*?

The *Jīvanmukta*

यदा सर्वे प्रमुच्यन्ते कामा येऽस्य हृदि स्थिताः ।
अथ मर्त्योऽमृतो भवति अत्र ब्रह्म समश्नुते ॥१४३

Yadā sarve pramucyante kāmā ye'sya hṛdi sthitāḥ|
Atha marṭyo'mṛto bhavati, tatra brahma samaśnute||

'When all the desires of the heart are burnt away, the individual becomes immortal while living, and attains Brahman even in this body.'

The characteristics of a person who is liberated in life have been discussed in diverse ways by our scriptures. The *Bhāgavata* speaks of such a state. *Vivekacūḍāmaṇī* (5.540) says: 'Persons who have had their life's purpose fulfilled by the realization of the Self, roam about in the world in strange attires—some with ordinary clothes, some clad in barks of trees, still others with the points of the compass as their dress (i.e., stark naked), some like madmen, some like boys free from the slightest tinge of lust and greed, and still others like ghouls.' Sri Ramakrishna also says this. He says that seeing him, people would remark thus: 'Someone remarked that I was a Brahmajnani. So the Vaishnava pundits wanted to test me. One said, "Why hasn't he beads, and a mark on his forehead?" Another of them replied, "They have dropped from him, as the dry branch from a coconut tree." It was there that I learnt this illustration of the dry branch of a coconut tree. The upadhis, limitations, drop when one attains Knowledge.'[2] Sri Ramakrishna also remarks that a person of knowledge cannot maintain his body for long: 'But in that state his body does not last many days. He remains unconscious of the outer world. If milk is poured into his mouth, it runs out. Dwelling on this plane of consciousness, he gives up his body in twenty-one days. That is the condition of the Brahmajnani.'[3]

Sri Ramakrishna had seen such men of knowledge in Dakshineswar.

Now, who is a *jīvanmukta*, 'the liberated in life'?

ननु जीवन्मुक्तः कः? यथा देहोऽहं पुरुषोऽहं ब्राह्मणोऽहं
शूद्रोऽहं अस्मीति दृढनिश्चयस्तथा नाहं ब्राह्मणो न
शूद्रो न पुरुषः किन्तु असङ्गः सच्चिदानन्द–स्वरूपः
स्वप्रकाशः सर्वान्तर्यामी चिदाकाश–रूपोऽस्मीति
दृढनिश्चय–रूपापरोक्ष–ज्ञानवान् जीवन्मुक्तः ॥

Nanu jīvanmuktaḥ kaḥ? Yathā deho'yaṁ puruṣo'haṁ brāhmaṇo'ham śūdro'ham asmīti dṛḍha-niścayaḥ tathā nāhaṁ brāhmaṇo na śudro na puruṣaḥ kiṁtu asangaḥ saccidānanda-svarūpaḥ svaprakāśaḥ sarvāntaryāmī cidākāśa-rūpo'smīti dṛḍha-niścaya-rūpa-aparokṣa-jñānavān jīvanmuktaḥ.

Nanu jīvanmuktaḥ kaḥ? Now, who is 'liberated-in-life'? *Yathā* just as *dṛḍha-niścayaḥ* there is the firm conviction that *deho'yaṁ asmi* 'I am the body' *puruṣo'haṁ* 'I am a man' *brāhmaṇo'ham* 'I am a Brahmin' *śūdro'ham* 'I am a Sūdra' *iti tathā* similarly *dṛḍha-niścaya-rūpa* the firm conviction of the form of *nāhaṁ brāhmaṇo* 'I am not a Brahmin' *na śudro* 'I am not a Sūdra' *na puruṣaḥ* 'I am not a man' *kiṁtu* but *asangaḥ* unattached *svarūpaḥ* of the nature of *saccidānanda* existence-knowledge-bliss *svaprakāśaḥ* self-effulgent *sarvāntaryāmī* all-pervading *cidākāśa-rūpo'smīti* of the form of space *dṛḍha-niścaya-rūpa-aparokṣa-jñānavān* (a person who has) such immediate knowledge is *jīvanmuktaḥ* the liberated-in-life.

Now who is the 'liberated-in-life'? Just as one has the firm conviction that 'I am the body', 'I am a man', 'I am a brahmin', 'I am a Sūdra', etc, so also he who has the firm conviction born of immediate knowledge that 'I am not a Brahmin', 'I am not a Sūdra', 'I am not a man', etc, but am the unattached all-pervasive Self of the form of space itself, is the liberated-in-life.

True Knowledge

The explanation of *jīvanmukti* given in *Tattvabodha* is simple yet gripping. Just as an ignorant person has attachment for his body and mind, the person of Self-knowledge will have attachment for his Self or Brahman. Just as an ignorant person thinks he is a brāhmaṇa or a man or a woman, the enlightened soul thinks that he is not a brāhmaṇa, not a man or a woman, not the body, not the mind, and so on. This firm conviction comes after the attainment of knowledge.

Sūta Samhitā (24, 25) says: 'He who knows that the whole universe has been projected in Me through *māyā* becomes an *ativarṇāśramin* or one who has transcended the four stages of life.'

The *Pañcadaṣī* (7.85) says: 'The difference between jiva and Brahman is due to the presence or the absence of the conditioning medium of the inner organ (*antaḥkaraṇa*)—which is the mind, intellect, etc. Otherwise the two are identical.'

What happens when one attains Self-knowledge is told beautifully in the same work (1.64): 'The direct realization of the knowledge of the Self, obtained from the guru's teaching, is like the scorching sun that dispels the darkness of ignorance, which is the root of misery and rebirth.'

Jīvanmukti-viveka

But for a few Advaitic scholars, almost all are agreed about *jīvanmukti.* Vidyāraṇya, a saint of the 14th century, has written a book on this subject, titled *Jīvanmukti viveka*.

In this great work, the author deals with all the points one has to think of about the question. Vidyāraṇya quotes authorities on the subject profusely and discusses the proofs of the existence of *jīvanmukti.* He then discusses the aspect of *prārabdha* karma, that karma which has begun to fructify (which we shall discuss soon). The next topic of discussion is the mind: whether the mind dissolves or remains after the attainment of liberation. The next consideration of Vidyāraṇya is the uses of the idea of *jīvanmukti*. Finally, post-*jīvanmukti* situation is discussed.

He who knows Brahman becomes Brahman—ब्रह्मवेद ब्रह्मैव भवति (*Muṇḍaka Upaniṣad,* 3.2.1)—is the best example of the state attained by the knower of Brahman. Such an individual transcends all limitations, dualities, and sorrow. This is the blessed state we all should have been in. But the world is so much in us that it entangles us unnecessarily to *māyā*.

References:

1. *Bṛhadāraṇyaka Upaniṣad,* 4.4.7
2. *Gospel,* p. 538)
3. Gospel, p. 151

Chapter 46

REMOVAL OF IGNORANCE

Attaining Self-Knowledge

We have come a long way in our discussion on the system of Advaita Vedanta. From bondage to liberation, the author of *Tattvabodha* has taken us a full circle. Having discussed liberation in life and the qualifications of a liberated individual, this section deals with how one becomes illumined.

Knowledge is of two types: direct (*aparokṣa*) and indirect (*parokṣa*). What we learn from others, books, and so on is indirect, but what we experience ourselves is direct. Direct knowledge is scientific, and that is the spirit of the age.

Swami Vivekananda as young Narendra was ever eager to know the Truth. He went to every great person of his times to ask the same question he had: 'Have you seen god?' Nobody replied properly. At last he came to Sri Ramakrishna. Swamiji tells about his experience: 'I crept near him and asked him the question which I had asked so often: "Have you seen God, sir?" "Yes, I see Him just as I see you here, only in a much intenser sense." "God can be realized," he went on; "one can see and talk to Him as I am seeing and talking to you. But who cares? People shed torrents of tears for their wife and children, for wealth or property, but who does so for the sake of God? If one weeps sincerely for Him, He surely manifests Himself" That impressed me at once. For the first time I found a man who dared to say that he had seen God, that religion was a reality to be felt, to be sensed in an infinitely more intense way than we can sense the world. As I heard these things from his lips, I could not but believe that he was saying them not like an ordinary preacher, but from the depths of his own realizations.'[1]

Experience, the Best Teacher

Swami Vivekananda was the only teacher, perhaps, to boldly state that we need not believe even if our guru said something unless we tested it. Such boldness is never heard of. Isn't this true rationality? Swami Vivekananda always stressed personal experience.

Swami Vivekananda says: 'Therefore it is certain that you won't be able to know the Atman, the Essence of Intelligence, through the mind. You have to go beyond the mind—for only the Atman exists there—there the object of knowledge becomes the same as the instrument of knowledge. The knower, knowledge, and the instrument of knowledge become one and the same. It is therefore that the Shruti says, "विज्ञातारमरे केन विजानीयात्— through what are you to know the Eternal Subject?" The real fact is that there is a state beyond the conscious plane, where there is no duality of the knower, knowledge, and the instrument of knowledge etc. When the mind is merged, that state is perceived. I say it is "perceived," because there is no other word to express that state. Language cannot express that state.

Shankaracharya has styled it "Transcendent Perception" (*Aparokṣānubhūti*). Even after that transcendent perception Avataras descend to the relative plane and give glimpses of that—therefore it is said that the Vedas and other scriptures have originated from the perception of Seers. The case of ordinary Jivas is like that of the salt-doll which attempting to sound the depths of the ocean melted into it. Do you see? The sum and substance of it is—you have only got to know that you are Eternal Brahman.'[2]

Tattvabodha now explains what happens in liberation:

ब्रह्मैवाहमस्मीत्यपरोक्ष-ज्ञानेन निखिल-कर्म-बन्ध-
विनिर्मुक्तः स्यात् ॥

Brahmaivāham asmi iti aparokṣa jñānena nikhila-karma-bandha vinirmuktaḥ syāt.

Aparokṣa jñānena by the immediate knowledge that *Brahmaivāham asmi iti* I am Brahman Itself *nikhila-karma-bandha* all bondages of karma *vinirmuktaḥ syāt* becomes freed from.

By the immediate knowledge that 'I am Brahman Itself' one becomes freed from all bondages of karma.

Bondages of Karma

'We read in the Bhagavad Gita again and again that we must all work incessantly. All work is by nature composed of good and evil. We cannot do any work which will not do some good somewhere; there cannot be any work which will not cause some harm somewhere. …Good and evil will both have their results, will produce their Karma. Good action will entail upon us good effect; bad action, bad. But good and bad are both bondages of the soul. The solution reached in the Gita in regard to this bondage-producing nature of work is that, if we do not attach ourselves to the work we do, it will not have any binding effect on our soul. We shall try to understand what is meant by this "non-attachment" to work.

This is the one central idea in the Gita: work incessantly, but be not attached to it. Samskara can be translated very nearly by "inherent tendency". Using the simile of a lake for the mind, every ripple, every wave that rises in the mind, when it subsides, does not die out entirely, but leaves a mark and a future possibility of that wave coming out again. This mark, with the possibility of the wave reappearing, is what is called Samskara. Every work that we do, every movement of the body, every thought that we think, leaves such an impression on the mindstuff, and even when such impressions are not obvious on the surface, they are sufficiently strong to work beneath the surface, subconsciously. What we are every moment is determined by the sum total of these impressions on the mind. What I am just at this moment is the effect of the sum total of all the impressions of my past life. This is really what is meant by character; each man's character is determined by the sum total of these impressions. If good impressions prevail, the character becomes good; if bad, it becomes bad.'[3] 'Liberation means entire freedom—freedom from the bondage of good, as well as from the bondage of evil. A golden chain is as much a chain as an iron one.'[4]

In order to get rid of this bondage, we should overcome our tendency of doing bad, and then try to do good alone. The tendency to do good also is bypassed in time when the Self is attained.

Liberation comes only from knowledge of the Atman. This Self knowledge does not depend either on our works, or worship, or sadhana, or anything. This is made very clear by our ancient teachers. Self knowledge is revealed when the mind is pure. If karma has nothing at all to do in the higher stages of Advaita sadhana, why is karma discussed? What is karma? All these will be discussed in the next chapter.

References:

1. Life of Swami Vivekananda, Vol. 1, p. 77
2. Complete Works, Vol. 7, p. 142
3. Complete Works, Vol. 1, pp. 53-4
4. ibid., p. 55

Chapter 47

KARMA

Karma: Its Ideal

'Karma' means action. 'Karma' also means fruits of action in a general sense, though the word '*karma-phala* is the correct term. The modern concept of karma and that of traditional India are different. In the modern concept of work, we work and earn money. There ends the matter. There is no other condition or sentiment involved. It is all physical.

In the Indian concept of work, however, the whole thing is spiritual. Physical work and earning money too have a spiritual connotation. We earn, not for livelihood, but to serve God. Everything is deified. To understand the ideal, we must see the way ancient India thought of human life. All life is sacred, said the sages, and the goal of all is liberation or attainment of knowledge. Whether or not one is conscious of it, all are working towards liberation from limitations. Knowing the ideal perfectly well, the sages classified human beings into groups. This grouping is called the caste system. A lot of mud-slinging has taken place and is taking place on caste. Much of it is done as a reaction, and also owing to ignorance of the facts.

Swamiji On Caste

Swami Vivekananda saw during his time how reformers tried to cry down caste. He said that caste is a social custom and religion has nothing to do with it. But the reformers did not understand that. The problem is in confusing privileges with caste. Even today there is the question of privilege in India as it is in other countries. Will a company director

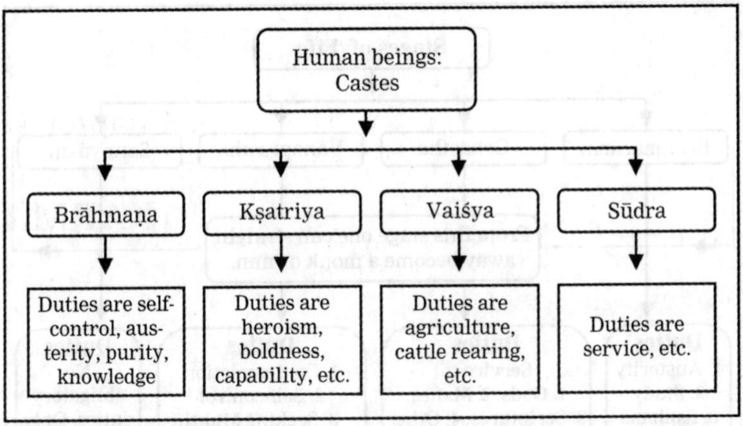

sit and eat with a sweeper or give him the same salary as he gets? So caste was a good system.

We shall quote Swamiji (3: 245): 'These conceptions of the Vedanta must come out, must remain not only in the forest, not only in the cave, but they must come out to work at the bar and the bench, in the pulpit, and in the cottage of the poor man, with the fishermen that are catching fish, and with the students that are studying. They call to every man, woman, and child whatever be their occupation, wherever they may be. And what is there to fear! How can the fishermen and all these carry out the ideals of the Upanishads?

'The way has been shown. It is infinite; religion is infinite, none can go beyond it; and whatever you do sincerely is good for you. Even the least thing well done brings marvellous results; therefore let everyone do what little he can. If the fisherman thinks that he is the Spirit, he will be a better fisherman; if the student thinks he is the Spirit, he will be a better student. If the lawyer thinks that he is the Spirit, he will be a better lawyer, and so on, and the result will be that the castes will remain for ever. It is in the nature of society to form itself into groups; and what will go will be these privileges.'

'Caste is a natural order; I can perform one duty in social life, and you another; you can govern a country, and

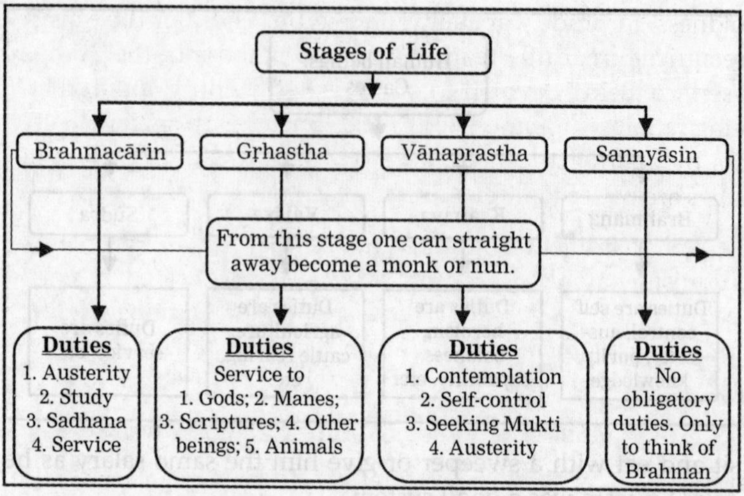

I can mend a pair of old shoes, but that is no reason why you are greater than I, for can you mend my shoes? Can I govern the country? I am clever in mending shoes, you are clever in reading Vedas, but that is no reason why you should trample on my head. Why if one commits murder should he be praised, and if another steals an apple why should he be hanged? This will have to go.

'Caste is good. That is the only natural way of solving life. Men must form themselves into groups, and you cannot get rid of that. Wherever you go, there will be caste. But that does not mean that there should be these privileges.'

What is Caste?

Hinduism divides human beings into four classes (*varṇas*) and four groups (*āśramas*): The four *varṇas* are *brāhmaṇa, kṣatriya, vaiśya,* and *śūdra*. Each group has certain obligatory duties. The *Bhagavad Gītā* (18. 46) gives the list of these obligatory duties of each class. 'The duties of the brāhmaṇas and others have been classified according to their respective tendencies. The natural duties of the brāhmaṇa are self-control, austerity, purity, forgiveness, straightforwardness, knowledge, and so on. The duties of the Kṣatriya are heroism, boldness, fortitude, capability, and so on. Those of the Vaiśya are agriculture, cattle-rearing, and trade. Those of the Śūdras is service. Being devoted to one's respective duty, the human being attains supreme good. The human being achieves success by adoring the Lord through his own duties. My own duties are better than those of others, though well performed.'

Apart from these duties for the four castes in general, Hinduism has also set apart specific duties for each stage of life. These stages are called *āśramas* or stations of life. The student, the householder, the retired person, and the renunciate are the four stages.

So karma directly depended on caste. Caste was a social division only and had little to do with religion.

Coming to the spiritual theory of karma, which concerns us here, our bondage and liberation are solely dependent on our actions. Our birth, life, suffering, death—everything depends on karma. So karma has meaning and can be controlled.

We shall use the question-answer method to discuss karma here. Swami Hariharānanda Araṇya has discussed karma brilliantly in his book on yoga.

1. What is Action and what are its Effects?

The constant activity of the *antaḥkaraṇa* or the inner

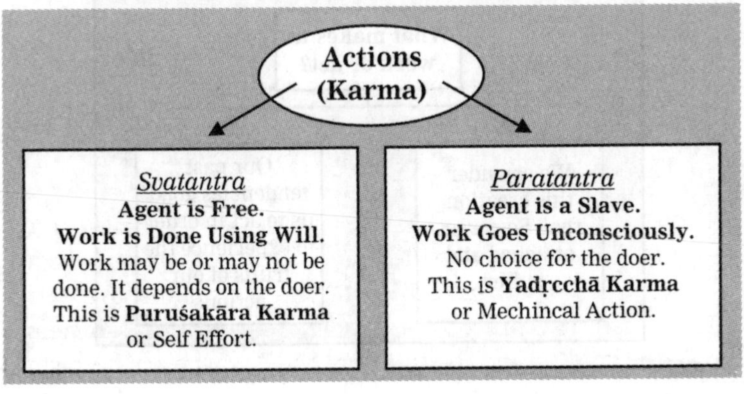

organ—the subtle body—with its expression through the gross body, is called karma. We have the mind, intellect, ego, memory, organs of action, sense organs, and life forces. All these 19 constituents function constantly, using the gross physical body as the instrument. Such actions are karma.

2. What are the two fundamental divisions of karma?

There are two types of actions: one done with knowledge and wilfully, and the other done without knowledge. Blood circulation goes on without our knowledge. But we lift a box with knowledge. This is the difference. We may or may not lift a box, but we apparently cannot stop our blood circulation wilfully. Thus there are two types of actions: where will (*icchā*) is involved—called *puruṣa-kāra;* where no will is involved—called *yadṛcchā*.

3. Let us forget actions which we cannot help doing. But why do we do wilful actions? What makes us work?

As the diagram indicates, we work for two reasons: (1) attachment for the world; or (2) to experience the fruits of our past deeds. But there is also a third reason: (3) the person seeking self-knowledge, performs selfless actions to purify himself. There is one more reason. (4) The enlightened person works for the good of the world.

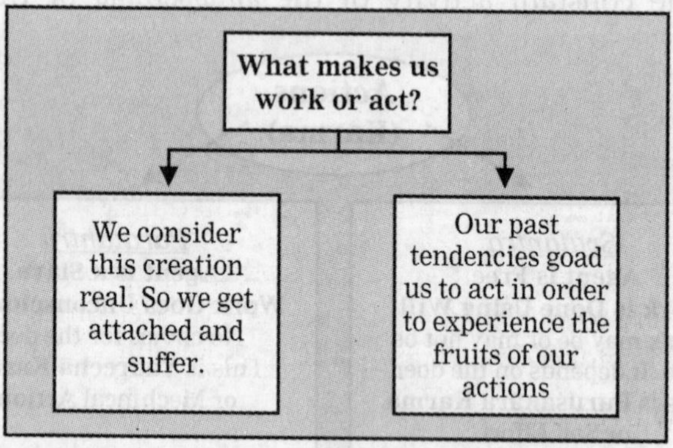

4. What is the process of the arousal of *puruṣakāra* or self-effort?

There are two instigators for the arousal of the desire to act.

A. Knowledge, which can be either born of memory or direct experience, leads to desire. Desire leads to determination that one must act. Determination leads to action. For example, if I have eaten a sweet yesterday, its memory brings its knowledge. Its pleasant taste makes me desire it again. Desire becomes strong and leads to the determination that I must eat it again. Then the action follows.

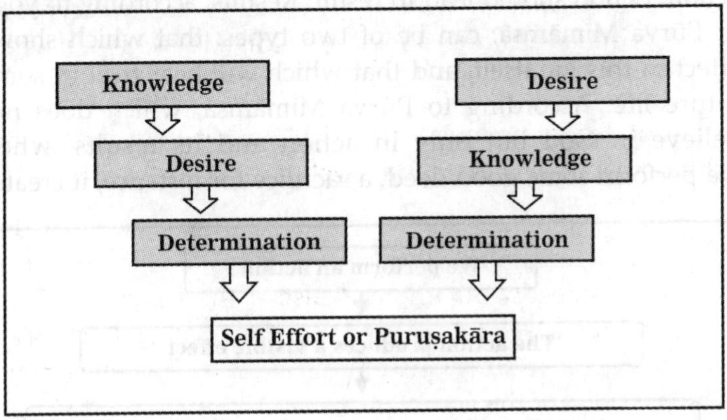

B. Desire may lead to knowledge. Knowledge in its turn may lead to determination, and determination may lead to action. For example, I may have the desire to know what a chocolate is. I procure it and eat it. I get the knowledge of it. Then the desire follows again and I may eat it again.

Two important points are to be noted here:

- Repeated desire leads to the formation of habit. I desire to smoke—and smoke. The desire comes again, and I smoke. Gradually, it becomes a habit.

- Even uncontrolled or mechanical actions (*yadṛcchā*) are, in the final analysis, Self Effort. Example:

Indian yogis can at will control their breathing. They can stop their heartbeat at will. They can enter underground and live there for days. So even breathing is self-effort, though unconscious.

5. What happens when we act—when self-effort is applied?

When we apply our self-effort, there is action (*karma*). Action leads to result (*karmaphala*).

Any action, from lifting a piece of paper to ruling an empire, needs self-effort according to Yoga. Self-effort leads to action. Action should lead to result. Results, according to yoga or Pūrva Mīmāṁsā, can be of two types: that which shows effect in this life itself, and that which will bear fruit in some future life. According to Pūrva Mīmāṁsā, which does not believe in God but only in action and its results, when we perform some good deed, a sacrifice for instance, it creates

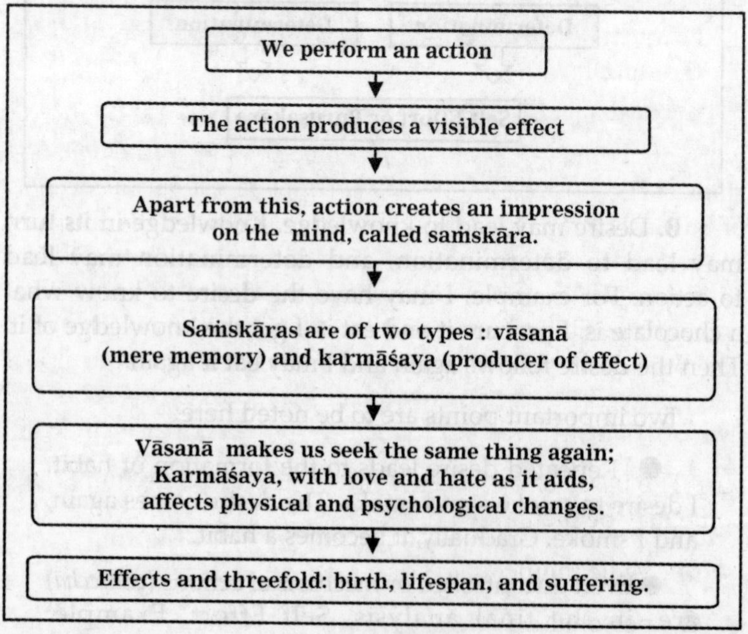

an *apūrva* bank balance of good effect. This will bear fruit either after death or after rebirth.

This implies two things: (a) That every action gives some fruit—good, bad, or neutral; and (b) there is rebirth. Indian sages did not concoct stories when they spoke about rebirth. They had to struggle very hard to arrive at such superb truths. Just as we cannot believe the rebirth theory at the very first instant, they too did not believe it. They had to strive much against accepting something which was naturally invisible, but true all right.

Rebirth is in the Vedas and Upaniṣads. In a glorious passage, the Bṛhadāraṇyaka Upaniṣad (4.4.3) says: 'तद्यथा तृणजलायुका तृणस्यान्तं गत्वा-अन्यमाक्रममाक्रम्यात्मानम् उपसंहरति एवं एव अयं आत्मा इदम् शरीरं निहत्याऽविद्यां गमयित्वाऽन्यम् आक्रममाक्रम्यात्मानमुपसंहरति, *tad-yathā tṛṇajalāyukā tṛṇasyāntaṁ gatvā*....' 'Just as a leech goes to the end of a blade of grass and, before relinquishing it, steps onto the next blade and then leaves the other behind, so also does the soul give up one body and take another, until it knows the Truth.' See p.267 in this book for the dualist's concept of rebirth.

In the *Bhagavadgītā* (2.22) it is said that the soul gives up worn out bodies and takes up fresh bodies just as they change clothes. Hinduism, Buddhism, Jainism, and even some schools of Sufism, believe in rebirth. The only objection to rebirth is, we cannot remember our past lives. To this, Swami Vivekananda gives a beautiful reply: 'Try and struggle, they would come up and you would be conscious even of your past life.' But he remarks elsewhere: 'Why, one life in the body is like a million years of confinement, and they want to make up the memory of many lives! Sufficient unto the day is the evil thereof!'

The bases of the sages' concept of rebirth are numerous. Some may be mentioned here:

- Vedic injunction;
- personal experience;

- inability to explain blindness or lameness at birth, for instance;
- evidence of the continuity of life;
- meaningfulness of life seen in this theory. Our view of life is very, very limited, like seeing a still photograph and guessing a whole movie.

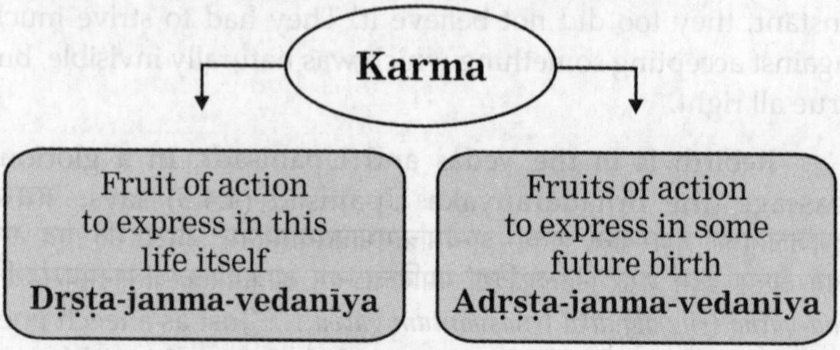

So rebirth explains the whys and why nots of numerous 'injustice' questions. 'Why should the Lord be unjust to me?' 'Why should he punish me so, even though I am a devotee?' 'Why are others happy while I alone am suffering?' All these questions can be answered only by the theory of rebirth. 'As we sow, so we reap,' is an immortal saying, true for all time to come. Everyone—the law, people, society—may forgive us our sins, but our conscience will not. It will definitely bear fruit one day or other. If I hurt, I am hurt. If I do good, I am blessed.

6. How many types of fruits of actions are there?

There are four types of fruits of action: good, bad, mixed, and neutral. Good fruits are called *śukla-phalas*; bad fruits are called *kṛṣṇa-phalas;* mixed fruits are called *śukla-kṛṣṇa-phalas*; finally, neutral ones are called *aśukla-kṛṣṇa-phalas*. This is according to Hariharānanda Aranya.

6. When do we reap the fruits of our actions?

We have already mentioned that there are two ways in which the fruits of action distribute themselves: either they bear fruit in this life itself, or they bear fruit in some future occasion.

7. How do we reap the fruits of actions on some future time?

In the *Gītā* (3.9-16), there is a description of the cosmic sacrifice. The whole cosmos is a huge sacrifice—work-result, result-work. Brahman is the source of the Vedas, Karma is born in the Vedas, sacrifice is born of karma, rain comes from sacrifice, food comes from rains, living beings are born of food. This is the eternal cycle of sacrifice going on. This cycle indicates that actions yield fruits. We are like little wheels within the cosmic wheel. When we work, we contribute a little to the cosmic sacrifice. And fruits have to come.

In order that work bear fruit on some future occasion, *karma-phalas* need the aid of love (*rāga*) and hate (*dveṣa*). With the activity of these two, the 'store' is called the *karmāśaya* or, in our terms, the unconscious shows effects. So the process is like this:

Any action of the subtle body—mind, sensory, motor, life force and other organs included—leaves an impression behind. If I see a flower, I can remember it five minutes later. Anything we do creates an impression. These impressions are called *samskāras*. These *samskāras* are of two types: (a) that which is of the nature of memory alone is called *vāsanā*; and (b) that which affects changes in the body-mind complex according to the fruits is called *karmāśaya*.

Vāsanās are apparently harmless because they only awaken memory. But they are the worst enemies of our lives. How? Suppose I eat a sweet. An impression is created in the mind: a *vāsanā*, as mere memory of the sweetness of the sweet, and a *karmāśaya*, as the producer of happiness, sorrow, or nothing. *Karmāśaya* awakens memory, so that it can produce the effect of the fruit of action—happiness, sorrow, etc. This *vāsanā* brings back the sweet to mind repeatedly. Memory is awakened repeatedly. That is all it does. If my will-power is strong, I resist the temptation to try the sweet again. If I am weak, I try it again and again. Thus it becomes a habit. Further, I get angry with those who stop me. That creates another *karmāśaya*. In this way, I am caught in the vortex of karma because love and hate reactions get involved.

Karmāśaya collects the impressions of good, bad, or neutral effects that actions produce. When we are about to die, they all come together, and create a full picture of what life is to be in the next birth. The *karmāśaya* then takes life out of this body and puts it in a place suitable to the actions performed. This is according to Yoga. According to Vedanta, there is God who is the distributor of the fruits of action.

Vāsanās are eternal. We have three important divisions of *vāsanās*: *jāti* or birth-*vāsanās; āyus* or lifespan-*vāsanās;* and *bhoga* or suffering/enjoyment-*vāsanās*. Hence we wish to be born, to live a long life, and not to die. Hence we wish to enjoy. All the countless births our soul has taken have been recorded in the mind.

Karmāśaya is more complex. If I eat a sweet, it creates a pleasant impression. If I eat it the second time, the previous experience is removed, and the later one is put in. One vital point is, whenever there is either love or hate (*raga* or *dveṣa*) involved, then alone the *karmāśaya* is stored. If there is no desire or aversion, love or hate, etc, there is no *karmāśaya*. Each time the action is performed in a slightly different manner, the reaction shown is in a slightly different manner, and the fruit too will be different. All this is collected afresh in the mind. Our present birth, therefore, is largely due to the previous birth.

Thus we have seen how action leads to fruits, how fruits lead to birth, lifespan, and enjoyment or suffering.

8. Is human life fatalistic then?

Our present birth, actions, suffering, enjoyment, lifespan,

death, all have been decided by our past lives. This is what karma theory says. Then, are we helpless puppets in the hands of our karmas?

Not at all! Read Swami Vivekananda: 'The doctrine of reincarnation asserts the freedom of the soul. Suppose there was an absolute beginning. Then the whole burden of this impurity in man falls upon God. The all-merciful Father responsible for the sins of the world! If sin comes in this way, why should one suffer more than another? Why such partiality, if it comes from an all-merciful God? Why are millions trampled underfoot? Why do people starve who never did anything to cause it? Who is responsible? If they had no hand in it, surely, God would be responsible. Therefore the better explanation is that one is responsible for the miseries one suffers. If I set the wheel in motion, I am responsible for the result. And if I can bring misery, I can also stop it. It necessarily follows that we are free. There is no such thing as fate. There is nothing to compel us. What we have done, that we can undo.'[1]

That precisely is the meaning of self-effort or *puruṣakāra*.

9. How does Karma lead to liberation?

In his *Karma Yoga* Swamiji has said that by performing actions our character is formed. That is, the hardships involved, blows we receive, knowledge we acquire--all this will lead us to purify our minds. While in the path of karma the mind becomes purified, the purified mind, purified intellect and the Self become one and the same (says Sri Ramakrishna). When the upper layers of the lake are crystal clear, we see the bottom. So also we see the Self through the purified mind, says Swamiji. So for him karma is a path to liberation.

According to Advaita, however, karma does *not* lead to *mukti* or liberation directly. Karma can never bring Self-knowledge because Self-knowledge is not something acquired: it is already there. We cannot work out our liberation or knowledge. It is not something that is earned. It is already there. What karma does is, it takes us to the path of knowledge.

Karma yoga is a step to Jñāna Yoga. The Advaitin gives a low place for karma in the process of spiritual development. Yet Advaita accepts karma as a vital factor in bondage and liberation. How is that?

We are bound because of ignorance. Ignorance goads us to seek the things of the world. We work towards seeking happiness and entangle ourselves to the world. Swamiji gives the example of a bullock tied to an oil mill of olden days: 'The bullock in the oil-mill never reaches the wisp of hay tied in front of him, he only grinds out the oil. So we chase the will-o'-the-wisp of happiness that always eludes us, and we only grind nature's mill, then die, merely to begin again. ...When man finds that all search for happiness in matter is nonsense, then religion begins. All human knowledge is but a part of religion.'[2]

After struggling for ages, we awaken to the truth that life is nothing but *māyā*. We begin to strive for knowledge. So karma, in a way, negatively helps us to know the Truth.

Secondly, karma also takes us to *jñāna* or knowledge. According to Śaṁkara, karmayoga or selfless action is the first stage of sadhana. This leads to purification of mind. Then comes *jñāna yoga* the path of self-knowledge.

We may note in passing that it was Swamiji who, for the first time perhaps, said that karmayoga can lead us directly to realization.

10. How many types of *karmaphala* are there?

We have seen that when we perform some action, it leaves an impression, and that this impression may bear fruit now or later. Depending upon the time of its fruition, *karmaphalas* have been divided into three broad classes: that which is bearing fruit now (*prārabdha*), that which is stored (*sañcita*) and those which will be performed in the future (*āgāmī*). The first one

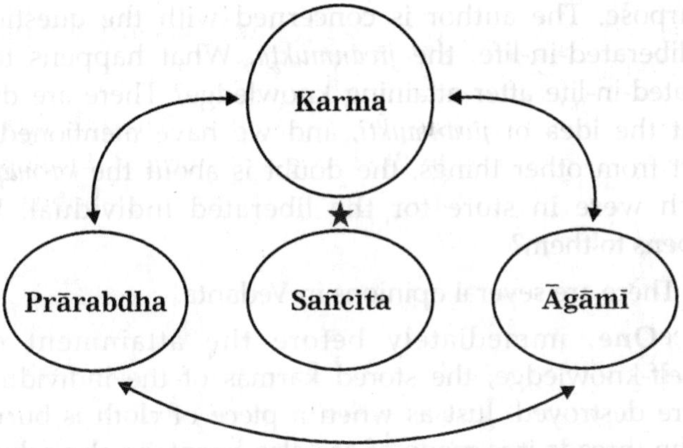

alone is *dṛṣṭa-janma-vedanīya*—the fruition is experienced in this life. *Sañcita* are stored-up fruits of action, the *karmāśaya,* which may or may not bear fruit in this life. *Āgāmī* are actions yet to be performed.

This will be dealt with in the next chapter.

कर्माणि कतिविधानि सन्तीति चेत, आगामि–सञ्चित–प्रारब्ध–भेदेन त्रिविधानि सन्ति ॥

Karmāṇi katividhāni santīti cet, āgāmi-sañcita-prārabdha-bhedena trividhāni santi.

Karmāṇi the fruits of action or karmas *katividhāni* are of how many types *santīti cet* if it is asked, *trividhāni santi* they are divided into three; *āgāmī-sañcita-prārabdha-bhedena Āgāmī, sañcita,* and *prārabdha.*

If one asks as to how many types are the fruits of action divided, (the answer is,) they are divided into three types: that which should yield fruit in the future, that which is stored, and that which has begun to yield fruit.

The author of *Tattvabodha* has taken up a new topic altogether. After he discussed the attainment of Brahman and *jīvanmukti,* he begins discussion on karma. This is done with a purpose. The author is concerned with the question of the liberated-in-life, the *jīvanmukta*. What happens to the liberated-in-life after attaining knowledge? There are doubts about the idea of *jīvanmukti*, and we have mentioned this. Apart from other things, the doubt is about the *karmaphalas* which were in store for the liberated individual. What happens to them?

There are several opinions in Vedanta.

One, immediately before the attainment of Self-knowledge, the stored karmas of the individual are destroyed. Just as when a piece of cloth is burnt the threads it is made of are also burnt, so also when ignorance goes, the effects of ignorance—mind, memory, past impressions—all are destroyed.

Two, the stored fruits of actions alone are destroyed, while other fruits remain. As for instance, that which has begun to bear fruit will continue to bear fruit. So far as future actions and their fruits are concerned, if at all the *jñāni* does actions after attaining knowledge, the effects of his good deeds go to his disciples, while the effects of his bad deeds (if any) go to those who insult and injure him.

Three, the *jñāni* sees everything as Brahman, lives and moves in Brahman. For us he is in a body, eating, working, and so on. What he is actually doing he alone knows. So though the ignorant feel that the person of knowledge is functioning, the *jñāni* will be immersed in the bliss of Brahman. He has no future or past actions. Those past deeds which have begun to bear fruit too are nothing for him. Whose body? Whose karmas? Whether the body remains or goes are of little consequence to him.

Four, according to Sri Ramakrishna, ordinarily a person gives up his body after 21 days of attainment of Self-knowledge. However, if a *jñāni* continues to live, he lives like a *paramahamsa*, or with a semblance of ego, or for the good of the world.

Five, a new concept of vijñāni has been introduced with Sri Ramakrishna's advent. We have discussed that earlier.

We have discussed the meaning and effect of karma above. For the ignorant millions, karma certainly has its effects. Yet, according to Sri Ramakrishna, Holy Mother, and Swami Vivekananda, karma will not have any effect for the devotee, if he or she ardently prays to God. God is beyond all rules and regulations. He can change rules according to his sweet will. This, again, is a new development in Indian spiritual thought. The ordinary idea was that we should suffer for our evil actions. Holy Mother and Sri Ramakrishna stress that if we earnestly pray, practise japa, perform good deeds, and seek God's grace, the evil karmas are countered or even nullified.

Even Vedanta asserts that God is the distributor of the fruits of action. In the *Brahma Sūtras* commentary (3.2.39), there is a discussion about the fruits of action. The doubt is raised as to who is the distributor of the fruits. The Advaitn answers that it is God who does this. If God is not the controller, then our *karma-phalas* cannot bear fruit of themselves. Because they are inert. The Pūrva Mīmāmsakas, those who believe in the Vedas as teaching sacrifices only, say that something called *apūrva* (unseen power) is created through the works, which lead the soul either to heaven or hell. But that is negated because the Upaniṣads, the standard references in such matters, themselves assert that God is the distributor of the fruits of action. 'That great birthless Self is the bestower of the food all round and the giver of wealth,' says the *Bṛhadāraṇyaka Upaniṣad* (4.4.24).

So while the ordinary, ignorant millions suffer from the fruits of their actions and go round and round, the *jñāni* and the *bhakta* make use of them to rise higher and higher in life.

References:

1. Complete Works, Vol. 1, p. 320
2. Complete Works, Vol. 7, pp. 103-4

Chapter 48

KARMA YET TO BE DONE

Āgāmī Karma

What we are is because of our past actions. That simply means that what we shall be depends upon our present actions. If we wish to be good and great, noble and divine, we should perform such actions. This is the greatness of Hinduism—it gives tremendous scope for improvement. People unfortunately think that Hinduism is a fatalistic religion. They do not know. There are some religions which damn those who have sinned to hell—eternal damnation. This is all unthinkable in Hinduism. Who is a sinner?—asks Hinduism. Everyone is the Atman. Sins, mistakes, etc, are all superficial coverings—dust covering the mirror. We have the capacity to wipe that dust out. This gives great hope for us mortals.

In order to attain knowledge, we need the help of work. the *Brahma Sūtras* (3.4.24), says that 'the Upaniṣads being our authority, we say that activities are necessary.' Knowledge needs the help of sacrifices because the scriptures say that duties help in burning away past sins. Even after enlightenment, says the *Gītā*, royal sages like Janaka performed actions. Their actions were for the good of the world.

For those who are seeking Self-knowledge, scriptures prescribe noble actions like worship, meditation, service, and so on. According to the scriptures, work can be classified into five types:

1. Desire-born actions are *Kāmya Karmas.*

These are the works all human beings perform day and

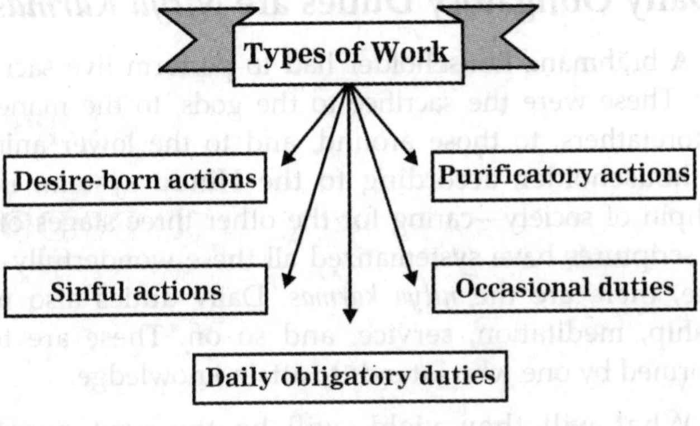

night. We work because we can earn money, merit, and so on. By earning merit, we know we shall get more money and more enjoyment. According to our scriptures, by performing sacrifices like *agniṣṭoma*, the soul will go to heaven. Owing to the force of one's merits, the soul can also become a god—even Indra, the king of the gods. Indra, Varuṇa, and others are offices. But after the fruits of actions are exhausted, the soul lands back into lower positions. Therefore our scriptures warn time and again that we should never perform desire-born actions. There may be momentary joy but the final result is endless misery.

2. Sinful Actions are *Niśiddha Karmas*

No sane individual advises us to perform sinful acts. In spite of ourselves, we commit sinful deeds and suffer. Everyone else may excuse us, but not our nervous system. They keep bothering us. According to some religions, the sinner is eternally damned. Not so in Hinduism or Vedanta. No one is condemned or damned here. According to Sri Ramakrishna, sins are nothing but the mountain of cotton. When we strike a match, off it goes. The 'match' is the name of the Lord or spiritual practice. So sins are not a big hurdle for a spiritual aspirant. But an aspirant seeking knowledge should by all means avoid committing sins.

3. Daily Obligatory Duties are *Nitya Karmas*.

A brāhmaṇa householder had to perform five sacrifices daily. These were the sacrifice to the gods, to the manes, to the forefathers, to those around, and to the lower animals. The householder, according to the Hindu system, is the lynchpin of society—caring for the other three stages of life. Our scriptures have systematized all these wonderfully well. These, then, are the *nitya karmas*. Daily duties also mean worship, meditation, service, and so on. These are to be performed by one who intends to attain knowledge.

What will they yield, will be the next question. According to all the scriptures, *nitya karma* will not give any fruit; but their purify the mind. But their non-performance will make us incur bad karma.

4. Occasional Duties are *Naimittika Karmas*.

Occasionally, certain responsibilities fall upon us. They have to be performed. Such duties are like the performance of some festival. They too will purify the mind.

5. Purificatory Actions are *Prāyaścitta Karmas*.

Knowingly or unknowingly, we commit errors in life. These are the sins. They have to be atoned. Scriptures have various rules of atonement. By performing them, we become freed from sins.

These are the five duties of every aspirant. We have been discussing the fit aspirant since the beginning of this book. He who follows the principles laid down in the performance or non-performance of these duties is a fit aspirant. These actions are not meant for the person of knowledge. The person who has attained knowledge is beyond rules and regulations.

The Person of Knowledge

Does a person who has attained knowledge work? Swami Vivekananda says: 'Great men like Avataras, in coming back

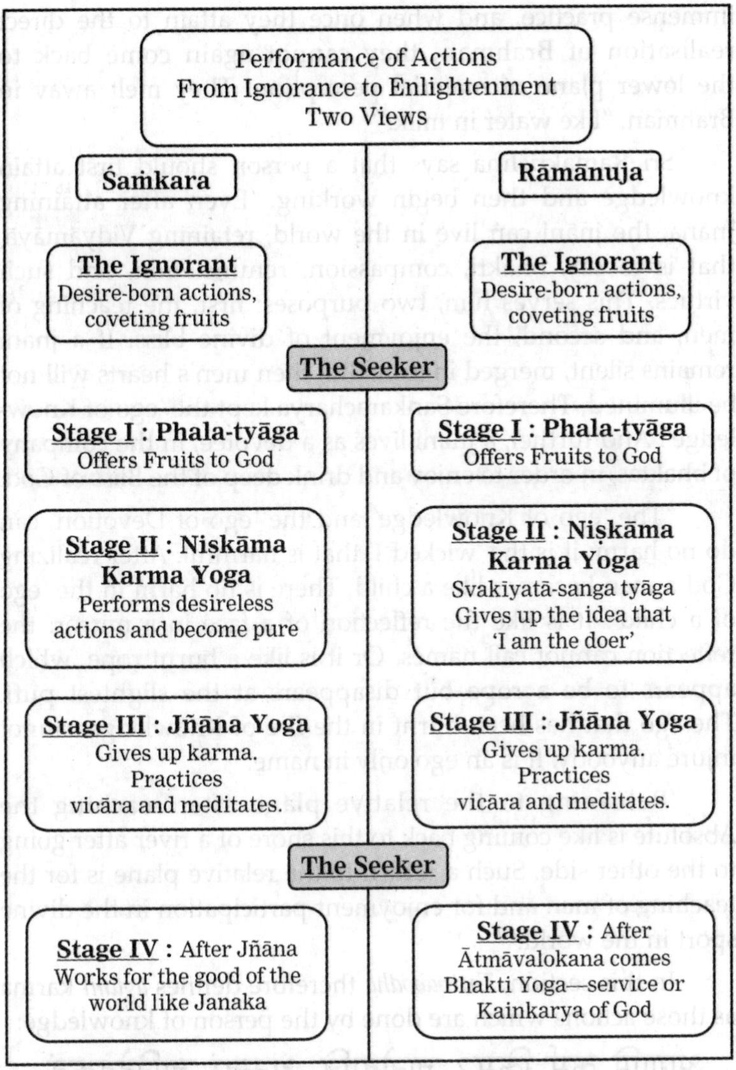

from Samadhi to the realm of "I" and "mine", first experience the unmanifest Nāda, which by degrees grows distinct and appears as Om, and then from Omkara, the subtle form of the universe as a mass of ideas becomes experienced, and last, the material universe comes into perception. But ordinary Sadhakas somehow reach beyond Nāda through immense practice, and when once they attain to the direct realisation of Brahman, they cannot again come back to the lower plane of material perception. They melt away in Brahman, "like water in milk."'[1]

Sri Ramakrishna says that a person should first attain knowledge and then begin working. 'Even after attaining Jnāna, the jnāni can live in the world, retaining Vidyāmāyā, that is to say, bhakti, compassion, renunciation, and such virtues. This serves him, two purposes: first, the teaching of men, and second, the enjoyment of divine bliss. If a jnani remains silent, merged in samadhi, then men's hearts will not be illumined. Therefore Sankaracharya kept the 'ego of Knowledge'. And further, a jnani lives as a devotee, in the company of bhaktas, in order to enjoy and drink deep of the Bliss of God.

"The 'ego of Knowledge' and the 'ego of Devotion' can do no harm; it is the 'wicked I' that is harmful. After realizing God a man becomes like a child. There is no harm in the 'ego of a child'. It is like the reflection of a face in a mirror: the reflection cannot call names. Or it is like a burnt rope, which appears to be a rope but disappears at the slightest puff. The ego that has been burnt in the fire of Knowledge cannot injure anybody. It is an ego only in name.

'Returning to the relative plane after reaching the Absolute is like coming back to this shore of a river after going to the other side. Such a return to the relative plane is for the teaching of men and for enjoyment-participation in the divine sport in the world."[2]

In this section, *Tattvabodha* therefore defines *āgāmi* karma as those actions which are done by the person of knowledge:

आगामि कर्म किम्? ज्ञानोत्पत्ति-अनन्तरं ज्ञानिदेहकृतं
पुण्यपाप-रूपम् कर्म यदस्ति तदागामी इति
अभिधीयते ॥

Āgāmī karma kim? Jñānotpatti-anantaraṁ jñānideha-kṛtam puṇya-pāpa-rūpam karma yadasti tadāgāmī iti abhidhīyate.

Āgāmī karma kim? What is *Āgāmī* karma? *Jñānotpatti-anantaraṁ* after the awakening of Knowledge *jñānideha-kṛtam* that which is done by the body of the person of knowledge *karma puṇya-pāpa-rūpam* actions of the form of sin and virtue *yadasti* whatever are there *tadāgāmī iti abhidhīyate* that is called *āgāmī* .

What is future karma? Those actions which are done by the body of a person of knowledge after the awakening of Self-knowledge—both good and bad—are called future actions.

Sri Ramakrishna says: "A man may keep this ego even after attaining samadhi. Such a man feels either that he is a servant of God or that he is a lover of God. Sankaracharya retained the 'ego of knowledge' to teach men spiritual life. The 'servant-ego', the 'knowledge ego', or the 'devotee ego' may be called the 'ripe ego'. It is different from the 'unripe ego', which makes one feel: 'I am the doer. I am the son of a wealthy man. I am learned. I am rich. How dare anyone slight me?' A man with an 'unripe ego' cherishes such ideas."[3]

'After realizing God, some souls perform work in order to teach men. Janaka, Narada, and others like them, belong to this group. But one must possess power in order to be able to teach others. The sages of old were busy attaining knowledge for themselves. But teachers like Narada went about doing good to others. They were real heroes.'[4]

'After attaining Knowledge one cannot do much work.'[5]

References:

1. Complete Works, Vol. 6, p. 499
2. Gospel, p. 860
3. Gospel, p. 860
4. Gospel, p. 857
5. Gospel, p. 791

Chapter 49

KARMA THAT IS STORED

Regarding how one should live in this world after attaining knowledge, Sri Ramakrishna says: 'First he should realize God. Then "he can swim in a sea of slander and not be stained." After realizing God, a man can live in the world like a mudfish. The world he lives in after attaining God is the world of vidyā. In it he sees neither woman nor gold. He finds there only devotion, devotee, and God.'[1]

Can the *jñāni* get attached to the world? Sri Ramakrishna says: 'A man is liberated after attaining Knowledge, after realizing God. For him there is no further coming back to earth. If a boiled paddy-grain is sown, it doesn't sprout. Just so, if a man is boiled by the fire of Knowledge, he cannot take part any more in the play of creation; he cannot lead a worldly life, for he has no attachment to 'woman and gold'. What will you gain by sowing boiled paddy?'[2]

Sri Ramakrishna is emphatic in saying again and again that 'A man may lead the life of a householder after attaining Knowledge. But he must attain Knowledge first.'[3]

Swami Vivekananda says: 'Religion is to be realised, not only heard; it is not in learning some doctrine like a parrot. Neither is it mere intellectual assent—that is nothing; but it must come into us. Ay, and therefore the greatest proof that we have of the existence of a God is not because our reason says so, but because God has been seen by the ancients as well as by the moderns. We believe in the soul not only because there are good reasons to prove its existence, but, above all, because there have been in the past thousands in India, there are still many who have realised, and there will be thousands in the future who will realise and see their own souls. And there is no salvation for man until he sees God, realises his own soul.

'Therefore, above all, let us understand this, and the more we understand it the less we shall have of sectarianism in India, for it is only that man who has realised God and seen Him, who is religious. In him the knots have been cut asunder, in him alone the doubts have subsided; he alone has become free from the fruits of action who has seen Him who is nearest of the near and farthest of the far.'[4]

सञ्चितं कर्म किम्? अनन्त-कोटि-जन्मानां बीजभूतम्
सत्कर्म जातं पूर्वजातं तिष्ठति तत सञ्चितं ज्ञेयम् ॥

sañcitaṁ karma kim? Ananta-koṭi-janmanāṁ bīja-bhūtam
satkarma jātaṁ pūrva-jātaṁ tiṣṭati tat sañcitaṁ jñeyam.

sañcitaṁ karma kim? What is *sañcita*? *Ananta-koṭi-janmanāṁ* Of infinite number of births *bīja-bhūtam* of seed-form *satkarma jātaṁ* born of good actions *pūrva-jātaṁ* born before *tiṣṭati* remains *tat* that *sañcitaṁ* stored *jñeyam* should be known.

What is *sañcita karma*? That which remains since infinite number of births in seed form, and are born of good actions are called *sañcita* fruits of action.

The fundamental problem with life is the *sañcita karma*—the bank holding our account. We suffer endless miseries, yet consider we are happy, because of the bank account—our own past deeds. Though *Tattvabodha* is dealing with the enlightened soul and his or her actions and results of actions, we have discussed with the ordinary mortals too in view. For us, the seeking people, *sañcita karma* is a real problem.

There are two ways out: 'either do not work, or give up fruits of work.' The first one we cannot do because, as Śrī

Kṛṣṇa says in the *Bhagavad Gītā* (3.5), no body can remain even for a moment without doing anything. Owing to the force of Prakṛti, everyone will have to work always. So the second way is the best. This is giving up the fruits of action. We perform actions because we want enjoyment. But enjoyments elude us always.

Swami Vivekananda says: 'All thought of obtaining return for the work we do hinders our spiritual progress; nay, in the end it brings misery. There is another way in which this idea of mercy and selfless charity can be put into practice; that is, by looking upon work as "worship" in case we believe in a Personal God. Here we give up all the fruits of our work unto the Lord, and worshipping Him thus, we have no right to expect anything from mankind for the work we do. ... The selfless and unattached man may live in the very heart of a crowded and sinful city; he will not be touched by sin.'[5]

True enjoyment is only in the Atman declare the scriptures. To attain that, saints say, we should first of all perform *karma yoga*, the yoga of surrendering the fruits of our actions. So this is the best means of overcoming sorrow.

Swami Vivekananda says:

> Even the lowest forms of work are not to be despised. Let the man, who knows no better, work for selfish ends, for name and fame; but everyone should always try to get towards higher and higher motives and to understand them. "To work we have the right, but not to the fruits thereof." Leave the fruits alone. Why care for results?... If you want to do a great or a good work, do not trouble to think what the result will be.[6]

In order that our bank balance may not accumulate adversely, the only way is to perform selfless action. But initially it is not possible. Swami Vivekananda gives us both the ideal and the practice of *karma yoga*.

'The ideal man is he who, in the midst of the greatest silence and solitude, finds the intensest activity, and in the midst of the intensest activity finds the silence and solitude of the desert. He has learnt the secret of restraint, he has controlled himself. He goes through the streets of a big city with all its traffic, and his mind is as calm as if he were in a cave, where not a sound could reach him; and he is intensely working all the time. That is the ideal of Karma-Yoga, and if you have attained to that you have really learnt the secret of work.

But we have to begin from the beginning, to take up the works as they come to us and slowly make ourselves more unselfish every day. We must do the work and find out the motive power that prompts us; and, almost without exception, in the first years, we shall find that our motives are always selfish; but gradually this selfishness will melt by persistence, till at last will come the time when we shall be able to do really unselfish work.'[7]

Through unselfish work, there will be no accumulation of *sañcita*, our minds will become purified, and we shall ardently seek the Highest. We quote from the *Pañcadaśī* (10.6,7).

'He who thinks "I am" is the agent. Mind is his instrument of action, and the actions of the mind are two types of modifications in succession, internal and external. The internal modification makes him the agent, while the external modification assumes the form of "this". It reveals to him the external things.'

References:

1. Gospel, p. 757
2. Gospel, p. 668
3. Gospel, p. 368
4. Complete Works, Vol. 3, p. 378
5. Complete Works, Vol. 1, p. 60
6. Complete Works, Vol. 1, pp. 33-4
7. Complete Works, Vol. 1, p. 35

Chapter 50

KARMA THAT'S TAKING EFFECT

Sage Bharata

There was a king in ancient times. His name was Bharata. When he became old, he went to the forest to do penances. He strove to attain the highest, and did sadhana day and night. One day, he saw a helpless deer give birth to a young one and die. He began to care for the young one. He became so attached to that animal that at the time of death, instead of thinking of the Atman, he thought of the fawn. As a consequence he had to take birth as a fawn in the next life. But karmas are not lost. So the deer remembered his past birth well, and did sadhana in that life also.

After sometime, the fawn died and was born a Brahmin. Here too the memory of the past remained. In time, the Brahmin attained the highest. The body remained until the *prārabdha karma* remained.

In this section, *Tattvabodha* discusses *prārabdha karma.*

प्रारब्धकर्म किमिति चेत्, इदम् शरीरम् उत्पाद्य इहलोके
एवम् सुखदुखादिप्रदं यत्कर्म तत्प्रारब्धम् भोगेन नष्टं
भवति, प्रारब्ध–कर्मणाम् भोगादेव क्षय इति ॥

Prārabdha-karma kimiti cet, idam śarīram utpādya ihaloke evaṁ sukha-duḥkhādi-pradaṁ yat karma tat prārabdham bhogena naṣṭam bhavati, prārabdha-karmaṇāṁ bhogādeva kṣaya iti.

kimiti what is *prārabdha-karma* prārabdha-karma *cet* if it is asked, *idam śarīram utpādya* having given birth to this body *ihaloke* in this world *evaṁ* in this manner *sukha-duḥkhādi* happiness, misery, etc *yat pradaṁ* that which gives *karma* action *tat* that *prārabdham* (is called) 'begun' *bhogena* through experience *naṣṭam bhavati* becomes destroyed, *prārabdha-karmaṇāṁ* of the fruits of action which have 'begun' (to bear fruit) *bhogādeva* through experience alone *kṣaya iti* destruction.

If one asks what prārabdha karma is, the answer is, that which gives birth to this body in this world and makes us experience happiness and misery is *prārabdha karma.* Such fruits of action are eliminated only through experience. This is because, their destruction is only through experience.

Bhogādeva Kṣayam

How do those karmas that have begun to yield fruit become destroyed? Both yoga and Vedanta are clear that they have to be experienced. That is the only way for their destruction. This is what *Tattvabodha* says here. *Karmaphala* can be destroyed either by experience, or by burning them through sadhana. Yoga says that the seeds of the fruits of action are burnt away by the force of sadhana. Thus they cannot sprout. Before the attainment of knowledge, the seeds are all weakened (*tanūkaraṇa*) and burnt (*dagdha*).

Vedanta follows this method partially, but says that so long as ignorance or *avidyā* remains, there are fruits of action, memory, mind, and so on. Once ignorance goes, nothing remains.

The ordinary mortal has to face the consequences of his or her past deeds. None can escape the law. Yet, by God's grace one can overcome suffering, assures Sri Ramakrishna.

In *The Gospel of Sri Ramakrishna,* we see a discussion about this. A devotee asks Sri Ramakrishna about this question, and Sri Ramakrishna replies in a beautiful way.

A Devotee: "Does the body remain even after the realization of God?"

Sri Ramakrishna: "The body survives with some so that they may work out their prarabdha karma or work for the welfare of others. By bathing in the Ganges a man gets rid of his sin and attains liberation. But if he happens to be blind, he doesn't get rid of his blindness. Of course, he escapes future births, which would otherwise be necessary for reaping the results of his past sinful karma. His present body remains alive as long as its momentum is not exhausted; but future births are no longer possible. The wheel moves as long as the impulse that has set it in motion lasts. Then it comes to a stop. In the case of such a person, passions like lust and anger are burnt up. Only the body remains alive to perform a few actions."[1]

Reference:

1. Gospel, p. 477

Chapter 51

HOW IS KARMA DESTROYED ?

Destruction of the Past

We are born, we live in this world, and we die—all this is predestined. The cause of this predestination is we ourselves. It all happens according to what we have done. In each birth we get to know about spirituality, God, Atman, and so on. In each life we get chances to improve ourselves. Yet the world is too strong and it drags us down always. So we continue running round and round the circle—birth, life, death. We keep on accumulating *vāsanās* and *karmāśayas*.

How can these *karmāśayas* and *vāsanās* be destroyed? According to the devotee, *vāsanās* can be destroyed through prayer. 'Heinous sins—the sins of many births—and accumulated ignorance all disappear in the twinkling of an eye, through the grace of God. When light enters a room that has been kept dark a thousand years, does it remove the thousand years' darkness little by little, or instantly?' asks Sri Ramakrishna.[1]

According to the yogi, *vāsanās* are destroyed when *kleśas* (pain-bearing obstructions) are controlled. The *kleśas* are five in number. Ignorance (*avidyā*), *jīva*-hood (*asmitā*), attachment (*rāga*), aversion (*dveṣa*), and clinging to life (*abhiniveśa*). These are the five pain-bearing obstructions. These *kleśas* can be in any of the four states: freely expressed, repressed, attenuated, or dormant. But they are all problematic. When the *kleśas* are burnt away, when they attain the *dagdha-bīja* state, problems end. When they are burnt, they cannot instigate the *vāsanās* and *vāsanās,* in their turn, cannot instigate the *karmāśaya*.

But how does the Vedantin look upon the past accumulations? Vedanta speaks of the fit aspirant for Advaita sadhana. While speaking of the fit aspirant, this school says that he or she has to undergo mental training by way of cleansing the mind of impurities. The impurities of the mind, which are desires and ambitions, may be cleansed. But the inherent tendencies, the past *samskāras,* remain. They can go only when the light of knowledge shines. That is what this section says:

संचितं कर्म ब्रह्मैवाहं इति निश्चयात्मक–ज्ञानेन नश्यति।
आगामि कर्मापि ज्ञानेन नश्यति। किञ्च आगामिकर्मणां
नलिनीदलगत–जलवत् ज्ञानिनां सम्बन्धो नास्ति ॥

sañcitam karma brahmaivāham iti niścayātmaka-jñānena naśyati. Āgāmi karmāpi jñānena naśyati. Kiṁca āgāmi-karmaṇāṁ nalinī-dalagata-jalavad jñāninām sambandho nāsti.

sañcitam karma the fruits of action which are stored *naśyati* will be destroyed *niścayātmaka-jñānena* by the decisive knowledge that *brahmaivāham iti* I am Brahman. *Āgāmi karmāpi* the future fruits too *jñānena* by knowledge *naśyati* are destroyed. *Kiṁca āgāmi-karmaṇāṁ* moreover, the future fruit-bearing karmas *nalinī-dalagata-jalavad* like water on a lotus leaf *jñāninām* with knowledge *sambandho* relation *nāsti* is not there.

The fruits of actions which are stored will be destroyed by the decisive knowledge, 'I am Brahman.' The karmas that are to bear fruit in the future too will be destroyed by knowledge. Moreover, future fruit-bearing actions have no connection with knowledge, like the water on a lotus leaf.

If water falls on the lotus leaf, it simply sits there and shines. Though the lotus leaf is in water all of its life, water does not seem to affect it or wet it in the least. This example has been used by Vedantins to their benefit in many cases.

In the present instance, the enlightened soul's actions have no effect on him—this is being discussed. The *brahmajñāni* will live in this world, if at all he lives after enlightenment, for the good of the world. He has no works, no attachment, no bondage, no duties. He is free. He is Perfect. He is called the *paramahamsa.* There may be some rare souls, who are ordained to be world teachers, who retain the 'ego of knowledge' or 'ego of devotion', according to Sri Ramakrishna, and work for the good of the world. The ordinary souls generally give up their body, he adds, after 21 days. The *Gospel of Sri Ramakrishna* records his words:

> It is said that sages like Dattatreya and Jadabharata did not return to the relative plane after having the vision of Brahman. According to some people, Sukadeva tasted only a drop of that Ocean of Brahman-Consciousness. He saw and heard the rumbling of the waves of that Ocean, but he did not dive into it.
>
> ... a man cannot preserve his body after attaining Brahmajnana. The body drops off in twenty-one days.
>
> There was an infinite field beyond a high wall. Four friends tried to find out what was beyond the wall. Three of them, one after the other, climbed the wall, saw the field, burst into loud laughter, and dropped to the other side. These three could not give any information about the field. Only the fourth man came back and told people about it. He is like those who retain their bodies, even after attaining Brahmajnana, in order to teach others. Divine Incarnations belong to this class.[2]

We have seen that the *sancita* karma of the *brahmajñāni* will be destroyed at the time of illumination, because knowledge burns all the products of ignorance. The body continues until the karma that had already begun to bear fruit lasts. The *brahmajñāni* himself is unaffected whether or not the body lasts. For us he is eating, walking, talking. What he does he himself knows. This is what Śankara says in his *Gītā* commentary.

Thus, as the *Upadeśa Sāhasrī* (19.25) says: 'A person of knowledge will immediately meet with the extinction of all types of bondages like the extinguishing of a lamp.'

References:

1. Gospel, p. 616

2. Gospel, p. 354

Chapter 52

DISTRIBUTION OF KARMA

Karma and its Effects

The soul was bound, and it is liberated in life now. What happens to its past, present, and future actions? In the *Brahma Sūtras* (4.1.13), it has been mentioned in this way: तदधिगम उत्तरपूर्वाघयो–रश्लेष–विनाशौ तद्व्यपदेशात्। That is, 'when Brahman becomes realized, there will be non-attachment and destruction of the subsequent and previous sins respectively, because it has been declared so.'

All the previous sins have no meaning for the illumined soul, and his subsequent actions, if at all they be sinful, will not affect him in any way.

It is said in the *Chāndogya Upaniṣad* (4.14.3):' यथा पुष्करपलाश आपो न श्लिष्यन्त एवमेवंविदि पापं कर्म न श्लिश्यत इति ब्रवीतु मे भगवानिति। Just as water does not stick to a lotus leaf, even so sin does not stick to a person possessed of this knowledge.'

Does the *jñāni,* the person of knowledge, perform sinful actions again? Sri Ramakrishna says: 'Those whose spiritual consciousness has been awakened never make a false step. They do not have to reason in order to shun evil. They are so full of love of God that whatever action they undertake is a good action.'[1]

In *Bhagavadgītā* (18.17), it has been said that an illumined person does not kill, though he may kill the whole world. This is because the idea that 'I am the doer' has absolutely left him. The *jñāni's* actions are all for the good of the world.

He is compared to the golden sword by Sri Ramakrishna, which cannot cut.

Yet, if perchance something is done by him—keeping this option open—which could be considered bad, what happens to the *karmaphala* of such an action? And what happens to his good deeds? This section discusses that:

किञ्च ये ज्ञानिनं स्तुवन्ति भजन्ति अर्चयन्ति च तान्प्रति
ज्ञानिकृतं आगामि पुण्यं गच्छाति; ये ज्ञानिनं निन्दन्ति
द्विषन्ति दुःखप्रदानं कुर्वन्ति तान्प्रति ज्ञानिकृतं सर्वं
आगामि क्रियमाणं यदवाच्यं कर्म पापात्मकं तद्गच्छति।

Kimca ye jñāninaṁ stuvanti bhajanti arcayanti ca tānprati jñānikṛtaṁ āgāmī puṇyaṁ gacchati; ye jñāninaṁ nindanti dviṣanti duḥkha-pradānaṁ kurvanti tānprati jñānikṛtaṁ sarvam āgāmi kriyamāṇaṁ yadavācyaṁ karma pāpātmakaṁ tad gacchati.

Kimca again *ye stuvanti jñāninaṁ* those who praise the people of knowledge *bhajanti* serve them *arcayanti ca* and worship them *tānprati* towards them *jñānikṛtaṁ* done by the persons of knowledge *āgāmī puṇyaṁ* future good fruits of actions *gacchati* go; *ye nindanti jñāninaṁ* those who insult the persons of knowledge *dviṣanti* hate them *duḥkha-pradānaṁ kurvanti* bring sorrow to them *tānprati* towards them *jñānikṛtaṁ* done by the perons of knowledge *sarvam* all *āgāmi* future *kriyamāṇaṁ* actions *yadavācyaṁ* which aren't to be mentioned *karma* actions *pāpātmakaṁ* sinful *tad gacchati* they go.

Again, the stored and to-be-done good fruits of actions go towards those who praise, adore, and worship the persons of knowledge. And the stored and could-be-done evil actions, which are sinful and are not to be mentioned, go to those who insult, bring sorrow to, and hate the perons of knowledge.

Transference

Can *karmaphala,* the fruits of action, be transferred from one person to another? This was believed to be impossible. But with the advent of Sri Ramakrishna, it has been *seen* that it is possible. The biographer of Sri Ramakrishna, Swami Saradananda, himself a person of realization, writes in *Sri Ramakrishna, the Great Master* [also translated as *Sri Ramakrishna and His Divine Play*]: 'When the Master came and lived at Shyampukur in Calcutta for treatment, he had one day a vision that his subtle body came out of his gross one and was walking up and down. Regarding this vision the Master said, "I saw that it had sores all over its back. I was wondering why they were there, and the Mother showed that it was because people came and touched my body after committing all kinds of sins because out of compassion for their sufferings, I had to take upon myself the results of the evil deeds. That is why this (showing his throat) is there. Why, otherwise, should there be so much suffering, though this body never did any wrong?"[2]

Swami Saradanandaji comments: 'The scriptures say that not only ordinary people but even those who have become liberated in life cannot but experience the result of actions of both kinds, good and bad, as long as their bodies last. Ordinary men experience the results of their good and bad actions themselves. Now, who experiences the results of the good and bad actions done through the body of the liberated? For, the liberated one cannot be that experiencer, as his ego has been burnt up by knowledge, and without an ego, there is no liability to enjoyments and sufferings springing from action. Who then can possibly be the experiencer? The results of actions are inevitable.

'Even the liberated ones cannot but do some actions, good and bad, till their bodies' fall like a dry leaf. The scriptures say that those unliberated persons who serve and love the liberated ones enjoy the results of the good actions of the latter, and those who hate them suffer the results of the bad actions done through their bodies. Who can say how great is the result of the loving and devoted service rendered to the incarnations of God, seeing that great results are attained through the service of even ordinary liberated persons?'[3]

References:

1. Gospel, p. 201

2. Swami Saradananda, *Sri Ramakrishna, the Great Master* (Chennai: Sri Ramakrishna Math), p. 379

3. ibid., p. 498

Chapter 51

THE LIBERATED

> 'The aim of the jnani is to know the nature of his own Self. This is Knowledge; this is liberation. The true nature of the Self is that It is the Supreme Brahman: I and the Supreme Brahman are one. But this Knowledge is hidden on account of maya.'
>
> **—Sri Ramakrishna**[1]

One who knows the Self is liberated in life. After the body falls off, he is liberated finally, which is called *videha-mukti*. Who is fit for liberation? Is it true that only a brāhmaṇa or persons belonging to a high caste are liberated? Sri Ramakrishna rejects this idea totally. 'Everybody will surely be liberated.'[2] "Hazra said that a man could not be liberated unless he was born in a brahmin body. 'How is that?' I said. 'One attains liberation through bhakti alone. Sabari was the daughter of a hunter. She, Ruhidas, and others belonged to the sudra caste. They were liberated through bhakti alone."[3]

Liberation: the Only Worthy Goal

'What is then worth having? Mukti, freedom. Even in the highest of heavens, says our scripture, you are a slave; what matters it if you are a king for twenty thousand years? So long as you have a body, so long as you are a slave to happiness, so long as time works on you, space works on you, you are a slave. The idea, therefore, is to be free of external and internal nature. Nature must fall at your feet, and you must trample on it and be free and glorious by going beyond. No more is there life; therefore no more is there death. No more enjoyment; therefore no more misery. It is bliss unspeakable, indestructible, beyond everything. What we call happiness and good here are but particles of that eternal Bliss. And this eternal Bliss is our goal.'[4] These are Swami Vivekananda's words.

Tattvabodha concludes the beautiful exposition of Advaita Vedanta with the following words:

तथा चात्मवित्संसारं तीर्त्वा ब्रह्मानन्दं इहैव प्राप्नोति
तरति शोकमात्मवित इति श्रुतेः ॥

तनुं त्यजतु वा काश्यां श्वपचस्य गृहेऽथवा ।
ज्ञानसंप्राप्ति–समये मुक्तोऽसौ विगताशयः॥

इति स्मृतेश्च ॥

Tathā ca ātma-vit saṁsāraṁ tīrtvā brahmānandaṁ ihaiva prāpnoti 'tarati śokam ātmavit' iti śruteḥ.
Tanuṁ tyajatu vā kāśyāṁ śvapacasya gṛhe'thavā|
Jñāna-saṁprāpti-samaye mukto'sau vigatāśayaḥ,
iti smṛteśca.

Tathā ca moreover *ātma-vit* one who knows the Self *saṁsāraṁ* this miserable world *tīrtvā* having crossed *brahmānandaṁ* bliss of Brahman *ihaiva* in this world itself *prāpnoti* attains *'tarati* crosses *śokam* misery *ātmavit'* the Self-knower *iti śruteḥ* as the Vedas say.

Tyajatu vā let the body be discarded *tanuṁ* the body *kāśyāṁ* in Banaras *śvapacasya gṛhe'thavā* or at the house of a lowborn; *jñāna-saṁprāpti-samaye* at the time of the attainment of knowledge *mukto'sau* he becomes liberated *vigatāśayaḥ* having killed all desires, iti *smṛteśca* say the Smṛtis also.

Moreover, one who knows the Self attains the bliss of Brahman, having crossed this miserable worldliness in this life itself. The Vedas say: 'One who knows the Self transcends sorrow.' Again, the Smṛtis also say that after the attainment of knowledge whether the body falls off in Banaras or in the house of a lowborn—it is all the same for the one who has destroyed all desires.

Swami Vivekananda says: 'Our main problem is to be free. It is evident then that until we realise ourselves as the Absolute, we cannot attain to deliverance. Yet there are various ways of attaining to this realisation. These methods have the generic name of Yoga (to join, to join ourselves to our reality). These Yogas, though divided into various groups, can principally be classed into four; and as each is only a method leading indirectly to the realisation of the Absolute, they are suited to different temperaments.

'Now it must be remembered that it is not that the assumed man becomes the real man or Absolute. There is no becoming with the Absolute. It is ever free, ever perfect; but the ignorance that has covered Its nature for a time is to be removed. Therefore the whole scope of all systems of Yoga (and each religion represents one) is to clear up this ignorance and allow the Atman to restore its own nature. The chief helps in this liberation are Abhyasa and Vairagya. Vairagya is non-attachment to life, because it is the will to enjoy that brings all this bondage in its train; and Abhyasa is constant practice of any one of the Yogas.'[5]

Unless the *jīva* attains *nirvikalpa samādhi* it cannot understand bliss. This is the clear verdict of all illumined souls and spiritual teachers. In *nirvikalpa samādhi,* there are no modifications of the mind at all, say the scriptures.

'The fullest realization of the divine mood, the finale of the spiritual drama, is very rarely seen in human life. When the Jiva, tightly bound by the fetters of his actions, gets liberated by the grace of God, he gets but a faint taste of this mood.

For, when the control of the internal and external sense organs of a man (i.e. jiva or self in bondage) becomes as easy and natural as his breathing; when, losing its identity in the love of the Supreme Self, his little I-consciousness merges for ever in the indivisible ocean of Existence-Knowledge-Bliss Absolute; when melted in the Nirvikalpa Samadhi, his mind and intellect get rid of all kinds of dross and assume Sattvika forms; and when the series of desires in his mind, scorched to ashes by the fire of the divine knowledge, can no longer give rise to new impressions and fruits of actions—it is then and then only that the sweet play of the divine mood starts in him and his life is blessed beyond measure. It is very rarely that one has the opportunity of meeting a person blessed with the full manifestation of the divine mood and enjoying unbreakable peace and contentment.'[6]

The bliss that is attained in samādhi is incomparable, say the scriptures and illumined souls. That is the supreme goal to be attained.

भिद्यते हृदय–ग्रन्थिः छिद्यन्ते सर्व सम्शयाः ।
क्षीयन्ते चास्य कर्माणि तस्मिन् दृष्टे परावरे ॥[7]

When that supreme One is seen, all doubts are removed, all problems are solved, all karmas are destroyed, and knots of the heart are cut asunder. This is the culmination of life.

सर्वात्मकोऽहं सर्वोऽहं सर्वातीतोऽहमद्वयः ।
केवलाखण्डबोधोऽहं आनन्दोऽहं निरन्तरः ॥

'I am the Self of all. I am everything. I am beyond everything. I am the One without a second. I am the one Consciousness. I am Bliss itself.'[8]

Conclusion

After the great attainment, whether or not the body lives is not the great one's concern any more. He feels like the sage in the *Vivekacūḍāmaṇī* (518):

I had been dreaming all the time and was travelling in the wilderness created by *māyā*. In this wilderness, all troubles like birth, death, and so on tormented me endlessly. The tiger called ego tortured me always. At last, by the grace of my teacher, I have attained the highest. I have been wakened from my dream. I am free.

References:

1. Gospel, p. 658

2. Gospel, p. 98

3. Gospel, p. 591

4. Complete Works, Vol. 3, p.128

5. Complete Works, Vol. 8, p. 152

6. Sri Ramakrishna, the Great Master, p. 784 (see p. 438-40) for details about nirvikalpa Samadhi.

7. Muṇḍaka Upaniṣad, 2.2.8

8. *Vivekacūḍāmaṇī*, 516

Om śāntiḥ, śāntiḥ, śāntiḥ.
Śrī Rāmakṛṣṇārpaṇamastu